Religious Interests in Community Conflict

Religious Interests in Community Conflict

Beyond the Culture Wars

Paul A. Djupe and Laura R. Olson
Editors

BAYLOR UNIVERSITY PRESS

Waco, Texas 76798

Book Design by Diane Smith
Cover Design by Cynthia Dunne, Blue Farm Graphics
Cover image used by permission of Jim Kalett/Photo Researchers

Library of Congress Cataloging-in-Publication Data

Religious interests in community conflict : beyond the culture wars / Paul A. Djupe and Laura R. Olson, editors.
p. cm.
Includes bibliographical references and index.
ISBN-13: 978-1-932792-51-5 (pbk. : alk. paper)
1. Church and social problems--United States. 2. Religion and politics--United States. 3. Social conflict--United States. I. Djupe, Paul A. II. Olson, Laura R., 1967-

HN39.U6R45 2007
322'.10973--dc22

2006032758

Printed in the United States of America on acid-free paper with a minimum of 30% pcw recycled content.

Table of Contents

❈

List of Tables and Figures

Tables

FIGURES

Acknowledgments

We began this project in an academic effort to contribute to theory building in religion and politics, but we also managed to have an enormous amount of fun working on the book that has resulted. Our field is very collaborative, and this book is as well. The two of us had worked together on other projects before beginning this book, and we had also worked with many of the volume's contributors. We believe the book has benefited from that close collaborative environment and hope that our combined insights will advance dialogue in the field.

No project of this magnitude would be possible without the generous support and assistance of many individuals. We are particularly grateful to the contributing authors who submitted to our tightly structured chapter outline with good humor and grace. Their insights and expertise combine to make this a book of which we are very proud. We would also like to thank Carey Newman of Baylor University Press, whose enthusiasm for and belief in this project encouraged us. Our colleagues at Denison University and Clemson University provided a warm and welcoming environment in which to work. We are especially grateful to several individuals who did not contribute to this volume but provided great insight and support in various forms: Wendy Cadge, Melissa Deckman, Booth Fowler, Chris Gilbert, John Green, Adam Silverman, Corwin Smidt, Jason Taylor, and Adam Warber. Finally, we are strengthened in every way by the love of our families—thanks for being there for us.

INTRODUCTION

Chapter 1

Toward a Fuller Understanding of Religion and Politics

Paul A. Djupe & Laura R. Olson

Religion and politics have been profoundly intertwined in the United States since before the founding of the republic, despite constitutional prohibitions against state intervention in religious matters. Religious interest groups lobby government alongside secular interest groups. Political candidates target specific religious constituencies for their votes. Clergy speak out on key issues of the day. The heavy religious overtones of the 2004 presidential campaigns again highlighted the important role of religion in the practice of American politics (Green, Smidt, Guth, and Kellstedt 2004; Pew Forum 2004). Much scholarly and popular attention has been rightfully paid to the macro-level relationship between religion and politics. Religion and politics, however, intersect just as profoundly at the local level as they do on the national stage—and over similar issues. The growing religion and politics literature has barely explored the specific nature of these local-level interactions, even though a local milieu would allow researchers greater perspective and validity in making causal claims. This is the approach we utilize in this volume.

Our project represents a systematic attempt to explore the political motivations, effectiveness, and interplay of organized religious interests as they confront public policy problems in their local communities. In other words, we are concerned with the degree of *representation* of religious interests in political conflicts. Accordingly, three guiding questions unite the volume's chapters. First, what motivates organized religious interests to confront public problems? Second, do religious interests cooperate with one another to confront public problems, and what barriers exist that might hinder them from doing so? Third, how effective are religious interests when they choose to confront public problems?

Motivated by both substantive and theoretical concerns, we have assembled an expert team of authors to explore the extent to which religious groups involve themselves in different types of community political debates. Each chapter offers an illustrative case study of a different policy problem in a different community. Significantly, each chapter is organized tightly around a common outline and we urged contributors to be as inclusive of religious interests as possible. With this common design, we are able to maximize the cumulative impact of our case studies and enhance our understanding of religion and politics in the United States. Thus, in the concluding chapter, we integrate the insights offered by the substantive chapters to comment on the extant theories of religion's effect on political behavior. We also offer a general theoretical interpretation of how religion and politics intersect at the community level.

Toward the goal of creating a meta-analysis in the concluding chapter, the case studies presented in the volume are designed to constitute a de facto sample including communities with diversity on several variables of interest. We include investigations of some of the most visible hot-button issues in American politics today, including gay marriage and race relations, along with ongoing concerns that sometimes fly below the mass media's radar, such as health care and homelessness. The chapters investigate a diverse range of communities, including those in which one faith dominates (such as Salt Lake City) and those which have considerable religious diversity (such as Cincinnati). The communities studied also span the gamut from rural to urban and are located in all major regions of the continental United States.

We are especially interested in the extent to which the full range of religious interests either comes together to address the issue of concern, or fails to do so. We are, therefore, interested in the concept of ecumenism—or the formal practice of working together across ecclesiastical dividing lines. This volume is not, however, merely a study of ecumenical cooperation. We are just as interested in circumstances characterized by a lack of cooperation among religious actors, and the cases presented in these chapters reflect both ecumenism and a lack thereof.

The volume itself is organized around four substantive themes: religion in the public square, social justice, race relations, and moral concerns. These substantive themes capture the diversity of issues about which organized religious interests have tended to express greatest concern in the past several decades. Each chapter is an investigation of an individual issue that falls under one of these broad rubrics of public discourse.

The Study of Religion and Politics in the United States

Research on the role of religion in American politics has proceeded along a wide range of avenues that tend to head off in different directions. One of the more interesting facets of the study of religion and politics in the United States is its diversity. Scholars conceive of "interests" at the individual, group, and governmental levels: citizens, clergy, churches, denominations, public interest groups, peak associations of denominations, elected officials, and others. Of course, this diversity is a blessing as well as a curse since it encourages us to understand one actor at a time.

Scholars have debated the extent to which the framers of the Constitution wished to establish a Christian nation; related questions about the meaning of the separation of church and state in the United States keep many constitutional experts busy (Dreisbach 2003; Jelen and Wilcox 1995; Witte 2005). A small body of literature also explores the effect of religion on the behavior of contemporary political elites (Benson and Williams 1982; Layman 2001; Leege, Wald, Krueger, and Mueller 2002; Oldmixon 2005). Meanwhile, scholars have noted that both voting behavior (Deckman 2004; Green, Guth, Smidt, and Kellstedt 1996; Green, Rozell, and Wilcox 2000, 2003; Guth and Green 1991; Kellstedt, Guth, Green, and Smidt 1994; Kohut, Green, Keeter, and Toth 2000; Layman 2001; Rozell and Wilcox 1995, 1997) and public opinion on key sociomoral issues are informed by religious beliefs (Byrnes and Segers 1992; Cook, Jelen, and Wilcox 1992; Deckman 2004; Green et al. 1996; Hunter 1991; Jelen 1995; Kohut et al. 2000; Layman 2001; Layman and Green 2005). Another strand highlights religious contexts, typically in churches, which have been shown to support political mobilization (Burns, Schlozman, and Verba 2001; Campbell 2004; Djupe and Gilbert 2003; Gilbert 1993; Harris 1999; Verba, Schlozman, and Brady 1995; Wald, Owen, and Hill 1988, 1990) and the development of social capital and civic skills (Djupe and Gilbert 2006; Djupe and Grant 2001; Putnam 2000; Verba, Schlozman, and Brady 1995).

Studies also have documented the fact that the pluralistic American interest group (Byrnes 1991; Hertzke 1988; Hofrenning 1995; Moen 1992) and social movement (Findlay 1993; Harris 1999; Morris 1984; Zald and McCarthy 1987) universes have long included religious voices among their ranks. Such religious interests span every major religious tradition and offer messages ranging from left-wing calls for social justice to conservative campaigns of the Prohibition era and late twentieth-century, Christian Right politics.

In the late 1960s, a team of prominent sociologists of religion led by Rodney Stark studied California clergy and found that they were not providing a sustained religious witness on the pressing issues of the time: social unrest, such as race riots; the assassinations of prominent religious and political leaders, and the mounting number of casualties in the Vietnam War (Stark, Foster, Glock, and Quinley 1971). This shocking conclusion belied a profound disjuncture between religious and public life in the 1960s. Significant changes have occurred since then as Christian conservatives have been drawn into politics, and the political activity gap between modernist and conservative religious groups has narrowed (Guth, Green, Smidt, Kellstedt, and Poloma 1997; Kohut et al. 2000). Significant events (such as the September 11, 2001, terror attacks and the war in Iraq), contentious issues (such as stem-cell research and gay marriage), and prominent organizations (such as the Republican Party and Bread for the World) continue to encourage religious voices to engage significant public problems.

Under what circumstances might organized religious interests get involved in addressing public problems at the local level and when are their efforts effective? Are religious groups able to work together or are there barriers that prevent cooperation? Researchers have arrived at different answers to these questions over the past several decades. Early research found few clergy willing to take part in politics. Hostile congregations stymied mainline Protestant clergy in Little Rock, Arkansas, when they tried to fight racism in the mid-1950s (Campbell and Pettigrew 1959). Clergy in a mill town in the South in the 1930s were likewise unwilling to take a stand against oppressive working conditions and labor agreements because they were under the economic thumb of the mill operators (Earle, Knudsen, and Shriver 1976; Pope 1942). On the other hand, more recent illustrations show that religious individuals and interests *are* willing to take a public stand on pressing issues—and evidently with increasing frequency (Crawford and Olson 2001a; Djupe and Gilbert 2003; Guth et al. 1997; Kohut et al. 2000; Olson 2000).

The current volume stems from conversations between the editors through our work and in person, as we attempted to remedy some of the problems with our work and test our conclusions more broadly and convincingly. Building on previous research on the political activity of clergy, Paul Djupe and Christopher Gilbert (2003) suggest a framework of four collections of forces that advance or inhibit clergy participation in public life: personal motivations, congregational resources, denominational culture and mobilization, and community needs. Even so, although Djupe and Gilbert took steps to identify the common connections among religious interests, their study of clergy in just two Christian denominations limits the generalizability of their research and means more studies are needed.

Research with different tacks has also been less than thoroughly satisfying. Laura Olson (2000), for instance, studied the activity of clergy in one city, which provides substantial depth about that case but also significantly limits the generalizability of her conclusions (see also Crawford 1995; Jelen 1993b). James Guth and colleagues (1997) surveyed clergy nationwide in eight denominations, providing them with a large and wide-ranging database. However, they focused exclusively on Protestants and incorporated little information about either clergy's local communities or the relationships they form with clergy of different faiths.

Moreover, individual studies of religious activism overwhelmingly have focused on one type of actor. Several studies examine specific denominations or religious traditions (for example, Byrnes 1991; Djupe and Gilbert 2003; Guth et al. 1997; Harris 1999; Leege 1988; Maisel and Forman 2001) but do not look beyond these ecclesiastical boundaries. Many excellent studies analyze religious interest groups and social movements (Byrnes 1991; Findlay 1993; Harris 1999; Hertzke 1988; Hofrenning 1995) but do not purport to cover the full range of the political activism of religious interests. Scholars tend to study either clergy (Crawford and Olson 2001a; Djupe and Gilbert 2003; Guth et al. 1997; Jelen 1993b) or the mass public (Green et al. 1996; Kellstedt, Green, Guth, and Smidt 1994; Kohut et al. 2000), but very rarely do they examine both (but see Djupe and Gilbert 2006).

While there are sensible reasons to limit the focus of a study to one type of actor at a time, in practice different types of religious actors are knit together to address public problems. The only other volume in the literature that addresses political activism and includes some religious interests at the local level in a systematic way (Sharp 1999) focuses primarily on abortion and gay rights.

The solution, we concluded, was to combine the strengths of all these approaches. By employing numerous community case studies, we multiply the depth that Olson (2000) was able to provide. We include a diversity of faith traditions as did Guth and colleagues (1997). We mandate a multifaceted definition of religious interests to maximize generalizability. Finally, we build upon a framework that can fully test Djupe and Gilbert's (2003) four-pronged theory of religious activism.

Data Sources and Research Design

The research of this volume has been designed to bolster internal and external validity. To establish internal validity, we explicitly asked each contributor to provide comprehensive coverage of as many different types of religious interests in a community as possible, to use multiple methods, and to use community conflict about a single issue to frame their investigation. The questions of why and how religious interests address each particular conflict, therefore, lie at the center of each chapter. To augment external validity, we include a nearly random selection of issues and communities with high internal validity. Thus, in the concluding chapter, we are able to conduct a meta-analysis that allows us to compose more confident answers to the three core questions that motivate the project.

The value of studying individual communities derives from the rich depth of study that such an approach affords. It is possible to study the full range of organized religious interests in an individual community because it is geographically bounded and because each author is well acquainted with the community under study. The chapters as a group constitute a wide-ranging sample themselves because they include many different political contexts.

Within each of four broad issue rubrics (moral concerns, religion in the public square, social justice, and race relations), our contributors study a diversity of community types: rural and urban communities from different regions of the country. Given the explanatory power that this diversity provides, we have the raw materials to make more confident conclusions about how organized religious interests work together (or find themselves at loggerheads) in addressing a broad range of public problems.

Moreover, the contributors to this volume employ a wide variety of research methods. Data are drawn from sources as diverse as surveys of clergy and citizens, in-depth interviews with religious leaders and politicians, and archival materials from the news media, religious organizations, and local governments. Although we have been ecumenical about the specific research methods employed by contributors, we explicitly required the authors of each chapter to employ some form of direct observation beyond the written record. Thus, we are able to take advantage of the particular methodological expertise of the contributing authors who have amassed a wealth of data to bear on their questions.

We place great confidence in the conclusions drawn from these community case studies. Validity is achieved primarily through exceptional clarity about the cues to which both researchers and their subjects are responding. For instance, it has been common practice in the study of clergy political activity to ask individual clergy if they have addressed certain issues, such as "race relations," in the past year (Djupe and Gilbert 2003; Guth et al. 1997; Olson 2000). Yet the exact meaning of an issue like race relations varies significantly from one community to another. Our approach in this volume allows us to move beyond the generalities of the term to three specific instances in which religious interests chose to take action around issues or events in their communities that involved race. In Cincinnati, as Anand Sokhey shows in chapter 9, the concept of race relations is tied specifically to the race riots of April 2001 and their aftermath. In chapter 7, James Guth and colleagues discuss how religious interests engaged the question of celebrating the Martin Luther King Jr. Holiday in Greenville, South Carolina. Meanwhile, Franklyn Niles documents the response of the religious community to a Ku Klux Klan rally in Siloam Springs, Arkansas, in chapter 10. Thus, we are able to illuminate the ways in which religious actors approach the broad and nebulous notion of race relations from three widely divergent contextual perspectives.

Another major strength of our local focus is that it allows the case studies to establish a more comprehensive and reliable sense of what is meant by the phrase "religious involvement in public life." Many observers talk frequently about the idea that religion is highly relevant to American politics and American public life, but the specific nature of this involvement is multifaceted and difficult to summarize concisely. As but one illustration of the difficulty inherent in defining "public religion," consider the fact that America's preeminent religious historian Martin Marty recently spent several years engaged in a major research project designed specifically to define this term and its parameters (see Blumhofer 2002; Marty 2000).[1] What does political activism of religious interests include? According to the chapters presented in this volume, it consists of activities ranging from protest marches to providing for the needy and from attending city council meetings to facilitating discussion and education groups (and see also Ammerman 2005; Chaves 2004; Wuthnow 2004 for other accounts of the range of such activity in the United States).

Lastly, we can conceptualize our collection of case studies as a sample of interest group systems: governmental jurisdictions in which religious interests pursue their goals interdependently. A focus on systems allows us to engage a growing literature on the study of interest groups that addresses representational patterns (Gray and Lowery 1995; Nownes and Freeman 1998). This linkage will be explored in great depth in the concluding chapter because of the analytical power it provides.

Looking Ahead

Part 1 of the volume addresses the most visible policy areas in which religious interests engage: moral concerns. In chapter 2, James Penning and Andrew Storteboom examine community conflict over a proposal by the Match-e-be-nash-she-wish Band of Pottawatomie Indians to build a $100 million casino in a rural, culturally conservative county in southwestern Michigan. Over time, conflict over the casino escalated both in scope and intensity until it involved local, state, and national governments. The chapter examines the roles of various interests and actors in the conflict, focusing in particular on the activities of clergy and churches. The chapter provides insights regarding the role of people of faith in community conflict, the escalation of community conflict, and the impact of federalism on community conflict.

David Damore, Ted Jelen, and Michael Bowers offer the first of two chapters that examine the role religious interests play in battles over gay rights. In chapter 3, Damore and colleagues present an analysis of Nevada's enactment of an amendment to the state constitution that defines marriage as a union between a man and a woman despite the fact that Nevada's political culture is widely regarded as highly libertarian and individualistic. Many observers attributed the passage of the amendment to the activities of the Church of Jesus Christ of Latter-day Saints, a prominent, but by no means dominant, group in Nevada politics. This chapter details the manner in which religious leaders advanced arguments in favor of the amendment in an environment that at first glance would appear hostile to them.

In chapter 4, Paul Djupe, Jacob Neiheisel, and Anand Sokhey examine the role played by religious interests in the battle over another proposed constitutional amendment, this time in Ohio. Addressing scholars' lack of understanding of local-level debate about gay marriage, Djupe and colleagues ask how local clergy inform the opinions of the faithful and the proximate. With whom do clergy and churches align themselves in this fight? Which organizations were active in mobilizing religious interests and which interests did they mobilize? Did clergy deemphasize homosexuality as an issue when their congregations disagreed with them, or did they speak prophetically in an attempt to change hearts and minds?

Part 2 addresses religious interests and their work to address social justice issues. In chapter 5, Sue Crawford explores the quiet work that religious interests have undertaken to address a policy crisis in the absence of an overt community conflict. She tells the story of a coalition that has worked to address health concerns in a rapidly changing urban area. The neighborhood population and the congregational memberships of neighborhood churches include sizable groups of two vulnerable health populations: the elderly and new immigrants. Congregations (represented by clergy) comprise the core of the coalition, but religious health system professionals, religious university professionals, and other nonprofit and neighborhood leaders also participate in the coalition. This chapter illustrates ways in which the work of the local health coalition benefits from ideas developed within broader religious institutions such as seminaries, large health system associations, networks of parish nurses, and the national health ministries association.

Laura Olson investigates a similar midwestern religious coalition in chapter 6, this one designed to address homelessness. For twelve years, the small city of Racine, Wisconsin coped with its burgeoning homeless population through the work of a network of churches that volunteered to shelter the homeless one night each week. This now-defunct network, which called itself the Racine Emergency Sheltering Taskforce (REST), represented a significant range of religious perspectives, including the dominant faiths of the Upper Midwest (Lutheranism and Catholicism), African-American Protestants, and evangelical Protestants. Because representatives of these churches were not required to meet in the same room with one another, theological conflicts were minimized and true ecumenical cooperation prevailed. This chapter documents the reasons why REST congregations chose to participate in a program that depended almost entirely on their own resources (in terms of volunteers, physical space, and money) and why these congregations were willing to overlook the theological differences that would otherwise have separated them.

Part 3 addresses religious interests and the public square. In chapter 7, James Guth, Lyman Kellstedt, Joshua Copeland, and Christine Rowland investigate a battle in Greenville, South Carolina, over whether to observe the federal and state Martin Luther King Jr. Holiday as a county holiday. The fact that Greenville County was one of the few counties in South Carolina to have offices open and employees working on Martin Luther King Day became the most hotly disputed issue in local politics. Religious organizations played a central role in the struggle, as both African-American and white mainline Protestant churches rallied as never before to put pressure on the Council to adopt the holiday. Part of the community's deeply conservative—and politically powerful—Bob Jones University constituency even supported the creation of an official county holiday. This religious mobilization was matched by the similar activation of key economic and political elites. A Citizens' Study Committee, consisting of leading conservative and liberal activists, produced a compromise proposal with widespread endorsement among community elites, though that was not the end of it.

In chapter 8, Quin Monson and Kara Norman examine another public-square controversy that erupted in Salt Lake City when the Church of Jesus Christ of Latter-day Saints purchased a section of Main Street from the city (located between the Salt Lake Temple and the LDS Church Administration Building) and converted it to a pedestrian plaza. The chapter outlines the contours of the controversy over free speech on the Main Street Plaza, describing it as emblematic of long-standing cultural and religious divisions between Mormons and non-Mormons in Salt Lake City and other parts of Utah. As was the case in the Greenville holiday dispute, the settlement of the Salt Lake City controversy was aided in large part by the work of a coalition: the Alliance for Unity, a civic institution that community religious and civic leaders formed to bridge the divide between Mormon and non-Mormon Utahns. This chapter aids our understanding of religion and community conflict by demonstrating the importance of nonreligious institutions in resolving conflicts, especially when religious and governmental institutions lie at the center of the conflict.

Part 4 examines religious interests and race relations. In chapter 9, Anand Sokhey explores the ways in which religious interests can come together to address racial unrest. In April 2001, riots wracked Cincinnati after police shot and killed Timothy Thomas, an unarmed African-American youth. After the riots were quelled, religious leaders played prominent roles in promoting racial reconciliation. Although many clergy became active in these reconciliation efforts in a plethora of ways, others remained silent. Sokhey conducted interviews and a mail survey of clergy in the Cincinnati area to document and explain the racial reconciliation activities that they undertook in the wake of the riots. Overall, Sokhey finds that clergy were deeply engaged in racial reconciliation activities, although he also validates, to an extent, an old finding of the "suburban captivity of the churches" (Winter 1966).

Finally, Franklyn Niles approaches race relations from a different perspective in chapter 10: how do religious interests respond when the Ku Klux Klan comes to town? This chapter investigates the causes and consequences of collective clergy behavior. It focuses on the strategies that the Siloam Springs Ministerial Alliance (SSMA) in northwest Arkansas used to mobilize parishioners to protest peacefully against the Ku Klux Klan, which held a rally in Siloam Springs in August 2000. According to clergy and city leaders, mobilization efforts were extraordinarily successful, with ministers estimating that 25 percent of their parishioners participated in protest activities including silent "prayer walks." Noteworthy about these mobilization efforts is that prior to the Klan rally, the SSMA had never engaged in organizing or promoting social protest. In fact, as of 1998 the Alliance was organizationally moribund. Why, despite years of inactivity and substantial organizational barriers, did the SSMA succeed in mobilizing parishioners to protest peacefully against the

Klan? How are collective interests identified and mobilized within a ministerial organization?

In chapter 11, we take stock of where we are as a subfield, since this volume was designed to take a systematic look at religion and politics theory. But we also need some standards of what these theories need to account for in order to pass muster. Thus, we start with a system-level perspective that draws on recent innovations in the study of interest group systems. In essence, theories should explain individual and group level behavior and the system-level representational patterns that result. That is, we should have a representational theory of religious interests. Instead of simply adding another voice to the cacophony, we review the literature with these criteria in mind. Then, we take advantage of the tightly controlled research design of the project by leveraging the findings of each chapter to make generalizable comments on how and why religious interests decided to address community problems and how effective their efforts proved. In the end, we find a lot to like in the religion and politics literature, but also suggest that a substantial shakeup is desirable.

Part I

MORAL CONCERNS

Chapter 2

God and Gaming

Community Conflict over a Proposed Indian Casino in West Michigan

James M. Penning & Andrew Storteboom

When a major commercial development is proposed for a small, rural community, conflict is likely. When that development is an Indian casino and the rural community is largely white as well as culturally and theologically conservative, conflict is nearly inevitable.[1] The focus of this study is on just such a casino proposal.

In late 1999, the 175-member Match-e-be-nash-she-wish Band of Pottawatomie Indians, also called the Gun Lake Band, proposed to build a casino in Dorr Township, Michigan, a largely rural community located in Allegan County, about twenty miles south of Grand Rapids, near the small city of Wayland. The proposed casino was to be large, covering 193,500 square feet (Knape 2003a) and costing approximately $100 million (Knape 2003b). It would include an entertainment lounge, a 300-room hotel, a sports bar, three restaurants, and two fast food outlets (Davids 2001; Wells 2002a: 2). According to the Band's estimates, it would draw nearly three million visitors a year and create 4,301 jobs, including 1,554 in the casino itself and 2,747 in the surrounding community (Friends of the Gun Lake Indians 2003: 1).

While estimates of the overall economic impact of the proposed casino varied, virtually all observers agreed that the impact would be profound, both on Allegan County and on surrounding counties. For example, an economic impact analysis funded by the Grand Rapids Area Chamber of Commerce suggested that over a ten-year period the casino would generate $1.2 billion in new money for Allegan County but cost adjacent counties $880 million (Knape 2003c: A1).

Such a major proposal was bound to generate conflict. But the vehemence of the conflict and its expanding scope amazed (and continues to amaze) participants both within Allegan County and across the state and nation. Ultimately, the casino controversy involved not only Dorr Township and Allegan County but also a wide variety of interest groups, state and federal courts, three Michigan governors, the State Legislature, Michigan's congressional delegation, and the federal government (including the federal courts, Department of the Interior, and two U.S. presidents). The dispute evolved from one that was initially perceived as a local community conflict into one with statewide and even national implications.

Our primary goal in examining the Wayland casino conflict is to examine the role played by religious interests in this conflict. Indeed, the conflict has notable implications regarding the mobilization of religious interests, the political effectiveness of religious interests, and coalition-building both among religious interests and between religious interests and other concerned parties. To facilitate the analysis, at the end of the chapter we utilize concepts pertaining to mobilization theory, economic and morality politics, and interest group theory.

We employ several different sources of data in our analysis of the Wayland casino controversy. First, we rely heavily on published sources, including newspaper accounts, scholarly books and papers, and Web sites of both proponents and opponents of the proposed casino. Second, we employ data obtained from personal interviews with a wide variety of participants in the controversy, including reporters, state legislators, Indians, businesspersons, clergy, and interest group leaders. Finally, we utilize data obtained from a brief questionnaire mailed to the senior pastors of all churches in Allegan County and nearby townships in Kent County. Questionnaires were mailed in two waves (during the first and third weeks of April 2003). Out of a total of 157 questionnaires mailed, 85 usable responses were received, for an overall response rate of 54 percent.[2]

The Great Wayland Casino War

Distant Drums (1990–1999)

In 1990 Michigan had virtually no casinos. Today, largely as a result of a series of actions that the federal government and Michigan voters took to remove legal impediments to casinos, Michigan has twenty-one casinos, ranking second among the states only to Nevada. According to the Michigan Legislative Service Bureau (LSB), "the contrast between the availability [of gaming] a decade ago and the current situation is astounding" (LSB 2001: 3). As Figure 2.1 indicates,

Figure 2.1

Casinos in Michigan
and Federally Recognized American Indian Tribes

with the exception of three commercial casinos operating in the city of Detroit, Indian tribes operate all of the casinos. In addition, nine American Indian tribes are currently looking to start new casinos in the state and many existing operations are expanding (Edison-Swift 2002: 1).

By 1998, Michigan Governor John Engler struggled with the issue of Indian casino gaming in the state. Personally opposed to casino gaming, Engler had witnessed the rapid expansion of Indian gaming in Michigan and had recently received four additional requests from Indian tribes for new casino compacts. Despite his distaste for casino gaming, Engler ironically found himself in the position of casino advocate, twisting the arms of legislators to get them to support four new casino compacts. Engler argued that he had little choice since, without the compacts, the tribes could build casinos without his permission and without guaranteeing the state a share of casino revenues. In exchange for legislative resolutions endorsing the four compacts, Gov. Engler pledged that he would not sign another casino compact except at the behest of both houses of the state legislature (Heinlein 2001: 4).

If Engler believed that these legislative resolutions would end the seemingly insatiable demand for new casinos in Michigan, he was sorely mistaken. In 1999, the Department of the Interior officially recognized the Match-e-be-nash-she-wish ("Gun Lake") Band of Pottawatomie Indians, paving the way for the Band's proposal to build a new casino in Allegan County. Although the Gun Lake Band owned eighty acres of land near the small village of Bradley, they considered that land sacred (Franklin 2000). Hence, the Band began looking for other property on which to build the proposed casino. The Gun Lake Band ultimately purchased an abandoned factory site (previously occupied by the AMPRO Corporation) along U.S. 131 in Dorr Township, near the city of Wayland (Shagonaby 2001). However, in order to use this land, located less than three miles from the original Indian settlement in Bradley, the Gun Lake Band would need approval from the U.S. Department of the Interior to place this land "in trust."

The initial local reaction to the casino proposal was muted, possibly because area residents did not yet fully appreciate the enormous size and scope of the casino project. Ironically, out-of-state interests were among the first to complain about the proposed Wayland casino. Specifically, Boyd Gaming, a multi-billion dollar

Las Vegas company with casinos in five states, got involved through its representative Kevin Flynn, a Chicago businessman and former owner of Blue Chip Casino in Michigan City, Indiana. Although Boyd Gaming, wary of potential competition from Michigan casinos, initially hired Flynn to fight proposed casinos in Battle Creek and New Buffalo, Michigan, the Wayland casino was soon added to his list. One publication reported that Illinois officials had linked Flynn's company to organized crime ("High Rollers" 1999). Regardless of the truth of these allegations, press reports stated that Flynn had signed a contract with Boyd Gaming, promising him $5 million if casinos were to be kept out of southwestern Michigan for three years. These reports prompted a review by the U.S. Attorney's Office, the Michigan State Police, and the Michigan Attorney General's Office, at least in part, to determine whether the contract violated state prohibitions against lobbyist contingency fees ("High Rollers" 1999).

One of the most notable actions taken by Boyd Gaming was to hire the Lansing lobbying firm, Cusmano, Kandler & Reed, Inc., with instructions to fight any legislative efforts to secure a compact for the Wayland casino. According to William Kandler, founder of the firm, his primary focus was on Democrats in the legislature, since more Democrats than Republicans were in the "unknown" or "undecided" categories ("High Rollers" 1999: 2).

Not all of the early opposition to the casino came from out-of-state economic interests; additional early opposition came from homegrown anti-casino groups such as the Michigan Alliance Against Casinos (MAAC), which were also concerned with the moral dimensions of gaming. Thus began a pattern—which continued throughout the casino controversy—of an uneasy alliance of economically and morally motivated groups fighting the proposal. According to David Moore, a MAAC leader, "This whole fight makes for very strange bedfellows . . . You get the gaming industry opposing itself, [and] people opposing it on religious grounds. It's been a very strange educational process for me and, I think, everyone else" ("High Rollers" 1999: 6).

First Skirmishes (2000)

In 2000, two years after Gov. Engler promised that he would not pursue any new casino compacts without state legislative approval, Sen. Joanne Emmons introduced a resolution in the Michigan Senate urging the Governor to negotiate a compact with the Gun Lake Band

(Heinlein 2001). A similar resolution was introduced in the House by Rep. Larry DeVuyst, a Republican representing the Alma area, the site of Michigan's largest Indian casino. DeVuyst argued that a casino compact could produce $200 million in revenues for the state over the next decade (Franklin 2000: 2). Emmons and DeVuyst introduced their resolutions during the final days of the legislature's lame duck session,[3] perhaps in hopes of gaining the support of retiring legislators. Fierce opposition, led by Rep. (now Senator) Patricia Birkholz of Allegan County stymied this move. Birkholz responded to DeVuyst's economic argument with a moral appeal, "We lost three library millages, but selling our souls for library money is not the answer" (Franklin 2000: 2).

In an effort to provide information about the proposed casino and, perhaps, reduce local opposition to the casino, the Gun Lake Band organized a town hall meeting in Wayland High School gymnasium in November of 2000. Casino opponent Todd Boorsma considered the timing of the meeting to be exceedingly suspicious because "it was scheduled for Wednesday, which is a church day, and was also on the opening day of deer season" (Boorsma 2003). Nonetheless, approximately a thousand citizens, most of whom were opposed to the casino, turned out for the meeting. Dorr Township supervisor Dan Kaczanowski and tribal spokesmen were peppered with questions concerning the possible negative impact of the casino on the community. According to Boorsma, the meeting had at least one significant consequence in that it provided a means for galvanizing opposition to the casino. Following the meeting, Boorsma collected names of casino opponents and used the names as a basis for establishing an anti-casino organization (and associated PAC) labeled West Michigan Gaming Opposition (WMGO) (Boorsma 2003).

Shortly thereafter, the Gun Lake Band organized a second town-hall meeting. As in the meeting, the second one was dominated by casino opponents. Many attendees worried that the casino would negatively affect their way of life. One local resident said, "We built a house in the . . . area because it was such a family friendly area . . . We don't want to see it changed" (Wells 2002b: 1). This meeting produced two significant consequences. First, the Dorr Township Board, apparently convinced that there was significant public opposition to the casino, changed its pro-casino stance to a neutral one. Second, tribal officials, upset over what they considered "racist" and "insulting" remarks made by crowds, cancelled future public meetings on the casino (Franklin 2000: 3).

The Battle Escalates (2001)

The year 2001 marked an escalation in the casino war, with conflict occurring not only in local government and the state legislature but also in the courts. In January, the Gun Lake Band sued the state in federal court, arguing that under the provisions of the federal Indian Gaming Regulatory Act of 1988 (IGRA), any state (such as Michigan) that permits any type of gaming must negotiate compacts with qualifying tribes. According to Band Chairman D. K. Sprague, Gov. Engler ignored federal requirements that a state must negotiate a casino compact within 180 days of a tribal request ("Casino Plan" 2001). In addition, the Band appealed to the U.S. Secretary of the Interior, Gale Norton, asking her to put pressure on the state to negotiate a compact (Davids 2001).

According to state Sen. William Van Regenmorter (now a state representative), a casino opponent, the Band's action was "premature" and did not follow proper procedure. Van Regenmorter also assumed that Secretary Norton, a Bush appointee, would not necessarily favor the establishment of a new casino in Michigan. According to Van Regenmorter, "Casinos raise a number of very significant moral issues, starting with greed and moving on to addiction and crime" (Davids 2001: 4). His sentiments were echoed by Rep. Patricia Birkholz who asserted that "I feel very strongly that as a whole it is a detriment to the fabric of the community." According to Birkholz, "between 95 and 97 percent of communications I receive [about the casino] are in opposition" (Davids 2001: 4–5).

On the other hand, tribal spokesman Ken Brock countered by touting the economic benefits of the casino for the Band, the local community, and the state. When asked about the problem of gambling addiction, Brock answered, "Because people have eating disorders, we don't close restaurants . . . If everything people did bad we banned from society we wouldn't have anything left in society" (Davids 2001: 4).

The year 2001 also witnessed a marked increase in organized group activity, both for and against the casino proposal. The Gun Lake Band circulated a petition throughout the community, garnering over a thousand pro-casino signatures (Stolarz 2001). It also gained the support of a variety of local business groups, including the Kalamazoo County and Wayland Area Chambers of Commerce.

On the other hand, casino opponents were able to obtain approximately twelve thousand signatures on their petitions, more than ten times the number obtained by casino proponents. Nonetheless, tribal spokesman Ken Brock downplayed the amount of opposition. According to Brock, "the only organizations opposed to the casino are the area's two legislators and the local Christian Reformed Churches . . . I can respect their moral position, but they can simply choose not to go" (Stolarz 2001: 2).

Brock may well have underestimated the size and scope of the anti-casino forces. According to the *Capital News Service*, as early as 2001, the casino was opposed by a loose coalition of groups, most of which objected to the casino on moral or religious grounds (Stolarz 2001). These groups, with a combined membership of over ten thousand, included West Michigan Gaming Opposition (WMGO); the Taxpayers of Michigan Against Casinos (TOMAC), a group fighting the New Buffalo casino; and the Citizens Exposing Truth About Casinos (CETAC), a Battle Creek organization (Stolarz 2001: 2). Moreover, as the following analysis demonstrates, religious opposition to the casino was by no means limited to a single denomination and a handful of state legislators.

In May 2001, the Band was dealt a setback when U.S. District Judge Robert Bell, in Grand Rapids, dismissed the Band's federal lawsuit, ruling that the Band had no legal basis to force the State of Michigan into negotiations for a compact until it had taken land into trust from the federal government (Wells 2002b). Perhaps in response to this ruling, the Band redoubled its efforts to locate a casino site and on June 5 announced the purchase of the AMPRO site discussed above. This action got the attention of the Grand Rapids Area Chamber of Commerce, which on June 20 announced its opposition to the proposed casino (Brown 2001).

Action on the casino now shifted to the Michigan House of Representatives where, on June 28, the House Regulatory Reform Committee unanimously approved a resolution sponsored by Rep. Larry DeVuyst, urging the State to negotiate a gaming compact with the Gun Lake Band ("Indian Casino" 2001). Indian spokesman Rex Hackler, applauding the Committee's decision, stated: "Clearly we're thrilled, but what it comes down to is there are three Democrats and three Republicans that recognized the tribe's rights and acted on fairness" (Reens 2001: 1). Opponents, however, cried "foul," noting that the resolution should have been handled by the House Gaming and Oversight Committee, a committee less favorable to casinos. Rep. (now Senator) Wayne Kuipers, an anti-casino member of the Gaming Committee, complained that "it was obvious it was sent to where it would get out of committee" (Reens 2001: 2). In any case, most observers agreed that this was a major setback for casino opponents who had shown up in force at the public hearing held by the Regulatory Reform Committee.

In July most House members from West Michigan, all Republicans opposing the casino, met with Republican Speaker of the House Rick Johnson, a supporter of the Wayland casino, urging him to delay the House vote on the committee recommendation until September. The legislators hoped that by delaying the vote, they could convince sufficient numbers of wavering legislators to kill the proposed resolution (Birkholz 2003; Kooiman 2003). While reports of the meeting vary, two things are beyond dispute. First, Speaker Johnson did, in fact, agree to delay a vote on the resolution until September. Second, virtually every attending legislator, except Speaker Johnson, believed that the speaker had agreed that the September vote was to be a single, final, up-or-down vote on the casino; no further House action would be taken on the proposal (Birkholz 2003; Jansen 2003; Kooiman 2003; Kuipers 2003).

The Gun Lake Band responded bitterly to this delay, with tribal chairman D. K. Sprague blaming the "religious right." According to Sprague, "In western Michigan there are Christian reform [sic] people, all Republicans with lots of money, and their favorite saying is, 'not in my backyard,' it's fine elsewhere." Sprague was confident the House would pass the resolution but claimed that House members had told him that last-minute, heavy lobbying by opponents had produced the delay (Melmer 2001).

West Michigan Senators and Representatives played *hardball politics* in the controversy, threatening to withhold their votes on a Republican-drawn redistricting plan if they were not given a delay on the casino (Melmer 2001). The dispute divided the Republican Party and fostered considerable ill will in the Party's legislative caucuses. Fulton Sheen, Republican Allegan County Treasurer (now state representative), attended a rally outside of the capitol, accusing the GOP-controlled legislature of "shoving the casino down our throats." And former GOP state representative and GOP district chairman Harold Voorhees asserted that his party was making a huge mistake by angering western Michigan Republicans (Melmer 2001: 2). Tribal spokesman Rex Hackler, however, accused opponents of racist motivation. According to Hackler, "At the last meeting on the casino, a bunch of people showed up and told members of the Gun Lake Band to 'go back where you came from' . . . Without using the words prejudice and racist, I can't describe these people . . . it's racism, pure and simple" (Melmer 2001: 2).

The tendency of each side in the casino dispute to demonize the opposition, a common occurrence in *morality politics*, added to the tension as the September deadline for a House vote on the casino resolution approached. Lobbying for and against the casino was fierce, both in the Michigan capital Lansing and at the local level. In mid-September, a group of approximately two thousand casino opponents, including "many ministers," held a rally in the Wayland High School gym, the site of the Band's original town-hall meeting (Boorsma 2003). Area churches were finally getting involved, and anti-casino signs began appearing both in front of private homes and area churches.

On September 26, 2001, the House voted on HR 167, a resolution urging Gov. Engler to negotiate a compact with the Gun Lake Band. The result was a narrow and perhaps surprising 52–51 defeat for the Band. While West Michigan legislators were jubilant, Indian officials did not share their joy, angrily pointing out that because the vote was held on Yom Kippur, the Jewish Day of Atonement, three Jewish Democratic representatives (likely casino proponents) were absent and did not vote (Friends of the Gun Lake Indians 2001).[4] The Band promised that it would negotiate with the federal government to place their land in trust, thereby possibly eliminating the need for state approval (Edison-Swift 2001).

Total War (2002–2005)

If casino opponents had any hope that the narrow House vote had finally ended the casino conflict, they were soon disabused of that notion; the Gun Lake Band continued to press its case in the courts and at the local, state, and national levels of government. Indeed, so confident was the Band of ultimate victory that in May 2002, it negotiated a five-year pact with Allegan County to provide 24/7 police coverage of the proposed casino. The first year's payment was to be $500,000 ("Tribe Seeks" 2002).

Casino opponents also increased their level of activity. In June 2002, the leading organization opposed to the Wayland Casino, West Michigan Gambling Opposition (WMGO), announced that it was merging with a leading Battle Creek group, Citizens Exposing the Truth About Casinos (CETAC), to form a new organization called Michigan Gambling Opposition (MichGO). CETAC, initially organized to oppose the proposed Firekeepers' Casino in Battle Creek, and the Wayland-oriented WMGO decided that they could be more effective, especially at the state level, by pooling their organizational resources. According to Todd Boorsma, founder of WMGO, "If people get the message out and people speak out . . . [casinos] can be stopped" ("Anti-casino" 2002).

Anti-casino forces also pressed their case before the August 2002 GOP state legislative primary, the most important primary in this heavily Republican area. Since Rep. Patricia Birkholz (R-Allegan County), a leading casino opponent, was running for the Michigan Senate, the local House seat was open. As one might suspect, the casino issue dominated the primary debate among the five GOP candidates for the House seat, producing considerable fireworks at candidate forums. Ultimately, the primary (and, later, the general election) was won by Allegan County Treasurer Fulton Sheen, perhaps the fiercest opponent of casinos in the group of candidates. The sole casino supporter among the GOP candidates lost badly, winning only 15 percent of the vote (Drake 2002).

With so much at stake, it is hardly surprising that the battle also continued in the courts. In September 2002, a Houston casino management firm, Kean-Argovitz Resorts Management/Michigan, filed a multi-million dollar breach-of-contract lawsuit against the Indians. According to the suit, the firm had "agreed to advance the tribe about $80,000 a month for administrative and legal expenses and up to an additional $100 million to buy a site and build a facility" but, due to the interference of a group of businessment from Mt. Pleasant, Michigan, the Band had changed its mind. The Michigan businessmen involved denied any wrongdoing and tribal officials refused to comment on the suit (Wells 2002b: D1).

Meanwhile, the Gun Lake Band received another bit of bad news from the courts. In September 2002, the United States Sixth Court of Appeals in Cincinnati turned down the Gun Lake Band's request to force the State of Michigan to negotiate a casino compact. In effect, the Appeals Court upheld Judge Bell's District Court ruling (discussed above) that a state does not have to negotiate with an Indian tribe until the tribe has land in trust. According to Sen. Birkholz, the Band was likely to appeal this ruling to the United States Supreme Court ("Appeals Court" 2002).

Regardless of the Band's decision to pursue an appeal to the Supreme Court, the appellate court's ruling highlighted the necessity of securing Department of Interior designation of the Wayland site as Indian land in trust. An important step toward achieving that status was to file an environmental impact statement, detailing the impact of the tribe's proposal on the community. On November 29, 2002, the Gun Lake Band published its environmental impact statement, specifying the proposed casino's location as well as its economic and social implications for the community. Not surprisingly, the environmental impact statement touted the benefits for the Wayland area. According to Sprague, the casino would "bring 4,300 badly needed jobs, local supplier purchases, economic development, and state revenue sharing, as well as proven regional recreational attraction to this area" (Wells 2002c). Tribal officials estimated that the casino would generate approximately $10 to $15 million per year in revenue for the state's school aid fund, as well as approximately $2 million annually for local governments (Harmon and Luke 2002; Luke 2002).

The Band's statement was welcome news for some local officials. John Campbell, chairman of the Allegan County Board of Commissioners, noted, "We've had the closure of the Plainwell Paper Company, the Life Savers Plant and the Pet Life Corporation . . . the great sucking sound we're hearing is jobs leaving Allegan County." According to Campbell, "I'm a conservative, pro-life, Republican Christian, but I have a different view. Two million dollars in revenue sharing is significant when you realize the deficit we've tried to erase for 2003 is $1.8 million" (Harmon and Luke 2002: A2). On the other hand, Hopkins Township Supervisor Mark Evans expressed concerns about traffic: "It's not going to be normal. We're not used to having 10,000 cars a day traveling through our community" (Harmon and Luke 2002: A2).

Casino opponents quickly responded to the Gun Lake Band's environmental impact statement in two different ways. First, opponents sought to persuade the U.S. Department of Interior to extend the mandatory thirty-day public comment period. Both area members of Congress, Vern Ehlers (R-Grand Rapids) and Pete Hoekstra (R-Holland) got involved, formally asking the Department of the Interior to extend the public comment period. Rep. Hoekstra acknowledged that this request was a stall tactic, admitting that "we need to put up roadblocks" to the casino (Harmon 2002a: A1). In addition, Peter Secchia, a powerful local businessman and former U.S. Ambassador to Italy, got involved. At a White House Christmas party for large donors, Secchia buttonholed President Bush's top political advisor Karl Rove, asking for his intervention in the casino dispute (Harmon 2002a: A1–A2). Ultimately this effort was successful as the Interior Department agreed to extend the comment period for an additional forty-five days (Tunison 2002). This agreement pleased MichGO's Todd Boorsma, who asserted that the Bureau of Indian Affairs could expect plenty of comments: "We are going to get letters from the whole community. . . . We're going to try to hit it at every angle" (Wells 2002c: 2).

In the second place, casino opponents challenged the validity of the Band's environmental impact statement by producing an alternative environmental impact statement. According to Congressman Peter Hoekstra, if opponents can demonstrate through their own environmental impact study that "severe damage" will be done to surrounding communities, "we might be able to get the Interior Department to say the impact is so severe that it won't allow this land to go into trust" (Harmon 2002a: A4). Consequently, the Grand Rapids Area Chamber of Commerce hired a Lansing consulting firm, Anderson Economic Group, to conduct its own independent impact statement.

The Anderson report, released in February 2003, challenged the methodology and conclusions of the Gun Lake Band's environmental impact statement, suggesting that the Band's statement was too narrowly focused and ignored the casino's impact on surrounding (non-Allegan) counties. According to John Brown, president of the Grand Rapids Area Chamber of Commerce, the Indians' report "greatly overstates the economic benefits that will flow from the casino and they virtually ignore the negative impacts regionally. . . . The tribe's methodology is critically flawed. . . . This will bleed tens of millions of dollars not only from the economy of Kent County, but from all of the surrounding counties, much to the detriment of legitimate businesses region-wide" (Wells 2003: D1). Indeed, the Anderson group study suggested that the casino would cost surrounding communities approximately $92 million dollars each year and blasted the

Band's conclusions, claiming that they "were based on incomplete or erroneous data" and "failed to account for two other proposed casinos in southwest Michigan" (Knape 2003a: A6).

Shortly after the Gun Lake Band released its November 2002 environmental impact statement, rumors spread through the state capitol that the legislature might revisit the Wayland casino issue during its December 2002 lame-duck session. In particular, opponents worried that House Speaker Rick Johnson might be inclined to push the Wayland casino through the House, perhaps using a voice vote to "gavel through" a request to Gov. Engler to negotiate a casino compact. Indeed, Rep. Birkholz was so concerned about this possibility that, in her words, "wherever I went, I carried around with me a written request for a roll call vote" on the casino (Birkholz 2003).

As concerns about a possible lame-duck casino vote mounted, casino opponents redoubled their efforts. The area's largest newspaper editorialized against the casino ("No Casino" 2002), church leaders urged their congregations to write their legislators, and lobbyists put on a full-court press. Nonetheless, the concerns of Rep. Birkholz and other opponents proved to be well-founded, since in early December Speaker Johnson did, in fact, call upon the House to endorse a Wayland casino compact. Johnson and the pro-casino forces scored an important victory when, on December 10, the House voted 58–47 to approve a resolution urging Gov. Engler to sign a compact with the Gun Lake Band. Although House opponents did their best to fight the measure by introducing forty-two amendments before the final vote, their best efforts fell short. Virtually every West Michigan legislator voted against the resolution (Harmon 2002b: A1). Two days later, the Michigan Senate followed suit in a 24–14 vote.

Casino opponents, many of them GOP stalwarts from West Michigan, were astonished and outraged at this turn of events. Todd Boorsma of MichGO, who had previously warned about the potential dangers of the legislature's lame-duck session, now complained about behind-the-scenes negotiations between the Governor, legislative leaders, and the Gun Lake Band that had produced a ready-made compact. Indeed, Boorsma and others referred to the compact as a "greased pig" (Harmon 2002c: A1). Prior to the House vote, Rep. Birkholz voiced similar concerns: "I think it's abhorrent they're doing it with no negotiation period, nothing for the Legislature to come back to oppose. They're being very shrewd." In her view, advocating the casino "is like selling your soul to the Devil" (Harmon 2002c: A2). Congressman Hoekstra expressed amazement at Speaker Johnson's decision to push for a casino vote despite the fact that thirty-nine of the fifty-eight members of the House GOP caucus had come out against the Wayland casino. According to Hoekstra, "Our leadership in Washington couldn't do that . . . We'd have a rebellion in the caucus. It would be ugly" (Harmon 2002d: A21). On the other hand, Rep. DeVuyst, author of the House resolution, defended his move to introduce the resolution during the lame-duck session, noting that "It's a . . . lot easier to work with people already involved than to start all over again next year" (Harmon 2002b: A21).

Speaker Johnson's decision to push for a House vote seemed likely to have long-term political repercussions. Certainly, his actions fractured personal relationships between West Michigan GOP legislators and the speaker. Each of the six West Michigan legislators interviewed for this study indicated that he or she believed that the speaker had broken his July 2001 promise to hold only a single, final vote on the Wayland casino and could, therefore, no longer be trusted. Sen. Kuipers complained that Johnson "reneged on his promise" (Kuipers 2003) while Rep. Kooiman speculated that "someone must have got to Johnson" (Kooiman 2003). On the other hand, Johnson's press secretary argued that he had promised to hold only one vote "last year," not in future years (Harmon and Luke 2002b: A21).

Anger over the speaker's action was not limited to the legislature. In December 2002, Peter Secchia, a powerful Grand Rapids businessman and GOP stalwart, asserted that "this is the worst bit of news for West Michigan in my 30 years of political activism" (Harmon 2002a: A1). Five months later, Secchia's anger had not cooled. In an e-mail to West Michigan legislators and businessmen, Secchia said that Speaker Johnson was dead meat in West Michigan for his backing of the Wayland casino. According to Secchia, "We had the votes to defeat the motion. . . . He [Johnson] told the lawmakers he wouldn't bring it up again, and then he brought it up in lame-duck . . . Rick Johnson just trampled our people. . . . When I say he's in deep doo doo over here, that's what I mean." Secchia urged Republican leaders to join him in the establishment of a political action committee that would support GOP candidates opposed to additional casinos. He also pledged to "vociferously oppose" any fundraisers held by Johnson in West Michigan ("Irate Secchia" 2002).

Clear partisan divisions were apparent in the two House votes and one Senate vote on the casino resolution. In 2001, for example, while Democrats in the House voted 37–10 in favor of the casino resolution, Republicans voted 42–10 against the resolution. Similarly, in 2002, House Democrats supported the resolution 41–8 while House Republicans opposed the resolution 41–15. In the 38-member Michigan Senate, Republicans were evenly split over the 2002 casino resolution, 11–11, while Democrats supported the resolution 10–3.[5]

Since the 2001 House vote was decided by a razor-thin, one-vote margin, it is difficult to attribute the 2002 reversal to a single factor. In aggregate terms, there was relatively little partisan shift over time, particularly among Republicans. Indeed, the number of GOP casino supporters increased by only one (and the number of opponents decreased by only one) between 2001 and 2002. However, other things being equal, this shift alone would have been sufficient to change the outcome of the vote on the resolution. On the Democratic side, support for the resolution increased by four votes while the number of opposing votes decreased by two. Thus, the total number of "yes" votes in 2002 totaled fifty-six, sufficient to ensure passage, even if the proposal had been a statute rather than a resolution.[6]

A variety of factors contributed to the success of the pro-casino effort in the Michigan legislature. One factor was the powerful argument, advanced by Gov. Engler, that since federal approval of the Band's request for land in trust was inevitable, the state could do nothing to prevent establishment of the Wayland casino. According to Engler, state approval of a compact would at least guarantee that the state would share in some of the casino's revenues (Engler 2002). A second factor working in the casino's favor was the political skill of its proponents. Proponents diligently worked behind the scenes to produce a compact and, with the assistance of Speaker Johnson, deftly manipulated the lame-duck session. Moreover, the draft of the compact they proposed to the legislature contained a provision designating eight percent of casino revenues for education, making it easier for wavering legislators to justify a pro-casino vote (Birkholz 2003; Luke 2002: 2). According to Rep. Barb Vander Veen, for some House members, tax revenues constituted "the bottom line" (Harmon and Luke 2002: A7). Perhaps most important, casino supporters spent huge amounts of money advancing their cause. Rep. Birkholz observed: "It was a decisive vote (in the House). They spent a lot of money and it paid off for them" (Luke 2002: 2). Among the most prominent financial backers of the casino were three politically connected businessmen from Mt. Pleasant, Michigan, who hoped to manage the casino: Sydney Smith, Barton LaBelle and James Fabiano Sr. Two of the three, LaBelle and Smith, were former Mt. Pleasant mayors, and each member of this triumvirate was a long time political backer of Gov. Engler (Harmon 2002c). Newspaper reports suggested that the trio were seeking a casino management contract with the Gun Lake Band which could provide them with up to $366 million over a seven-year period (Wells 2002a).

Not surprisingly, the Mt. Pleasant triumvirate was willing to spend freely to promote pro-casino political interests. In 1998, for example, the three poured the maximum of $3,800 each into Gov. Engler's reelection campaign and gave thousands of dollars to Engler's favorite candidates, including three GOP Supreme Court justice candidates (Wells 2002a: 2). Furthermore, according to *The Detroit News*, the trio, using both a corporation and political action committee they established (the 21st Century PAC), gave a total of $160,000 to persuade state legislators to support the casino (Hornbeck, Cain, and Heinlein 2002).[7] This total included contributions to forty-five of the fifty-one House members who supported the 2001 casino resolution and forty-five of the fifty-six House members who supported the 2002 resolution. Of course, it is difficult to demonstrate a causal relationship between contributions and casino votes. Indeed, some legislators receiving "Mt. Pleasant" money actually voted against the casino. In 2002, for example, five legislators receiving such money voted "no," and three failed to vote (Hornbeck 2002).

According to *The Detroit News*, although there is no evidence that the contributions were illegal, "campaign finance watchdogs say it smacks of influence peddling and violates the spirit of state laws." Rich Robinson, Executive Director of the Michigan Campaign Finance Network, a nonpartisan group focusing on campaign spending, complained, "It looks to me as though the intent of these contributions was to reinforce 'yes' votes on the compact. To reach that conclusion, we have to connect dots. There is always plausible deniability. But these are dots the size of beach balls that are six inches apart" (Hornbeck, Cain, and Heinlein 2002: 1).

Following the House and Senate votes on the concurrent casino resolution, public attention shifted to Gov. Engler, a term-limited executive serving his last two weeks in office. Most observers expected Engler to sign the resolution both because he had previously indicated that a casino compact would benefit the state and because of his close political ties to the Mt. Pleasant triumvirate. As December 2002 drew to a close, some casino opponents hoped that the governor might choose not to sign the resolution. Sen. Van Regenmorter expressed such hope: "I think there's a chance he might not sign it . . . I know he has been getting a lot of phone calls in opposition from a pretty broad spectrum of people." Similarly, Rep. Birkholz stated: "I know there is a fair amount of pressure on him. A lot of people have been very upset by this," and noted: "He has several other contentious issues on his desk" (Tunison 2002: A20).

Gov. Engler chose to end the suspense with a last-minute (December 30) letter to Majority Leader DeGrow and Speaker Johnson in which he stated his belief that not only would a casino compact be in the state's best interest but that, in any case, under federal law there was little the state could do to prevent the establishment of the casino. According to Engler, "The reality is that the Gun Lake Tribe will inevitably open a casino" (Engler 2002: 5). Nevertheless, Engler stated that he would refuse to sign the resolution because of public perception that he had participated in unsavory dealings with legislators and the Mt. Pleasant triumvirate to push through the casino. The governor explained: "My history with these men from Mt. Pleasant and their relatively recent involvement in the efforts of the Gun Lake Tribe has led to whispers, inaccurate accusations, and speculation about my role with respect to the compact. Contrary to claims that have been made, neither I nor anyone in my administration was involved in negotiating the Gun Lake Tribe's compact, securing votes for its passage, or has any financial interest whatsoever in the tribe's casino venture" (Engler 2002: 6).

Engler's surprising refusal to sign the resolution left incoming Democratic Governor Jennifer Granholm with a difficult problem. In his parting letter, Gov. Engler had urged Granholm to sign the resolution. Nevertheless, some legislators believed that an unsigned concurrent resolution becomes null and void at the end of a legislative session, possibly making Granholm's signature ineffective (Roelofs 2003). Even if that were not the case, some observers thought it would be unwise for the new Democratic Governor, who had won a narrow victory the previous November, to alienate large blocks of West Michigan legislators and voters, particularly in a year in which the state was facing a major budget deficit. The governor's immediate response was to delay action on the issue, pending further study (Roelofs 2003).

These decisions of Govs. Engler and Granholm regarding the casino compact seemed to spark renewed anti-casino activity on the part of people of faith in the Allegan County area. Sen. Kuipers, for example, had complained that "pastors don't seem to be against gambling anymore" and noted that "churches engaged late in opposing the casino" (Kuipers 2003). Nonetheless, Rep. Sheen, who also had been disappointed at the early lack of church mobilization on the casino issue, now saw serious church activity, noting that "hundreds" of "CasiNO" signs had sprouted in church lawns throughout the area. According to Sheen, "most churches don't like taking positions on social issues but they did on this one" (Sheen 2003).

Among Allegan area clergy, sentiment proved to be overwhelmingly against the proposed casino. As Table 2.1 reveals, among the eighty-one Allegan area ministers who gave their views on the casino issue, fully 89 percent either "opposed" or "strongly opposed" the Wayland casino. In contrast, only 5 percent expressed either "support" or "strong support" for the casino. Table 2.1 also reports the (median) ministers' estimates of their congregants' attitudes toward the proposed casino, with the data suggesting that the responding ministers saw little difference between their congregants' attitudes and their own.

Contrary to the assertions of Band Chairman Sprague, most of the opposition did not come from Christian Reformed congregations;

Table 2.1

Clergy and Estimated Congregant Opinions on the Proposed Wayland Casino

Opinion	Allegan Area Clergy Self-Reported Opinion	Clergy Estimate of Congregant Opinion (median %)
Strongly Support	1%	0%
Support	4	2
Uncertain	6	5
Oppose	24	40
Strongly Oppose	65	40
N	81	71

Source: Allegan area casino survey, 2001.

rather, opposition was spread across more than twenty different denominations. While the largest single group of anti-casino clergy responding to our survey was Christian Reformed (26 percent), at least nineteen other denominations were involved, including United Methodist (12 percent), non-denominational (12 percent), Reformed Church in America (11 percent), Baptist (7 percent), Assemblies of God (5 percent), Lutheran (5 percent), and Wesleyan (4 percent).

Not only did the Allegan area clergy tend to express strong opposition to the casino, they also reported that they had engaged in a wide variety of casino-related political activities. From Table 2.2, we see that the activities in which they most frequently engaged fell in the "church-related activities" category. For example, fully 68 percent of the responding clergy indicated that they had discussed the casino proposal with their congregants and 35 percent indicated that they had included the proposal in a sermon. This approach is understandable in that clergy spend the bulk of their workday at church and/or interacting with congregants. On the other hand, "non-church-related" activities" proved somewhat less common among the clergy surveyed, although clergy engagement in certain types of activities was also relatively frequent. The most frequently reported non-church activities were writing a letter to a public official (29 percent), speaking with a public official (28 percent), and working with an "outside" organization (22 percent).

In order to further clarify the sources of clergy activity regarding the casino, Allegan County clergy were divided into three roughly equal groups representing (1) conservative and/or fundamentalist denominations, (2) mainline Protestant or Catholic denominations, and (3) Christian Reformed and Reformed Church in America (CRC/RCA) denominations.[8] Table 2.2 reports the casino-related political activities of each group. There we see that clergy from conservative/fundamentalist denominations led the charge, proving far more likely than their mainline Protestant or CRC/RCA counterparts to engage in almost every type of political activity examined. Perhaps reflecting the moral zeal of their nineteenth-century predecessors, these clergy reported that they had frequently engaged in such actions as discussing the proposal with their congregants (73 percent), preaching a sermon on the casino (47 percent), writing a letter to a public official (43 percent), or circulating a petition (41 percent). Mainline clergy proved somewhat less likely than their conservative counterparts to engage in most types of political activities. Per-

Table 2.2

Percentage of Allegan Area Clergy Engaging in Casino-Related Political Activities by Denominational Category

Political Activity	Conservative/ Fundamentalist	Mainline/ Catholic	CRC/RCA	Total
Church-Related Activities				
Discussed the proposal with congregants	73%	68	61	68
Included the proposal in a sermon	47	20	32	35
Formed a church discussion group	10	20	3	10
Non-Church Activities				
Wrote a letter to a public official	43	19	23	29
Spoke to a public official	33	30	7	28
Worked with "outside" organization	37	24	7	22
Circulated a petition	41	10	10	21
Attended an informational meeting	33	10	21	
Contributed money	21	5	3	10
Wrote a letter to a newspaper	10	10	3	7
(N)	(30)	(22)	(31)	(83)

Source: Allegan area clergy survey, 2003.

haps surprisingly, CRC/RCA clergy tended to be the least politically engaged in the casino controversy. One can only speculate why CRC/RCA clergy proved to be the least politically engaged, but it may in part reflect the pietism of clergy from those denominations. Previous research (Smidt and Penning 2004) has indicated both that CRC and RCA clergy have recently demonstrated a declining interest in political activity and that they tend to place a higher emphasis on sanctification and evangelism than on cultural transformation.

Ministers were not the only church members involved in the casino controversy. Indeed, the ministers surveyed reported receiving large numbers of contacts from their congregants regarding the proposed casino, with most of the contacts coming from casino opponents. For example, Table 2.3 reports that the vast majority of responding ministers (86 percent) reported receiving no contacts from congregants who were casino supporters and only a small minority (4 percent) reported receiving more than ten contacts from supporters. In contrast, congregant contacts opposing the casino proved far more frequent. While 28 percent of the ministers reported receiving no supporting contacts from congregants, 25 percent reported receiving more than ten supporting contacts.

On January 12, 2003, the Allegan Ministerial Alliance, a group of about eighteen ministers, held an anti-casino meeting at Christ Community Church in the city of Allegan. The meeting included not only clergy and congregants but also state legislators and Dr. Rex Rogers, president of Cornerstone University (and author of a noted anti-gambling book). At the meeting, the ministers voted unanimously to appeal to local and state government officials to block the Wayland casino. "This issue has been on our hearts and minds for a long time," said Pastor Patrick White of Christ Community Church. According to White, "We decided we needed to make some noise" (Meehan 2003: D4).

One upshot of the gathering was that clergy met with elected officials, including Sen. Birkholz and Rep. Sheen, in an effort to mobilize anti-casino forces. Sen. Birkholz was given a letter of clergy opposition and asked to hand-deliver it to Gov. Granholm.[9] In addi-

Table 2.3

Congregant Contacts with Clergy Regarding the Casino and the Direction of those Contacts

Clergy Estimate of the Number of Congregant Contacts Regarding the Casino	Supporting the Casino	Opposing the Casino
0	86%	28
1–5	6	21
6–10	3	16
11–50	4	25
N	80	75

Source: Allegan area clergy survey, 2003.

tion, the ministers lobbied the Allegan County Commission. "I hope (county board members) take a stand against the casino," said the Rev. Joe Phipps, president of the Ministerial Association and pastor of the First Presbyterian Church in Allegan (Meehan 2003: D4). Nevertheless, County Board Chairman Jon Campbell said that the Board had not taken a position on the issue because, in his opinion, casino issues are the province of state and federal, not county, governments (Meehan 2003).

Perhaps belatedly, the local religious community began to mobilize itself in other ways as well. Bulletin announcements appeared in dozens of churches, asking congregants to write public officials and pray for the defeat of the Wayland casino (Kooiman 2003). In addition, as noted previously, petitions were circulated in the churches, with literally thousands of congregants adding their signatures to anti-casino petitions (Boorsma 2003; Sheen 2003).

Furthermore, a limited but noteworthy number of congregational governing boards took action to help block the proposed casino. As Table 2.4 indicates, 15 percent of the ministers responding to our clergy survey reported that their congregation's governing board had passed an official resolution opposing the casino. Virtually none reported that their board had officially endorsed the casino. Far less common among governing boards were such actions as sponsoring a letter-writing campaign, permitting the circulation of petitions, or permitting the use of church facilities for anti-casino rallies. Nonetheless, even these relatively low levels of activity may

Table 2.4

Church Governing Board Activity in Opposition to the Casino

Type of Activity	Percent	N
Official resolution opposing casino	15	13
Letter-writing campaign	4	3
Permitted circulation of petition	4	3
Called for prayers against casino	1	1
Discussion of casino after worship service	1	1
Permitted use of facilities for rally	1	1

Source: Allegan area clergy survey, 2003.
Note: There was no official governing board support for the casino among respondents.

be viewed as significant, given that many of the Allegan churches stem from the fundamentalist and evangelical Protestant traditions which have frequently looked askance at the involvement of official governing boards in "political" issues. The patterns noted above concerning the varied degree of political activity among clergy from different religious traditions also seems to characterize the decisions of governing boards, although the small "N's" involved make it difficult to draw firm conclusions. Nearly one-fourth of the governing boards of conservative/fundamentalist churches officially opposed the proposed casino (data not shown). In contrast, only small percentages of mainline churches (9 percent) or CRC/RCA churches (7 percent) took official stands regarding the casino.

It is important to note, however, that while clergy and congregants from most local churches tended to oppose the casino, not all did. MichGO's President Boorsma, for example, complained that a few local churches refused to include anti-casino announcements in their bulletins (Boorsma 2003). Sen. Kuipers noted that a few churches actually sponsored church outings for senior citizens to area casinos, a practice hardly compatible with anti-casino zeal (Kuipers 2003). These churches, however, constituted only a small minority of the area religious community. According to Rep. Kooiman, church involvement in the casino controversy varied greatly, with those congregations located nearest to the proposed site tending to be the most actively involved in the anti-casino movement (Kooiman 2003).

Over time, the casino controversy tended to foster increased cooperation, not only within the local religious community, but also between local churches and "outside" groups—both religious and non-religious. In February of 2003, for example, the Grand Rapids Area Chamber of Commerce formed a coalition, the Community Partnership for Economic Growth, designed to help fight the Wayland casino. The group included a variety of local political and economic heavyweights, including eleven state legislators and prominent businesspersons. Perhaps symbolizing the growing partnership between political, economic, and religious leadership, the new group was collectively headed by Helen Brinkman, a Kent County assistant prosecutor, Mark Jandernoa, a local businessperson, and the Rev. Robert Dean, Grand Rapids city commissioner and pastor of New Life Church of God in Christ (Kirkbride 2003: A6).

The Allegan County religious community also sought support from "outside" groups. According to Rep. Kooiman, for example, an appeal was sent to churches in surrounding counties for help in pursing the fight. In addition, former Michigan Rep. Harold Voorhees, a public relations officer with a Lansing-based Christian Right group, Citizens for Traditional Values (CTV), helped to get that organization involved in the movement. Voorhees worked with Boorsma in the effort, getting him to speak at several CTV meetings. While CTV did not specifically involve itself in the Wayland controversy, it did distribute "thousands of bulletin inserts," produced by the Michigan Department of Public Health, warning of the dangers of gambling (Voorhees 2003).

Perhaps the organization which played the most important role in coordinating the efforts of churches and other organizations was Boorsma's MichGO. Early in the casino controversy, Boorsma's organization invited Tom Grey, head of the Chicago-based National Coalition Against Legalized Gambling, to speak and provide organizational direction. In addition, MichGO worked closely with the culturally conservative Michigan Family Forum (Boorsma 2003).

Throughout the year 2004, the casino issue remained unresolved. All eyes were focused on four political venues. First, participants in the casino controversy awaited the casino compact decision of Gov. Granholm, who had stated her personal opposition to gaming during the 2002 election campaign and had delayed signing a compact for nearly two years. Second, participants in the controversy awaited the decision of the U.S. Department of Interior on the Band's request to place the Wayland land in trust. Third, participants continued to look to the courts for resolution on a number of legal issues, including the validity of unsigned concurrent legislative resolutions. Finally, in an ironic twist, participants speculated about the possibility that the state legislature might revisit the casino issue during the 2004 lame-duck session.

Like the seemingly interminable case of Jarndyce and Jarndyce (J&J) in Dickens's *Bleak House*, the casino dispute has dragged on with no final resolution in sight but with a variety of unexpected developments. In March 2004, casino backers were elated when the U.S. Department of Interior ruled that the casino would have "no significant environmental impact on the land set aside for the casino," thus paving the way for a possible decision to take the land in trust (Knape 2004b: A1). Sprague was elated, calling the decision "historic."

Said Sprague, "After three years of exhaustive studies and hundreds of pages of documentation, we are very pleased with this decision" (Knape 2004b: A1).

Casino opponents, of course, saw the situation differently. Boorsma blasted the federal ruling as shortsighted (Knape 2004b: A6). Furthermore, opponents redoubled their political activity, forming a new PAC, "23 Is Enough," aimed at stopping the Wayland project and capping the number of casinos in Michigan at twenty-three. The new organization attracted a Who's Who list of prominent local backers, including former President Gerald Ford, former U.S. Ambassador to Italy Peter Secchia, Amway (now Alticor) Corporation cofounder Richard DeVos, and former Perrigo Corporation chairman Michael Jandernoa (Hogan 2004a). The PAC set an initial goal of raising $150,000 to fight casino expansion and succeeded in raising approximately half that amount in short order (Knape 2004a). "23 Is Enough" also sent out questionnaires with four "gaming" questions to virtually every (state) House candidate in Michigan, with the goal of making endorsements before the August primary election (Hogan 2004a: 3).

While casino advocates tended to emphasize economic arguments, opponents continued to utilize a combination of economic and moral appeals. Some backers of "23 Is Enough," including Ambassador Secchia, for example, stressed "the adverse economic impact of the proposed Allegan casino" (Hogan 2004a). On the other hand, former Grand Rapids Mayor John Logie expressed worries about people "living 'close to the edge' who might be impoverished by casino gambling" (Knape 2004a: 3). Others expressed concerns over reports that Station Casinos, the Las Vegas-based investor in the Wayland Casino had recently agreed to pay $38 million to settle a lawsuit alleging improper dealings in Missouri. Jandernoa complained, "We would be getting Las Vegas money in here and by the looks of it, it's not West Michigan. West Michigan is a community based on ethics" (Roelofs 2004a: B1–B2).

The fall 2004 election added a new and important dimension to the Allegan casino controversy when Michigan voters, concerned over the rapid expansion of casino gaming in the state, passed Proposal 1, a constitutional initiative which requires that all new (non-Indian) casinos must be approved by both a local vote and a statewide vote of the people (Penning 2005). Proposal 1 attracted solid support statewide, receiving 58 percent of the vote. Support for Proposal 1 was particularly strong in West Michigan counties (including Allegan, Kent, and Ottawa counties) affected by the proposed Wayland casino, with approximately two-thirds of the voters in those counties supporting the anti-casino initiative.

Encouraged by this anti-casino vote, as well as by Gov. Granholm's delay in signing a casino compact, Michigan Senate Majority Leader Ken Sikkema (a Republican representing the Grand Rapids suburb of Wyoming) used the 2004 lame-duck session of the legislature to introduce a Senate proposal to rescind the Senate's 2002 approval of the Wayland casino. On December 8, the Senate voted 24–11 to do just that. The vote was conducted without roll call so that individual votes were not recorded (Roelofs 2004b).

To achieve this legislative victory, Sikkema skillfully orchestrated the GOP caucus in Lansing. Over soft drinks and catered Chinese lunch, Sikkema polled his caucus on the afternoon of the Senate vote. According to Sikkema, "The feedback was encouraging." Sikkema spokesman Ari Adler observed, "It was several things coming together. With the vote on Proposal 1, it was pretty clear that people in Michigan, and especially West Michigan, are interested in halting gambling" (Roelofs 2004b). Sikkema himself cited three factors in the Senate's decision: "This compact has not been signed by the Governor, an economic study was done that shows a negative economic impact, and the voters overwhelmingly voted to curtail the expansion of gambling" (Hogan 2004b: A4).

So is the Wayland casino proposal dead? Probably not. Jandernoa of "23 Is Enough" asserted, "We believe that the Senate action dealt a significant blow. . . . There has never been a tribal casino approved without support of the House and Senate" (Hogan 2004b: A1). Gov. Granholm's office was less sure about the matter, putting out a statement that "It's a complicated matter that is still under review by our administration." Sprague defiantly responded that "our fight for fairness is far from over and we will prevail." Sprague noted irony in the fact that "Senate Majority Leader, Ken Sikkema, . . . strong-armed this resolution through the Senate on December 7th, which commemorates the greatest of all sneak attacks" (Hogan 2004b: A1). While Sprague was off by one day, there was indeed a degree of irony in the Senate vote, namely, that legislative leaders had used lame-duck sessions both to approve and defeat the casino resolution. Undoubtedly, the tribe will continue its fight. Casino opponent, Peter Secchia, admitted as much, noting that "they have the money to make this rear its head up as many times as they want" (Roelofs 2004b).

As 2005 approaches, casino proponents and opponents await action from the U.S. Department of the Interior, Gov. Granholm, and various courts. In addition, the Michigan House of Representatives will likely revisit the casino compact issue during its 2005 session (Hogan 2004b: A4). Regardless of the ultimate resolution of the casino dispute, one thing is certain: gaming in Michigan will likely remain both a controversial and a permanent part of the state's political landscape.

Analysis and Conclusions

While this paper is essentially a case study of a single community conflict, its implications extend far beyond the immediate case at hand, providing important lessons about the role of religious interests in community conflict. Several theoretical perspectives contribute to our understanding of this subject. One set of perspectives that help us understand the role of religious interests in the Wayland casino dispute are theories pertaining to *group mobilization*. Political scientists have long studied political mobilization (Salisbury 1969; Walker 1991), although, until recently, few have directed their attention primarily at the mobilization of religious interest groups (Guth, Kellstedt, Green, and Smidt 2002). While the mobilization literature is complex, the general consensus is that group mobilization tends to be a function of environmental factors, including, most particularly, the presence of grievances or concerns, the availability of resources, and the presence of committed and effective leadership (Morris 1998: 2). As James Gimpel puts it, grassroots groups are often "formed from a complex mixture of widespread popular discontent and the political entrepreneurship of leaders who transform this discontent into the kind of pressure that will generate policy change" (1998: 103).

Clearly, as public awareness of the Wayland casino proposal grew, discontent over its potential consequences for the community grew. It is also clear that people of faith, particularly clergy and congregants from conservative denominations, played an important and growing role as this controversy progressed. Nonetheless, it was not always easy to mobilize conservative Christians in Allegan County, even in the face of controversy over an ostensibly "moral" issue such as a proposed casino. Indeed, the local religious community did not fully mobilize until the latter stages of the Wayland casino controversy. This finding challenges popular perceptions of religious groups as tightly organized, readily mobilized armies of Christian soldiers who are ready to attack perceived evil at the slightest provocation. In the casino controversy, the opposite was true; the religious community was slow to mobilize and difficult to organize and lead.

In part, this may reflect a natural tendency of clergy and congregants, particularly those from conservative, evangelical traditions, to avoid political and social engagement. As Daniel Hofrenning points out, "many—even most—citizens do not join a religious organization for political purposes" (1999: 1). It is therefore understandable that they might express "ambivalence" about church involvement in politics. In addition, for at least some of the local churches the delay in political mobilization may have reflected ambivalence about the gaming issue itself since some churches contained congregants who may have been supportive of the casino proposal.

In the Wayland casino case, however, the most important reasons for the relatively tardy mobilization of the local religious community relate to its organizational fragmentation and its leadership limitations. With the possible exception of the Allegan Ministerial Alliance, the local religious community consisted of a wide variety of congregations of disparate size, location, theology, and denominational affiliation. At the beginning of the casino controversy, these congregations had difficulty communicating with each other to discuss the casino proposal and to coordinate their actions. Furthermore, until the emergence of Rev. White of Christ Community Church in Allegan as an anti-casino leader, area churches suffered from a leadership vacuum which inhibited prompt, coordinated action.

In the second place, the role of religious interests in the casino conflict can be understood through the lens of *economic and morality politics*. It is clear that the battle over the Wayland casino was fought on both economic and cultural/moral grounds. As one might expect, with so many jobs and so much money at stake, individuals and groups differed over the proposed casino based on their perceived economic self-interest. Thus, for example, the Allegan Area Chamber of Commerce, seeing the casino as creating jobs, favored the proposal, while the Grand Rapids Area Chamber of Commerce, seeing the casino as a eliminating jobs (harming the city's convention, hotel, and entertainment businesses), opposed the proposal.

In this light, one might view the casino controversy as an example of "economic politics," politics involving clashes over money and resources. Students of interest groups have long recognized that economic interests (such as business, the professions, and labor) constitute some of the most powerful groups in America (Gray and Lowery 1992; Thomas and Hrebnar 1999). Moreover, since participants in economic conflicts frequently perceive their personal material well-being to be at stake, such conflicts may well generate considerable interest group activity and may produce a good deal of ill will among participants. Clashes between economic interests have a tendency to be social-class based, dividing participants along economic lines such as management vs. labor and/or rich vs. poor (Olson, Guth, and Guth 2003: 88). Yet economic conflicts may also be relatively amenable to compromise. Since money tends to be a fungible resource, clashing economic interests, at least under the best circumstances, may well be able to solve their differences through the give-and-take of the bargaining process.

The casino proposal also generated conflict over cultural (lifestyle) and moral issues. Some casino opponents, for example, worried that the proposed casino would lead to commercial and residential sprawl, threatening to destroy Allegan County's relatively slow-paced, rural way of life. As the casino conflict escalated, even greater opposition came from persons and groups concerned about the moral dimensions of gaming, including its alleged contribution to such social pathologies as alcoholism, crime, and family breakdown. Thus, people of faith, including clergy, laypersons, and allied organizations, played a central role in opposing the proposed casino. However, one should also note that not all religious interests opposed the casino. Indeed, as *The Detroit News* reports, the cultural and religious center of the Gun Lake Band is a Methodist mission church located near Wayland in the small village of Bradley (Heinlein 2001: 1). Moreover, as we have seen, certain non-Indian religious groups also supported the casino.

In this sense, the casino controversy may be viewed as a classic example of "morality politics," which involve "culture wars"-style (Hunter 1991) clashes over people's most fundamental beliefs, moral values, and norms of interpersonal conflict (Tatalovich and Daynes 1988: 1). As one might expect, religion tends to play a particularly important role in such politics (Meier 1994; Olson, Guth, and Guth 2003; Wald, Button, and Rienzo 2001).

As Wald (2003) points out, throughout American history conflicts over moral issues, such as abortion and school prayer, have often overshadowed economic conflicts, such as the distribution of federal funds or government regulation of the economy. Morality politics frequently produces fierce conflicts because participants tend to be true believers seeking to defend their basic values (Oldfield 1996). For such individuals, compromise is difficult or impossible since it threatens fundamental moral principles (Hofrenning 1999: 9). Morality politics lends itself to demonizing opponents; they are perceived not simply as wrong but as evil people seeking to corrupt society. Thus, morality politics has a tendency to foster simplistic argumentation (Olson, Guth, and Guth 2003), and politicians may be tempted to manipulate morality politics for their own ends (Wald 2003: 35).

As we have seen, the great Wayland casino war rapidly escalated from a relatively narrow, community-focused conflict into one with statewide and even national implications. Battles were fought in a variety of political venues, and the emotional tenor of the debate as well as the level of political activity seemed to grow more heated over time. A variety of reasons accounts for this escalation. One reason is that, like a good tennis match, the controversy lasted a long time, with each side scoring key points. On each side, hopes were raised and dashed with amazing regularity, leading to considerable bitterness and anger on the part of participants. Equally important, however, was the fact that the controversy contained elements of both "economic" and "morality" politics. As we have seen, the interest group literature suggests that each type of politics has the potential to generate considerable conflict between opposing forces. The Wayland controversy suggests that when both economic and morality politics are at work, a kind of negative synergy may occur, leading to the political equivalent of total war. Certainly, the casino controversy generated unusual alliances between economic and religious interests, leading, at the very least, to a wider conflict than might otherwise have been the case.

A third set of theoretical perspectives, which might collectively be labeled *interest group theory*, may also help us better understand why, despite the delay in mobilization of religious interests in the Wayland community conflict, religious groups were able to score some notable political victories. In general, this literature suggests that group effectiveness frequently functions as a complex interaction between structural factors (for example, political institutions), group resources, and the presence of countervailing groups (Gray and Lowery 1992; Thomas and Hrebnar 1999).

In the case of the Wayland casino controversy, political structures, particularly America's federal system, certainly influenced the activities and effectiveness of religious interests. A major reason for the complexity of the casino conflict is that it was fought both at different levels of government (local, state, and federal) and within various institutions at the same levels of government (legislative, executive, and judicial). Clearly, this analysis underscores the well-established view that federalism provides opponents of policy proposals with multiple venues for delaying and perhaps even defeating such proposals. It also, of course, demonstrates the importance of persistence in public policy-making.

The casino war also demonstrates that group resources matter. According to Thomas and Hrebnar (1994), group effectiveness is often a function of the availability of such resources as money, political and organizational skills of leaders, membership size and cohesiveness, lobbyist/policy-maker relations, and timing. Religious interests in the Allegan area possessed some, though not all, of these resources. For example, while area churches could not match the financial resources of the Indian tribe and its wealthy backers, they were able to pursue their objectives in a variety of other ways. Thousands of clergy and congregants signed petitions, wrote letters, contacted public officials, and attended a variety of informational meetings and public forums. Clergy preached on the casino issue and frequently discussed the issue with their congregants. On the other hand, one might argue that the anti-casino forces suffered from poor timing as their tardy mobilization, noted above, may have inhibited their efforts to organize effectively and mobilize financial and human resources.

Finally, the Wayland casino controversy illustrates the importance of interest group counter-mobilization. As we have seen, every escalation on the part of one side in the casino controversy seemed to produce a counter-escalation on the other side. Perhaps as a result, religious interests found it necessary to join forces with non-religious (primarily economic) interests. Indeed, perhaps the area churches were most effective when they were able to work in conjunction with secular groups—both non-profit, anti-casino groups such as MichGO and business groups such as the Grand Rapids Area

Chamber of Commerce. For the most part, these alliances between religious and economic interests were not planned in advance or formally coordinated. Rather, leaders of each type of group gradually recognized that they were fighting on the same side, even if their motivations differed. Thus, for example, while there is evidence that church leaders attended meetings of economic interests (such as Chamber of Commerce meetings), there is relatively little evidence of any structural ties between the two types of groups. Rather, the cooperation between moral and economic interests tended to be informal, based on personal relationships and ad hoc communication networks. Nonetheless, even this informal coordination proved remarkably effective, since legislators and other decision-makers found themselves pressed by constituent groups with two different but remarkably powerful sets of arguments. The combined attack proved difficult to resist, particularly among officials sharing the conservative values which dominate West Michigan. One can certainly conclude that even if the Wayland casino is ultimately approved and built in Dorr Township, the alliance of religious and economic interests can justifiably claim considerable success in delaying implementation of the casino proposal for three or more years.

Chapter 3

Sweet Land of Liberty

The Gay Marriage Amendment in Nevada

David F. Damore, Ted G. Jelen, & Michael W. Bowers

In 2002 the voters of the state of Nevada passed the second of two referenda (Question 2) required to amend the Nevada Constitution to define "marriage" as a union between a man and a woman. As a result, Nevada became one of a handful of states to amend their state constitutions to ban gay marriage. Since 2002, the controversy over gay marriage has become a new front in the ongoing culture wars (Fiorina 2005). Most notably, in 2004 President George W. Bush pushed the issue to the forefront of the national policy agenda by calling for an amendment to the U.S. Constitution to codify the heterosexual definition of marriage. Meanwhile, ballot initiatives in over a dozen states further sought to define marriage exclusively as a union between a man and a woman.

Against this backdrop, we explore the politics of the gay marriage conflict via detailed examination of the campaign to amend Nevada's constitution to prohibit same-sex marriages. Because Nevada was an early entrant in the debate over same-sex marriages, the state provides a useful case for examining the dynamics of the controversy. Indeed, factors central to the policy outcome in Nevada have proven equally important in subsequent campaigns in other locales. In particular, the case of Nevada allows three key points to be illustrated:

- Employment of the strategy of reactionary preemption (defined below) allowed opponents of gay marriage to succeed in defining the issue, mobilize support, and secure resources prior to the emergence of any organized opposition.

- The campaign to constitutionalize a heterosexual definition of marriage demonstrates the influence that organized religious minorities can wield—even in a locale well known for its libertarian political culture and in an era of increased acceptance of gay rights (Brewer 2003; Loftus 2001; Wilcox and Norrander 2002; Wilcox and Wolpert 2000).
- In contrast to some studies of religious activism that suggest religious particularism may limit the effectiveness of ecumenical coalitions (Jelen 1991; Reed 1994; Wilcox 1992), the same-sex marriage campaign was propelled by an alliance that included numerous religious particularists: Mormons, evangelical Protestants, and (in 2002) Roman Catholics.

We begin with an overview of the institutional tensions that exist among federalism, the Full Faith and Credit Clause of the U.S. Constitution, and the prerogative of states to define marriage within their borders, all of which have been key to the gay marriage controversy. Next, we move to an in-depth narrative of the initiative campaigns of 2000 and 2002 and conclude with a discussion of the implications that the Nevada case has for our understanding of the relationships among religion, politics, and group mobilization in an era of direct democracy.

Data and Methods

Given that our goal is to develop a comprehensive case study of the conflict over gay marriage in Nevada, our method is descriptive, and we rely on data from a number of sources. Prominent here are news reports of the Question 2 campaign as presented by the state's two largest newspapers, the *Las Vegas Review-Journal* and the *Las Vegas Sun*. These sources also provide information regarding public opinion on the issue and the salience (as measured by the number of stories, letters, and editorials) of gay marriage in the larger political environment in Nevada between 2000 and 2002. We also draw on material gleaned from the Web sites of both opponents and proponents of the gay marriage amendment, financial disclosure reports obtained from the Nevada Secretary of State's office, and materials (such as legislative histories) available at the Nevada Legislature's Research Library.

Gay Marriage, Institutional Tension, and Reactionary Preemption

The origins of the conflict over same-sex marriages are embedded in the institutional arrangements that structure the governing process in the United States. Specifically, the dispute stems from the power held by the states under the system of federalism to set the qualifications for marriages performed within their boundaries. This autonomy creates the potential that some states, but not others, could decide to sanction same-sex marriages. Consequently, because of the Full Faith and Credit Clause of the U.S. Constitution (which obliges states to recognize the public acts, records, and judicial proceedings of every other state), if even one state decides to allow same-sex unions, all fifty states would be required to recognize the legitimacy of those unions, effectively legalizing same-sex marriages.[1] From the perspective of opponents of same-sex marriage, the Full Faith and Credit Clause creates a loophole that would allow one state to dictate the definition of marriage for all states, even if most states have no interest in sanctioning same-sex marriages.

In 2003 and 2004 several state governments (most visibly, Massachusetts) moved to accommodate individuals who wished to marry a same-sex partner.[2] In response to these actions, opponents of same-sex unions have employed a strategy that we label *reactionary preemption.* The strategy is reactionary in the sense that opponents of gay rights seek to protect the status quo in the face of attempts by homosexuals to petition the government for equal rights and protections. It is preemptive because it establishes barriers that would protect against local-level policy changes if gay rights were expanded by governments in other locales.

Nationally, employment of this strategy resulted in the Defense of Marriage Act (Public Law 104–99), which was passed by Congress and signed into law by President Bill Clinton in 1996.[3] In 2004 the U.S. Senate began the process of proposing an amendment to the federal Constitution that would recognize only marriage between a man and a woman. Meanwhile, the House of Representatives took up action on the Marriage Protection Act, which seeks to limit the federal courts from hearing cases arising from the Defense of Marriage Act. At the state level, the politics of reactionary preemption have taken the form of legislation, ballot initiatives, and proposed constitutional amendments designed to codify the heterosexual definition of marriage.[4] In the case of Nevada, the ballot initiative process was used to amend the state's constitution so as to recognize only marriages between a man and a woman even though state statutes already defined marriage in Nevada as such (N.R.S. 122.020[1]).

The Ballot Initiative Process in Nevada

In a 1962 constitutional amendment to its longstanding initiative process, the voters of Nevada approved a bifurcated procedure treating proposed statutes and proposed constitutional amendments differently. A proposed *statute*, once it has received the requisite number of signatures, must be presented to the next session of the legislature. The legislature is required to take up this bill prior to all other measures except appropriations bills. The legislature then has forty days to approve or disapprove the proposal. Should the governor approve and sign the proposal, it becomes law. Should the legislature disapprove or take no action, the proposal is submitted to the voters at the next general election. If voters approve, it becomes law; if they do not, it fails. Any proposal so approved by the voters cannot be amended, annulled, repealed, or suspended by the legislature for three years. In cases where the state legislature disapproves a proposed statute, the legislature may propose its own measure to be submitted to the voters along with the initiative proposal. If both receive a majority, the one receiving the most positive votes in the general election is adopted (Article 19, Section 2, Paragraph 3).

If the initiative proposes a *constitutional amendment*, it does not go to the legislature. Instead, once the required number of signatures has been obtained, the question bypasses the legislature and goes directly to the next general election ballot. If it is approved, it is scheduled for a second general election two years later and must be approved in this election in order to be added to the constitution. Although Nevada requires only a simple majority for passage—not a supermajority as do some states—it is the only state that requires initiative-proposed constitutional amendments to be passed in two successive general elections in order to be ratified (National Conference of State Legislatures 2004).

Although the ballot initiative process was originally conceptualized as a mechanism for checking government power and infusing public opinion into policy-making, citizens and interest groups in Nevada increasingly are using ballot initiatives to circumvent the state legislature and create public policy unilaterally. Consistent with this trend, opponents of gay marriage used the process to constitutionalize a definition of marriage reflective of their preferences. It is against this backdrop that we now turn to an analysis of the successful campaign in 2000 and 2002 for Question 2, a proposed constitutional amendment banning same-sex marriages in Nevada.

Gay Marriage, Mormonism, and Nevada Politics

At first blush, Nevada might seem an odd venue for a battle in the ongoing culture wars. The fastest growing state in the Union long has championed the libertarian values of limited government, fiscal conservatism, and individual freedom. To wit, Nevada is the only state that allows legalized prostitution (in its rural counties). The state's dominant industries—gaming and tourism—have projected Las Vegas, Nevada's largest city, as an international party destination. Indeed, the Las Vegas Convention and Visitors Authority's official tag line of "what happens in Vegas stays in Vegas" clearly reflects a laissez-faire attitude towards behaviors and activities that may be stigmatized elsewhere yet coveted by many of the state's thirty-five million annual visitors.

Perhaps not surprisingly, Nevada is not a haven for marriage or traditional family units. The state ranks near the top nationally in the percentage of unmarried couples, and over twelve percent of Nevada's unmarried households contain children (United States Census Bureau 2003). Nevada also ranks fourth in the number of same-sex couples, with over five thousand lesbian and gay couples making their home in the Silver State (United States Census Bureau 2003). Because of liberal divorce laws that allow a couple to legally dissolve their marriage in as little as a week's time, Nevada has the highest rate of divorce among the fifty states: 6.8 per 1,000 citizens (United States Census Bureau 2003).

The transient nature of the state's population also hinders widespread political activism. Most notably, while Clark County, which contains nearly 70 percent of the state's population (United States Census Bureau 2003), gains upwards of twelve thousand residents monthly, over seven thousand people move out of the area each month (Clark County Demographics Study 2004). As a consequence, 30 percent of Clark County residents have lived in Nevada for fewer than five years, and just 15 percent of the state's residents over the age of 25 possess undergraduate or post-graduate degrees (United States Census Bureau 2003). More telling, during 2000 and 2002 fewer than 60 percent of the state's age eligible voters were registered to vote, and in the 2000 presidential election just over 41 percent of age-eligible voters turned out to vote (Nevada Secretary of State, Elections Department 2000).[5]

The disengagement of many Nevadans from politics provides an advantage to citizens and groups who are willing to absorb the costs and resources to affect political outcomes. With respect to Nevada's Question 2, members of the Church of Jesus Christ of Latter-day Saints and a group that called itself the Coalition for the Protection of Marriage were the driving force behind the campaign to amend the state's constitution to provide that "only a marriage between a male and female person shall be recognized and given effect in this state."

The political activism of members of the LDS Church and their resulting ability to push a statewide ballot initiative largely stem from the group's historically privileged position in the state. Mormons were the first white settlers in southern Nevada and consequently have played a significant role in the development of the state's economy, politics, and culture since the 1850s. Most notably, after opening the first Nevada branch of the LDS Church in 1915, prominent church members such as E. Parry Thomas quickly ingrained themselves in the Las Vegas financial community. In this position, Thomas and other Mormons proved influential in the development of the Las Vegas Strip through their control of local banking institutions (Willis 1998).[6]

Mormon economic influence in the early development of Las Vegas, coupled with the Mormon belief that its members should be involved in political, governmental, and community affairs, has produced a high concentration of Mormon public officials in the state. Indeed, while Mormons comprise 7 to 10 percent of the population in Clark County (as compared to two percent nationally), they exert a sizable influence on school boards, city councils, and county commissions throughout the state, as well as in the state legislature and in the Nevada delegation to the U.S. Congress.[7] As a consequence, the LDS Church has been able to affect and benefit from the flow of the state's ever-increasing development while remaining a dominant force in shaping community standards and values (Willis 1998).

The advantaged position of Mormons in Nevada also has served to minimize the backlash against the faith from other doctrinally conservative denominations. Although Mormons have not typically been accepted by many other Christian groups and have for centuries been the victims of intense and occasionally violent persecution ("Baptist Crusade" 2000; Ostling and Ostling 1999), the commonalities between Mormonism and other Christian groups provided the linchpin for amending Nevada's constitution to forbid same-sex marriages. Most notably, the leader of the Coalition for the Protection of Marriage, Richard Ziser, is not a member of the LDS Church, but rather is active in Canyon Ridge Christian Church, a nondenominational evangelical church in Las Vegas.

The 2000 Campaign

The wording of Question 2 and the subsequent campaign for its passage largely mirrored the effort of the Proposition 22 ballot initiative in California, which amended the California Family Code so that only a marriage between a man and a woman would be seen as valid and recognized in the state. California voters passed Proposition 22 in March 2000 with 61 percent of the vote. LDS Church leaders actively encouraged members to donate to the anti-same-sex initiative in California. Similarly, in 1998, members of the LDS Church contributed over $1.1 million to defeat gay-marriage proposals in Alaska and Hawaii (Jensen and Olson 2002; Willis 2000b).

Consistent with these efforts, the Nevada branch of the Church of Jesus Christ of Latter-day Saints threw its well-oiled grassroots fundraising machine behind the campaign for Question 2 (Willis 2000b). Although, as church spokesperson Will Stoddard explained, the LDS Church has "never held any ill will of any kind against those who profess to be homosexuals or have those tendencies," the church encouraged members to circulate petitions to qualify the amendment for the ballot, make financial contributions, and volunteer their time in support of the initiative (Willis 2000b). At the same time, mindful of its tax-exempt status, the church minimized its formal rolc in the initiative campaign by prohibiting the circulation of petitions on church property or at church meetings.

With the help of the LDS Church, the Coalition for the Protection of Marriage easily qualified the petition banning same-sex marriage in Nevada for the 2000 general election ballot. After collecting nearly two and a half times the required number of signatures, the petition was submitted to the Nevada Secretary of State for approval in mid-June and qualified for the ballot on July 7. Polls conducted in June 2000 indicated an easy victory for the amendment with 61 percent of the statewide sample of 637 likely voters favoring the proposal, compared to 30 percent in opposition and 9 percent undecided. Consistent with the higher concentration of Mormons outside of the state's population centers, support for the amendment topped 69 percent in rural areas. In comparison, 57 percent of likely voters in Clark County supported the measure (Vogel 2000). A second poll conducted in September indicated similar levels of support (Whaley 2000a).

Despite overwhelming support for the petition, the Coalition for the Protection of Marriage mounted an aggressive fundraising campaign. Through their network of churches and socially conservative activists, the group raised almost $750,000 by the end of August 2000 (Nevada Secretary of State 2004a). Their war chest swelled to over $1.6 million by the end of October (Nevada Secretary of State 2004b).[8] All told, the group spent nearly $1 million on the campaign for Question 2 during 2000.

Most of these resources were spent on an aggressive television and radio advertising campaign that sought to define the gay marriage conflict in terms of states' rights and the sanctity of marriage. The Coalition for the Protection of Marriage argued that the amendment was necessary to close a legal loophole that could require Nevada to recognize same-sex marriages conducted in other states, even though the state already had a law on the books mandating that only marriages between a male and a female were to be recognized. The group also used tag lines such as "Marriage: The way it's always been. The way it should be" and "Protect Marriage. Vote Yes on Question 2" to accentuate the traditional values frame.

Although Coalition leaders denied that their motivations were discriminatory, information gleaned from the group's Web page indicates that the Coalition was as much interested in combating the "homosexual agenda" as it was with protecting the heterosexual definition of marriage. Consistent with the politics of reactionary preemption, the Coalition's Web page notes: "we didn't pick this battle: homosexual activists and their lawyers filed the lawsuits. They want this issue decided in the courts, so that the citizens won't have a chance to participate in it," and accuses homosexual activists of venue shopping for "a judge who will rule in their favor" and "force same-sex marriage on the other states."

Additionally, the group argued that efforts were "being made to force the homosexual agenda of normalization and acceptance into our school systems nationwide." The group also contends that because the American Psychiatric and Psychological Associations and the National Association of Social Workers have concluded that homosexuality is genetically determined, "gay activists have politicized these three professional associations." According to the Coalition, studies suggesting a genetic basis for homosexuality "are not based on scientific research, but on an openly ideological agenda enforced by gay and lesbian caucuses" that "have been conducted by self-appointed homosexual activists, and their 'conclusions' have been puffed by the media."

To the degree that opposition to Question 2 emerged, it began to take shape in September 2000 with the formation of Equal Rights Nevada, a group consisting of about two dozen ministers of various denominations, liberal activists, and lesbian Mormons (Snedeker 2000). A variety of concerns motivated the actions of these individuals. Some, such as Rev. Valerie Garrick of the United Church of Christ, saw the amendment as unnecessary because Nevada already had a law defining marriage as between a man and a woman. Others felt that the initiative had nothing to do with the protection of marriage, but instead sought to constitutionalize discrimination that would result in second-class citizenship for gays and lesbians (Snedeker 2000). In arguing this point, Nevada ACLU director Gary Peck succinctly characterized the initiative as "anti-gay, derisive, unnecessary and bad for everyone in Nevada" (Rogers 2000). Still other opponents feared that the initiative campaign was part of a larger agenda that social conservatives designed to impose their morality on society (Sebelius 2002).

Equal Rights Nevada also gained the support of a number of religious groups such as the Clark County Ministerial Association and the National Conference for Community and Justice's Interfaith Committee (Willis 2000b). Perhaps most notably, Catholic Bishop Daniel Walsh, who oversees the Las Vegas Diocese, instructed his priests not to circulate signature petitions because, according to diocese Chancellor Bob Stoeckig, "[H]e was concerned that this particular measure would be used to foster ill will against homosexuals" (Willis 2000b). Later in the fall, the diocese issued a statement clarifying that while the Catholic Church perceives homosexuality as morally wrong and sees marriage in terms of a union between a man and a woman, the ballot initiative was a redundancy of existing state law that might result in a backlash against gay people (Ryan 2000).

Other religious groups, however, sought to downplay the issue out of fear of financial or member backlash. As Rev. Phil Hausknecht, a Lutheran minister who opposed the measure, explained, a "lot of pastors are afraid to make a statement about Question 2 because they are afraid of dividing their congregations and of losing financial support" (Willis 2000a). Indeed, Hausknecht noted that his decision to articulate his opposition to the amendment on discriminatory grounds did not sit well with some in his congregation and probably cost him some members (Willis 2000a).

Opposition to the amendment also benefited from the support of the typically conservative and reactionary *Las Vegas Review-Journal*, the state's largest newspaper. In 2000 the paper published five editorials or commentaries opposing the measure and only one supporting it. In the same year the *Review-Journal* printed over twenty letters on the topic, evenly split between supporters and opponents. Question 2 also received ample news coverage in the weeks leading up to the election, with the *Review-Journal* averaging about two Question 2 stories per week between the middle of September and Election Day. Consistent with the paper's editorial position, many of these stories were sympathetic to opposition forces and as such provided them with a forum to disseminate their message. The state's other major paper, the more liberally oriented *Las Vegas Sun*, also opposed the amendment.

However, because Equal Rights Nevada raised only $38,000 in 2000—equivalent to just 2 percent of the total raised by the Coalition for the Protection of Marriage (Nevada Secretary of State 2004d)—the group's ability to counter the Coalition for the Protection of Marriage's message of state rights and protection of traditional values was limited. Realizing that they could not compete with the Coalition's media buys, Equal Rights Nevada attempted to attract unpaid media attention by holding a series of news conferences and issuing press releases. The group also concentrated its efforts in Clark County, where pre-election polls indicated lower levels of support for the measure, and targeted young voters, whom polls indicated were more accepting of same-sex marriages, by linking opposition to Question 2 to a medicinal marijuana initiative also appearing on the ballot.[9]

Despite these efforts, the leaders of Equal Rights Nevada appeared to be resigned to their fate, a point driven home by a poll conducted in the week before the election showing that support for Question 2 had increased to 66 percent statewide. The five-percent increase was attributed to the Coalition's aggressive advertising buys in the weeks leading up to the election (Whaley 2000c). In discussing the failure of opposition forces to reduce support for the initiative, Liz Moore, a spokesperson for Equal Rights Nevada, suggested that the inability of like-minded individuals to coalesce, particularly in Las Vegas's gay community, was a function of the transient nature of southern Nevada life (Willis 2000c). Nonetheless, the group planned to continue and hoped to redouble its efforts in 2002. They were heartened by the suggestion of many analysts that the measure might prove to be the spark needed to politically mobilize Nevada's gay community (Willis 2000c).

In the end, Question 2 easily passed in 2000 with 69.5 percent of the vote, just below the 70 percent threshold that proponents of the measure hoped to garner. For opponents of the initiative, the only silver lining came in the form of exit polls indicating that a majority of voters between the ages of 18 and 29 opposed the measure. In contrast, 75 percent of voters over age 65 supported Question 2 ("Key Findings" 2000). Voters in Clark County, who had been the target of the bulk of the Coalition's media blitz, supported the initiative at a rate of 70 percent.

Although most analysts agreed that the presence of Question 2 on the ballot was likely to increase turnout among conservative voters (Whaley 2000b), evidence of the spillover effects of the initiative on other races on the Nevada ballot in 2000 was unclear. Most candidates competing in Nevada's state and national legislative races did not address the issue, presumably in order to avoid offending voters on either side (Kanigher 2000b). Exceptions occurred in a debate between candidates for one of Nevada's State Senate seats, in which the candidates were asked directly to state their positions on Question 2 (Kanigher 2000a) and to share their views on Reform Party presidential candidate Pat Buchanan, who had voiced his support for Question 2 during a campaign visit to the state (Wagner 2000). Only one candidate, Lois Tarkanian, a Democratic candidate for the Clark County Commission and the wife of former University of Nevada, Las Vegas men's basketball coach Jerry Tarkanian, publicly suggested that her defeat resulted from Question 2's mobilization of conservative voters who supported her Republican opponent (Packer 2000).

The 2002 Campaign

As noted above, the initiative process in Nevada requires that a proposal be passed by a majority of voters in succeeding general elections. This requirement helped to keep the issue of same-sex marriage on the state's political agenda through 2001 and into 2002. Most notably, the issue reemerged in response to the Nevada Family Fairness bill proposed by Democratic Assembly member David Parks. The proposed legislation would allow non-married couples to designate their partner as a "reciprocal beneficiary," thereby assuring hospital visitation rights to same-sex couples. In its original form, the bill gained the tentative support of Coalition for the Protection of Marriage leader Richard Ziser.

After the legislation was expanded to include inheritance rights, healthcare decision-making, and the ability of designees to make funeral arrangements for their partners, as well as requiring both partners to formally dissolve such arrangements, the measure drew the opposition of numerous religious organizations. Consistent with the politics of reactionary preemption, opponents to the legislation—most notably the Catholic and LDS Churches—argued that the bill created a legal entity that would be harmful to the protection and promotion of marriage; that it contradicted the people's will as expressed by the Question 2 vote in 2000; and, in the words of Coalition spokesperson Ziser, that it was a "backdoor method" for creating civil unions in Nevada (Hill 2001).

Opponents of the Nevada Family Fairness bill were able to fill the audience at the bill's hearing with over three hundred people. In response, the Assembly Judiciary Committee killed the bill. A similar proposal to extend domestic partner benefits to Clark County employees also was quickly scuttled. The only victory for proponents of gay rights in 2001 resulted from the decision of the state's largest and most politically powerful union, the Culinary Union, to offer domestic partner benefits.

By the spring of 2002, the issue's partisan underpinnings began to crystallize as both the Nevada Democratic and Republican Parties addressed Question 2 in their party platforms. The Democratic platform formally opposed the measure, while the GOP platform supported the ban on same-sex marriages in the state. At the same time, many well-known Democrats, including U.S. Senator (and Mormon) Harry Reid, voiced their support for the initiative, while prominent

Republicans such as incumbent Governor Kenny Guinn remained quiet. Also, in contrast to 2000 (when many politicians sought to downplay the issue), the issue of same-sex marriages permeated the debate in many legislative primary and general election campaigns. In light of the heightened attention to the issue, polls taken in July 2002 showed that support for the initiative had waned a bit, with only 55 percent of respondents supporting the initiative, 38 percent opposed, and 7 percent undecided (Riley 2002).

Not surprisingly, the Question 2 campaign in 2002 was a replay of the 2000 effort. Again, the initiative's proponents, the Coalition for the Protection of Marriage, were able to draw on their vast fund-raising network to increase their campaign war chest by another half-million dollars in addition to the $700,000 they had remaining from the 2000 effort (Nevada Secretary of State 2004b). In total the group spent nearly $1.2 million to disseminate its message in 2002.

In addition to the continuing support of the LDS Church and various evangelical Protestant denominations, in 2002 the group gained the backing of the Catholic Church—a move that gave further credence to the group's claim of ecumenism. As mentioned above, the Nevada Catholic Church opted not to support the measure in 2000 on discriminatory grounds, but changed its position in 2002 because by then it had decided that the proposal "would best preserve the definition of marriage held by the Catholic Church" (Riley 2002). In changing its position, however, the church maintained its concern that Question 2 might serve to generate hatred towards homosexuals: "some will use this initiative to advance attitudes that foster ill will against homosexual persons, their parents, and their families" (Riley 2002).

The primary opposition group to Question 2, Equal Rights Nevada, was able to raise around $75,000 in 2002, nearly double its 2000 take (Nevada Secretary of State 2004c). However, the group's resources again proved no match for the Coalition's media buys. As a consequence, in the months leading up to the November general election, television and radio airwaves and billboards throughout the state were filled with appeals to "protect marriage" and ensure that judges from other states did not dictate policy in Nevada. Unable to match the Coalition's spending, Equal Rights Nevada again sought to attract media coverage by holding press conferences and disseminating press releases to state and national media outlets. The group also gained the support of a number of religious denominations that saw the initiative as bigoted and discriminatory (Babula 2002).

In the end, however, Equal Rights Nevada's message, which sought to define the same-sex marriage issue in terms of equality and fairness, never gained traction. Nor was the group ever able to get Nevadans to analyze how the legislation would exactly protect heterosexual marriage. As a consequence, the Coalition's frame of protecting marriage and ensuring that Nevadans determine state policy defined the entire same-sex marriage debate. The only aspect of Equal Rights Nevada's message that seemed to resonate was the contention that Question 2 was part of a larger agenda that sought to impose the religious values of social conservatives on the rest of the state's population.

To this end, while Coalition spokesperson Richard Ziser was careful to focus his media comments on the states' rights and sanctity of marriage aspects of the issue, his actions behind the scenes gave credence to his opponents' claim that Question 2 was part of a larger, more divisive effort. For example, following Ziser's testimony that helped derail the "Nevada Family Fairness" bill in 2001, in 2002 the Coalition circulated a petition among candidates for elective office that reached beyond the scope of Question 2. The pledge sought to gain the guarantees of signers to oppose all spousal-equivalent rights for unmarried couples; to acknowledge that domestic partnerships, civil unions, or reciprocal beneficiary arrangements should be reserved only to married heterosexual couples; to support the belief that marriage is the strongest foundation for raising children; and to oppose any government recognition of "marriage imitations" such as civil unions or domestic partnerships (Morrison 2002a).

The Coalition also shifted the focus of its advertising campaign from an exclusively positive message to one that became increasingly negative. The centerpiece of the more aggressive message was a television spot in which the bride and groom who had dominated earlier spots were replaced with an image of a gloved hand holding a flashlight and opening a dictionary to remove the definition of marriage and replace it with something else. Opponents saw this advertisement as essentially equating opposing Question 2 to criminal activity (Neff 2002b). Later in the campaign Ziser further fanned the flames of controversy by circulating e-mails warning that if same-sex marriages were approved, the validity of same-sex relationships would be taught in Nevada schools, which some perceived as implying that same-sex marriage encourages pedophilia (Neff 2002a).

These actions earned the Coalition for the Protection of Marriage the scorn of many, including two of the state's most prominent political consultants, Democrat Billy Vassiliadis and Republican Sig Rogich. The two, who long have been active in Nevada politics and boast an impressive client base, jointly hosted a $100-per-person fundraiser for Equal Rights Nevada in October 2002. They decided to take this action because they saw the Question 2 campaign as fostering intolerance and divisiveness in order to increase the overall political clout of religious conservatives and their agenda (Sebelius 2002). Later, Vassiliadis and Rogich, taking advantage of their media appeal, publicly challenged the Coalition to support hospital visitation rights for same-sex partners, a move that Ziser dismissed as a publicity stunt.

The Coalition's Spanish-language advertising campaign also prompted the public opposition of Miss Nevada, Teresa Benitez, to Question 2. Benitez's involvement with the anti-Question 2 movement stemmed from a Spanish-language billboard that encouraged the state's large Hispanic population to "Protect *Your* Marriage" (as opposed to the English slogan "Protect Marriage"). Benitez felt that the switch in wording was intentionally designed to mislead and play on the fears of the Hispanic community. In response, Benitez cut a Spanish-language radio advertisement that characterized Question 2 as encouraging hate and intolerance, a move that also sought to offset the almost completely pro-amendment presentation of the issue in Nevada's Spanish-language media outlets (Pratt 2002).

While the efforts of Vassiliadis, Rogich, and Benitez probably had little effect on the outcome in 2002, their actions did provide opposition forces with a windfall of free media coverage. The willingness of the trio to offer public opposition to a ballot question that had passed with 70 percent of the vote in 2002 also indicates that passions surrounding the same-sex issue ran high on both sides. Unfortunately, this zeal translated into a number of nasty episodes throughout the 2002 campaign.

Most notably, "Yes on Question 2" signs were stolen or vandalized throughout the fall. The most egregious acts of vandalism occurred prior to the September 3 primary election when Question 2 signs and those of various Mormon candidates were plastered with "Mormon bigot" stickers or defaced with swastikas. Similarly, the garage door of one Question 2 supporter had "bigot" spray-painted across it. In response, Coalition spokesperson Ziser publicly blamed Equal Rights Nevada for the vandalism, noting that "the opponents of Question 2, who can't afford to put up their own signs, have to vandalize ours" (Neff 2002c). At the same time, a homosexual couple who refused to accept Question 2 literature subsequently had "faggot" spray-painted on their front door (Morrison 2002b).

In the end, despite endorsements against Question 2 by both the *Las Vegas Review-Journal* and the *Las Vegas Sun*, Question 2 easily passed with 67 percent of the vote in 2002. Although this margin of victory was slightly smaller than it had been in 2000, support for the amendment remained above the 60 percent level suggested by polls taken prior to Election Day (Whaley and Vogel 2002). As was the case in 2000, polling data suggested that undecided voters broke in support of the amendment.

Given the media and public attention that Question 2 garnered throughout 2002, many observers were quick to point to the mobilization effect of Question 2 as responsible for sizable gains for the Republican Party in Nevada's 2002 elections. Indeed, while the Democrats lost all six state constitutional offices and the race for Nevada's newly created U.S. House seat, none of these contests were particularly competitive. At the same time, Question 2 did appear to help Republican candidates running in down-ticket races that traditionally receive scant attention. For example, three candidates for the state's Board of Regents who signed the aforementioned pledge circulated by the Coalition for the Protection of Marriage won their races, prompting one victorious candidate to note that it is "hard to argue coincidence when all three who signed [the pledge] won their race" (Knight 2002). In one of these contests, the winning candidate, a long shot who was outspent by more than a two and a half-to-one margin, felt that gaining the endorsement of Ziser's group was crucial to his victory (Knight 2002). Indeed, all candidates who signed the pledge may have benefited from a mailer produced by the Coalition touting the names of candidates who supported the measure.

Discussion

In the above discussion we have attempted to provide a thorough accounting of the 2000 and 2002 ballot initiative campaigns to amend the Nevada state constitution to prohibit same-sex marriages. This analysis raises implications for our understanding of three important themes: the conditions under which religious minorities can dominate the policy process, the ability of diverse religious groups to find common ground in the face of doctrinal differences, and the consequences for group mobilization in an era of direct democracy.

First, it is not clear why such an amendment passed with relative ease in a state whose political culture is so aggressively libertarian. Although we cannot offer a definitive answer to this question, we argue that the lack of a clear connection to the tourist industry may be decisive. Socially conservative Nevadans tolerate gambling and prostitution in large part because the state's economy and the local economies of rural communities (in the case of prostitution) depend considerably on the availability of these activities for nonresidents of the state. Lacking an obvious connection to salient economic issues in the state, opponents of gay marriage were able to avert confrontation with the state's powerful gaming and entertainment industries (see especially Ralston 2000) and exert almost total control over the debate over gay marriage in Nevada.

Perhaps more puzzling is why the LDS Church became an essential component of a strong ecumenical coalition, given that members of other doctrinally conservative religious traditions have traditionally disdained Mormons. Indeed, despite the LDS Church's support of traditional moral values and its recent public relations campaign to be accepted as part of mainstream Christianity, many Protestant denominations do not consider Mormons to be Christians (Willis 1998). Moreover, several analysts have suggested that evangelical-Catholic coalitions are difficult to form and maintain, due in large part to doctrinal differences between the traditions (Guth, Green, Smidt, Kellstedt, and Poloma 1997; Jelen 1993a; Reed 1994; Wilcox 1992). The case of Question 2 thus poses a counterexample to the hypothesis that religious particularism limits the effectiveness of religiously motivated political activism. Doctrinal differences among different stripes of theologically conservative Christians have often inhibited the attainment of common political goals (see especially Wilcox 1992). The nature of the referendum process may have exacerbated the difficulty of forming a coalition of Mormons and evangelicals. Without an explicit partisan cue (which would have existed in an election between candidates), the aggregating effects of party identification were not available to ameliorate the potentially fragmenting effects of religious pluralism. Identification of Question 2 with a political party could have provided necessary cover for doctrinal differences among supporters. Given the non-partisan nature of the referendum process, Mormons' success in garnering support for Question 2 is all the more remarkable.

The LDS Church's success with the Question 2 matter is all the more noteworthy given the multiple constraints experienced by religious leaders who attempt political activity. For many (perhaps most) churchgoing Americans, religious denominations are not primarily political bodies; indeed, political activity on the part of religious leaders can occasion resentment on the part of the laity (Crawford and Olson 2001a; Djupe and Gilbert 2003). Such considerations are likely to be particularly salient within doctrinally conservative denominations, which are often characterized by an individualistic theology (Guth et al. 1997; Jelen 1993b). Obviously Mormon leaders in Nevada were well aware of these constraints and largely avoided formal or institutional roles for the LDS Church in the campaign. Similarly, the explicit use of coalitional framing (for example, naming the organization the "Coalition for the Protection of Marriage") allowed the LDS Church to employ religiously based social capital without occasioning countermobilization from within or outside of the Church. Moreover, it seems clear that Mormon Coalition members took pains to avoid having opposition to gay marriage framed as a "Mormon issue." The selection of the non-Mormon Richard Ziser as the Coalition's spokesperson was the most visible aspect of this ecumenical strategy. The LDS Church also cautiously avoided overtly backing the initiative and instead encouraged its members to support and work on behalf of the initiative campaign outside of the church context.

On this point, we argue that the substantial economic and political influence of the LDS Church in Nevada, as well as the church's role in anti-gay marriage campaigns in other states, led to the realization that Mormons were simply too numerous and too politically powerful for other social conservatives to ignore. As a consequence, it is unlikely that a coalition of Nevada's Baptist, Catholic, and other traditionalist denominations would have prevailed so easily in the gay marriage fight without the considerable resources that Mormons have to offer (see also Jensen and Olson 2002).

In the end, it appears that the proponents of Question 2 in Nevada learned to avoid the fragmenting effects of religious particularism by using their shared beliefs (including collective opposition to gays—a highly unpopular, visible, and salient outgroup—and widespread support for "traditional values") to formulate and sustain a powerful coalition. Indeed, the experience of Nevada, as well as subsequent initiatives in other states in 2004, suggests the possibility that gay rights may provide the common ground for successful ecumenical political coalitions among social conservatives.

The Question 2 ballot initiative campaign in Nevada also offers insight into the dynamics of group mobilization and information flows in an era of direct democracy. Perhaps because of its proximity to California (where initiatives are quite common and often well publicized) and its relatively easy qualification requirements, the process is being used increasingly to arbitrate a range of economic, social, and political questions in Nevada. While opponents argue that the process weakens legislatures and allows interest groups to control policy-making, proponents contend that the process is an indispensable tool for ensuring responsiveness, particularly in the face of legislative inaction. Consistent with this point, one constant theme in the Coalition members' comments was that they were simply exercising their rights via the democratic process—and that had the Nevada Legislature acted on the Nevada Protection of Marriage Act during the 1999 session, the initiative campaign would not have been necessary.

At the same time, using the initiative process to craft public policy ensures few protections for minorities, meaningful deliberation, or distance between public opinion and governmental decision-making (which was so prized by the framers of the U.S. Constitution). These concerns have even greater import when the delineation of rights is at stake and the group in question lacks the organizational acumen to mount an effective counter-campaign. Indeed, the decision of Mormons and social conservatives to use their influence to place Question 2 on the ballot shifted the onus to their opponents, who faced significant organizational barriers. Thus balanced group competition was unfeasible in this situation.

The resources of the LDS Church, while formidable, were certainly not unlimited, and the fragmented, individualistic political culture of Nevada undoubtedly contributed to the effectiveness of the Question 2 campaign. Political resources are more or less useful depending on the context in which they are deployed, and Nevada's political context clearly facilitated the success of a referendum campaign spearheaded by a minority religion. The transient nature of the population of Southern Nevada undoubtedly inhibited the development of effective opposition to Question 2. Put simply, many residents of the Las Vegas area lack strong social or organizational ties to the community, which in turn denied Question 2. The Question 2 referendum was a clear case of "minorities rule," wherein an intense, well-organized minority can have disproportionate influence over political outcomes (see Dahl 1956). In the Question 2 campaign, as in most other political battles, time, place, and circumstance were important to the final result.

When effective opposition failed to mobilize, the information environment surrounding Question 2 became a textbook example of John Zaller's (1989, 1992) model of one-way information flows: because the Coalition for the Protection of Marriage possessed the resources to flood the airwaves with its message, the information reaching voters reinforced the same attitude. Absent countervailing messages to neutralize the intensity of the Coalition's message, the potential for persuasion was significant. Indeed, the one-way information flow that characterized the Question 2 campaign ensured that the marriage protection and state's rights frames championed by the measure's proponents defined the terms of the debate over same-sex marriage in Nevada. Without sufficient resources to disseminate its messages, the opposition's counter-frame of fairness and equality never gained traction.

Given these dynamics, it is not surprising that aggregate opinion polls taken before and during the Question 2 campaign in 2000 and 2002 showed that undecided voters broke in support of the amendment, a point not lost on Equal Rights Nevada campaign manager Liz Moore, who noted in response to the Coalition's media buy that because "they own the TV airwaves, voters are only hearing one side of the story" (Whaley 2000c).

More broadly, while Question 2 may serve as a catalyst for political activism in Nevada's gay community, attempts to mobilize heterosexuals who support gay rights may prove difficult. Because the gay rights movement by its nature seeks particularized benefits, those who are sympathetic to but not part of the gay community may have little incentive to exert time and resources to secure outcomes that provide no personal benefit. Thus, it may not be surprising that same-sex marriage continues to fare poorly at the ballot box, even in situations where gay rights activists have the resources to mount an effective campaign.[10] As a consequence, until the political climate proves more hospitable to homosexuality, gay rights activists may have to settle for small legislative victories. To this end, in 2003 the Nevada Legislature quietly and unanimously passed legislation that allows unmarried couples to visit each other in the hospital and make decisions about funeral arrangements and organ donation.

Conclusion

As noted at the outset of this chapter, since the final passage of Question 2 in Nevada in the fall of 2002, the controversy surrounding gay rights and same-sex marriages has only increased. In 2004 alone, thirteen states addressed same-sex marriage via ballot questions (Lisotta 2004). At the national level, social conservatives in Congress, with the support of the White House, are pressing for an amendment to the U.S. Constitution to ban same-sex marriages.

At the state level, opponents of same-sex marriage have followed the playbook of the Coalition for the Protection of Marriage and the strategy of reactionary preemption. Specifically, in reaction to the perceived threat that same-sex marriages pose to the values held by social conservatives, anti-gay marriage groups use preexisting grassroots networks to coordinate the actions of like-minded individuals and raise the funds necessary to mount aggressive advertising campaigns. Access to these resources allows opponents of gay marriage to push the issue to the forefront of the agenda and effectively frame it to their advantage before any opposition can mobilize and offer a counter-message.

Also, as the Nevada case shows, using the initiative process to place wedge issues such as same-sex marriage initiatives on the ballot has important spillover effects in terms of voter turnout and agenda setting. As mentioned above, the strong performance of Republican candidates in Nevada in 2000 and 2002 in a state that is more or less evenly divided between Republicans and Democrats was due in part to Question 2. Indeed, perhaps not content simply to be a kingmaker, Coalition for the Protection of Marriage leader Richard Ziser ran unsuccessfully for the seat held by Democratic U.S. Senator Harry Reid in November 2004.

Chapter 4

Clergy and Controversy
A Study of Clergy and Gay Rights in Columbus, Ohio

Paul A. Djupe, Jacob R. Neiheisel, & Anand Edward Sokhey

"[I]f Issue 1 had not been on the ballot, John Kerry would have won Ohio."
—*Democratic strategist Greg Haas (quoted in Shapiro 2004)*

In 2004, voters in eleven states voted on various forms of a constitutional amendment banning same-sex marriage, and the proposals passed by comfortable margins in all eleven states.* Ohio was among these eleven states. Its voters passed constitutional amendment Issue 1, a measure pushed by the Cincinnati-based group Citizens for Community Values, which has a history of conservative activism in local politics (Bischoff 2004a: A20). Meanwhile, Ohio was the "Florida" of the 2004 presidential election campaign, so enormous attention and resources were focused on the state. Afterward, commentators credited Christian conservatives, mobilized in part to vote for Issue 1, with deciding Ohio for George W. Bush (Shapiro 2004; Zajac and Jones 2004).

In this chapter, we describe the constellation of religious interests involved in the Issue 1 debate. Although the presidential campaigns stayed away from the issue of same-sex marriage, just about every other organization seemed to weigh in on the issue in 2004. Therefore, we ask several basic questions: What links were interest groups involved with Issue 1 able to forge with churches? Did clergy engage the issue in and out of their congregations? In general, were religious and political interests integrated in the fight over same-sex recognition in Ohio?

We use multiple methods to reweave the tapestry of the Issue 1 campaign. Newspaper accounts are a crucial resource, as they documented elite activity and added perspective as the campaign progressed. News coverage cannot cover the full extent of grassroots involvement, however, which is the focus of our effort. Clergy can be critical nodes in wider information networks, delivering content from interest groups to their constituencies. Further, they can report, with some authority, the distinct perspectives of their congregations. And, of course, religious leaders have their own interests. For these reasons, we surveyed Columbus-area clergy. Details of the sample and survey procedure can be found in the appendix.[1]

Introduction to Issue 1

As the battle lines were being drawn in the 2004 presidential contest between George W. Bush and John Kerry, another battle was already raging within the swing state of Ohio—the struggle to qualify a proposed amendment to Ohio's constitution for inclusion on the November ballot. The amendment that later became known as Ohio Issue 1 was proposed by initiative petition:

> Be it Resolved by the People of the State of Ohio:
> That the Constitution of the State of Ohio be amended by adopting a section to be Designated as Section 11 of Article XV thereof, to read as follows:
>
> Article XV
> Section 11. Only a union between one man and one woman may be a marriage valid in or recognized by this state and its political subdivisions. This state and its political subdivisions shall not create or recognize a legal status for relationships or unmarried couples that intends to approximate the design, qualities, significance, or effect of marriage.

The 55-word amendment was authored by Cincinnati attorney David Langdon, sponsored by the Cincinnati-based group Citizens for Community Values, and backed by several organizations that labored to gather the signatures required to place the proposed amendment on the ballot. Langdon had been involved in Cincinnati politics for some time, often working with the Alliance Defense Fund (ADF), a think tank with a history of religious litigation. Langdon had filed an *amicus curiae* brief in a federal case involving the public display of the Ten Commandments (*ACLU v. Ashbrook* 2002); he had also been fighting to shut down a domestic partner registry in Cleveland Heights, Ohio. In early 2004, Langdon experienced a serious setback in his pursuits to put a stop to the registry when he failed to convince a common pleas judge that the registry stood in violation of the federal Defense of Marriage Act (P.L. 104–99; Galbincea and Theis 2004: A1).

Spearheading much of the effort to qualify the amendment for the ballot was the Ohio Campaign to Protect Marriage and its chair Phil Burress. A self-proclaimed former pornography addict, Burress underwent a born-again religious experience in 1980, and in 1991 rose to the position of president of the organization Citizens for Community Values (CCV), a "nonreligious, nonprofit educational organization that raises about $1.2 million a year from churches and individuals" to "campaign against pornography, promiscuity, and other elements it sees as a threat to the moral fabric of society" (Bischoff 2004a: A20). At the helm of CCV, Burress protested against the Robert Mapplethorpe photography exhibit in Cincinnati in the 1990s and worked to shut down pornography shops and strip clubs all over Cincinnati. Citizens for Community Values, which also has a lengthy history of combating what Burress describes as the "prohomosexual agenda," helped enact a citywide ban on laws protecting homosexuals from discrimination in 1993 (Bischoff 2004a: A20).

Despite repeated attempts by opponents of the amendment to keep it off the November ballot, Ohio Issue 1 became the only statewide referendum when it was certified on September 29, 2004. The last attempt by opponents of the amendment to prevent it from coming before the voters was denied by the Ohio Supreme Court on October 21. This last-ditch lawsuit sought to remove the proposed amendment from the ballot on the technical grounds that it did not include a summary of the issue as required by Ohio law. The decision of the Ohio Supreme Court was 6–1, with the only dissent coming from Republican Justice Paul E. Pfeifer (Johnson 2004a: 10D). With Issue 1 securely on the ballot, the battle for the hearts, minds, pocketbooks, and votes of the citizens of Ohio began.

A Profile of Ohio and Its Capital City

As the epicenter of a hotly contested race for the presidency, Ohio consistently has found ways to live up to the slogan that formerly adorned the state's license plates: "The Heart of It All." However, while the heart beats on, Ohio has not been in sound economic health for some time. Centers of industry along Lake Erie and the Ohio River have been shutting down, and once-booming steel towns such as Youngstown are now shells of their former selves. Once known for its family farms, Ohio (like many other states) is moving away from such family-oriented enterprises and toward corporate farming. Meanwhile, housing developments have sprung from the ashes of what were once family farms as the cities and their suburbs expand into rural Ohio.

The inhabitants of these rural areas share similar cultural and ethnic backgrounds and have resisted suburban encroachments upon their tight-knit communities. The most diversity in Ohio can be found in urban centers such as Cleveland and Columbus. Within Franklin County, home of the state capital, the percentage of white inhabitants is roughly 76 percent, compared to 85 percent statewide. Within Columbus city limits, the percentage of white inhabitants drops to about 68 percent. Columbus also has higher levels of education and per capita income than the rest of Ohio (United States Census Bureau 2005). In addition to hosting a more affluent and racially diverse population than most of the state, Columbus is home to a fairly large gay community. Citing the overwhelmingly conservative ideals that dominate in other cities such as Cincinnati, gay men and lesbians have moved to Columbus in hopes of finding acceptance. The emergence of Ohio Issue 1 as the only statewide issue on the November ballot, however, lowered such hopes (Thomas 2004: 1B).

Throughout the fall campaign season, organizations on both sides of Issue 1 worked to raise money and spread their messages. As of the October 21 filing deadline for reporting campaign contributions, supporters of Issue 1 reported just $50 in contributions, while opponents of the amendment declared $117,000 in raised funds. Among those contributing to the fight against Issue 1 were the Human Rights Campaign, a prominent national interest group working for gay, lesbian, bisexual, and transgender rights. Talk show host and former news anchor and mayor of Cincinnati Jerry Springer also joined the fight against the constitutional amendment (Johnson 2004a: 10D).

Groups on both sides of the issue raised money for their respective campaigns in several ways. They raised funds over the Internet and through door-to-door grassroots efforts. They also collected contributions from various organizations with vested interests in the proposed amendment. Although groups that lobbied on behalf of the gay marriage ban reported raising and spending few funds early on, by the end of the campaign, the Ohio Campaign to Protect Marriage reported spending a total of nearly $672,000 in its campaign for the amendment's adoption. The main opposition group, Ohioans Protecting the Constitution, spent $790,000 (Brown 2004: B3).[1]

Both sides raised and used funds to reach voters through radio and television spots. Radio ads urging Ohioans to vote for Issue 1's passage featured Ohio's Secretary of State, Republican J. Kenneth Blackwell.[2] Ads run by the opponents of Issue 1 focused on the potential effects that the amendment could have for seniors (Theis 2004b: B4), Ohio's economy, and unmarried couples. Such ads labeled the proposed amendment as "extreme" and emphasized the impact Issue 1 could have on all unmarried couples before ending with the ominous "It could hurt you" (Siegel 2004). Opponents, including large employers such as the insurance company Nationwide and retailing giant The Limited Group, argued that the law would negatively affect their ability to offer benefits to employees. Others argued that the gay marriage ban would create a perception that Ohio is an unfriendly place for business ("Why We Are Against Issue 1" 2004).

Despite this heavy television and radio campaigning, we suspect that the more significant contact with voters was direct. It was reported that Issue 1 supporters from the Ohio Campaign to Protect Marriage (OCPM) placed phone calls to 3.3 million households, playing a taped message from Secretary of State Blackwell that asked voters to support the amendment. OCPM also claimed to have registered 54,400 new voters and (importantly) distributed 2.5 million church-bulletin inserts to nearly 17,000 churches across the state (Siegel 2004). Such inserts asked voters to "protect marriage," quoting the book of Matthew: "For this cause shall a man leave father and mother, and shall cleave to his wife and the two shall be one flesh."

Indeed, religious leaders and faith-based organizations from across Ohio came out to pledge their support for Issue 1. Even though supporting a particular candidate running for political office can threaten a church's tax-exempt status, speaking out on nonpartisan issues, such as Issue 1, is permissible (up to a point). To encourage such participation in the advocacy of Issue 1 from the pulpit, groups such as the ADF assured clergy of the legality of advocating for the amendment. The ADF's analysis of federal tax law concluded that "unless a church has an extensive history of lobbying efforts . . . it is extremely unlikely that simple efforts to defend marriage, such as preaching about marriage, or making petitions available to be signed would be seen as a 'substantial' portion of church resources."[3] The ADF also made a more ironclad promise to provide legal aid to any church approached about their involvement in issues relating to marriage (read: Issue 1). Although it is unclear whether such announcements by groups such as the ADF actually spurred involvement among clergy in the campaign to pass Issue 1, many clergy across the state of Ohio did indeed publicly pledge their support for the amendment.

Many news stories noted the involvement of clergy in the battle over Issue 1. For example, ministers of several predominantly African-American Baptist churches in the Cleveland area spoke at a news conference on October 12 in support of the proposed amendment (Tinsley 2004: B1). Other ministers, led by the Rev. Rod Parsley of World Harvest Church, a prominent Columbus megachurch, toured the state in support of Issue 1 (Shapiro 2004: 6A). Both the Christian Coalition of Ohio and the Catholic Conference of Ohio demonstrated support for Issue 1, with the Christian Coalition making pro-Issue 1 yard signs available to voters through a network of distribution centers. The Catholic Church also stood behind proposed constitutional amendments banning gay marriage in Ohio and Michigan (Haga 2004). However, this is not to say that all clergy supported the amendment. Eighty-three ministers from the Cleveland area publicly announced their opposition to Issue 1 (Johnson 2004c: 1A). Nevertheless, the sheer volume of media coverage of clergy support for Issue 1 does seem to suggest that many religious leaders publicly approved of the proposed amendment.

Political leaders also took up public positions in the Issue 1 debate at various stages of the fall campaign season. The Ohio Democratic Party opposed the amendment's passage (Theis 2004b: B4); U.S. Representative Sherrod Brown, Columbus Mayor Michael B. Coleman, Franklin County Commissioner Mary Jo Kilroy, and U.S. Senate candidate Eric D. Fingerhut all spoke out against the amendment (Johnson 2004b: 1A). Issue 1 exposed a rift in the Republican Party, however. More than twenty GOP state lawmakers advocated the amendment's passage, but Ohio Governor Bob Taft came out against the amendment in mid-October ("Why We Are Against Issue 1" 2004). U.S. Senators Mike DeWine and George Voinovich and Attorney General Jim Petro also publicly announced their opposition to Issue 1. On the other side of the issue, Auditor Betty Montgomery, Treasurer Joseph T. Deters, and Secretary of State Kenneth Blackwell publicly pledged their support for the gay marriage ban (Johnson 2004b: 1D).

Not to be left out of the fray, many social and economic interest groups took sides on the issue, each citing different reasons why the proposed amendment could affect their interests. AARP-Ohio spoke out against Issue 1, reasoning that the amendment would hurt older couples who did not wish to marry because of the loss of benefits they would incur by doing so (Theis 2004b: B4). The League of Women Voters of Ohio (Bischoff 2004b: A1; Theis 2004a: T51) and many labor unions also announced their opposition to the issue (Theis 2004b: B4). The Columbus Partnership, a civic organization consisting of twenty-seven of central Ohio's largest employers, expressed concerns about the proposed amendment, citing the possible detrimental impact it could have on Ohio's economy. In the end Columbus Partnership did not officially take a position, although several members of the partnership, including the Ohio State University and The Limited Group, did formally oppose the amendment (Johnson 2004c: 1A). The university in particular feared Issue 1 because of the potential problems it might create in offering benefits to all of its employees.

While organizations and politicians on both sides of the issue mounted myriad efforts to present their ideas to the people of Ohio, several polls were conducted in an attempt to gauge voter support. From October 14–17, ABC News surveyed 1,072 registered Ohio voters, including 789 individuals who were identified as likely voters (Bischoff 2004b: A1). The results of the poll, released on October 19, showed that the race for the amendment's passage was indeed a close one, with 48 percent of those polled supporting Issue 1 and 45 percent opposed (with a 3.5-point error margin of error). The findings of this poll, however, were disputed since it had used a summary of the proposed amendment rather that the exact wording of Issue 1. Other polls, such as the ones conducted by the University of Cincinnati, the *Columbus Dispatch*, and Phil Burress (chairman of the Ohio Campaign to Protect Marriage), showed the amendment winning easily all over the state (Bischoff 2004b: A1). The *Dispatch*'s famed and respected mail survey polled 2,858 randomly chosen Ohio voters and predicted that the amendment would pass with 63 percent of the vote (with a 2-point margin of error) (Rowland 2004: 1A).

When the amendment was finally put to a vote in the November 2 General Election, the figure estimated by the *Dispatch* poll was remarkably close to the actual vote. Issue 1 received 62 percent of the vote statewide and went into effect on December 2, 2004. All but one county (Athens, home of Ohio University) passed the amendment (Thomas 2004: 1B). However, the vote was remarkably close in urban centers such as Franklin County (housing Columbus), where only 52 percent of voters favored Issue 1. In Cincinnati, proponents of the amendment tasted both victory and defeat after the election, as voters simultaneously repealed the city's ban on laws protecting homosexuals from discrimination (Spencer 2004). Not to be deterred, David Langdon, author and proponent of Issue 1, renewed his efforts to stop Cleveland Height's domestic partner registry, citing the new amendment as a new justification (Galbincea and Theis 2004: A1).

Precisely what implementation of the amendment will mean for Ohioans has yet to be fully determined since it will likely depend on interpretation in the courts. Already the effects of the amendment are being felt in ways that proponents of Issue 1 continually downplayed throughout the campaign. On March 24–25, 2005, charges were reduced in two separate domestic violence cases because Ohio's domestic violence laws contained language contradictory to the new amendment. Cleveland Municipal Judges Stuart Friedman and Lauren C. Moore both ruled that the language of Ohio's domestic violence law, which includes the phrase "person living as a spouse," stands in opposition to the amendment (Albrecht 2005: A1; Iacoboni 2005: B2).

Experts on both sides of the issue have speculated about the changes individuals and businesses will face as a direct result of Issue 1. Some commentators predict that Ohio's economy will suffer in the wake of the amendment's passage, while others maintain that it may bring new businesses to the state because of the family-oriented image that the measure purportedly reinforces (Spencer 2004). For the present time, businesses and universities that offer benefits to same-sex partners say that they will continue to do so until ordered to stop. The Ohio State University, Ohio University, and Miami University have all issued statements stating that they would go to court if necessary to retain the right to give benefits to same-sex couples (to date, Miami University has been sued by a state lawmaker—Johnson 2005). On December 2, 2004, the day after these universities announced their defiant stance with regard to the amendment, the American Civil Liberties Union led protests all over the state (Galbincea and Theis 2004: A1). Despite the defiant attitude of Ohio universities and some cities such as Cleveland Heights, Issue

1 represented a serious setback for gay rights advocates and same-sex couples across the state. Meanwhile, analysts for both political parties began to see Issue 1 as a crucial factor in Bush's victory in Ohio (Shapiro 2004: 6A).

Survey Results

We now turn our attention to what religious leaders in Columbus, Ohio were saying about the same-sex marriage amendment. In the fall of 2004, just after the election, we sent surveys to clergy of all of the more than nine hundred churches listed in the Columbus-area yellow pages. The survey asked about levels of clergy engagement in politics and the 2004 elections; it also asked clergy to describe the political tone and other attributes of their church and community. Thus, this sample of area religious elites can give us a sense of the degree to which religious interests are linked to clergy and churches, as well as the levels of political engagement among these clergy and churches.

Details of the sample (and its representativeness) are discussed in detail in the appendix, but we note here that our sample is certainly *not* representative of Ohio. To be more candid, the sample also may not be perfectly representative of the information church members were hearing in Columbus (since the unit of analysis for the sample is the church, which is not weighted by church size or the number of clergy in each church).

To begin, we note that Columbus-area clergy were almost universally highly interested in the politics of Issue 1. As Figure 4.1 shows, three-fifths of sample clergy report being interested "a great deal" in Issue 1, with only a handful showing little interest. Surely some of these clergy were interested because of Issue 1's central part in a national drama, its implications for the presidential campaign, and its intrinsic moral component. They may also show interest because the issue engaged their congregation, which, of course, may have been a result of their own efforts.

We asked clergy if issues of homosexuality came up for discussion in their congregation and why. Specifically, using a set of twelve source categories, we asked how such issues first came up and then what sources had motivated subsequent discussions. The results are presented in Table 4.1 (sorted by the source of the first generated discussion). Just a few clergy (14 percent) reported homosexuality never coming up in their congregation, but for most it did. Forces outside

Figure 4.1
The Interest and Involvement of Columbus Clergy on Issue 1

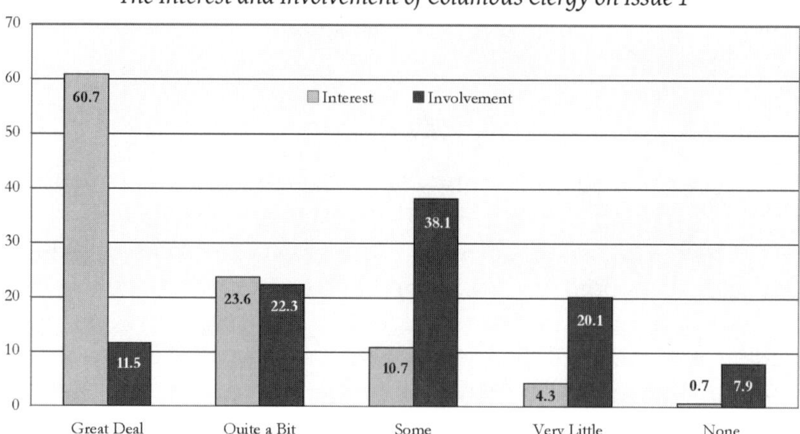

Source: 2004 Columbus Clergy Issue 1 Study.
Note: Interest: "How interested were you in Ohio's Issue 1, placing a constitutional ban on same-sex marriage?" and *Involvement:* "How actively involved were you with promoting, opposing, or discussing Issue 1?" Both coded: 1=a great deal, 2=quite a bit, 3=some, 4=very little, 5=none.

the church initially generated most of the discussion. A plurality of clergy mentioned denominational conflict as generating discussions of homosexuality in their congregation (95 percent of these are mainline Protestant clergy), with another 6.5 percent indicating that the denomination had advocated study of the issues. About a fifth indicated they (personally) initiated discussion of homosexuality, either by preaching (16.5 percent) or encouraging lay study of the issues (2.9 percent). About a tenth noted that "political events in the nation" led to discussion of homosexuality in their church, and very few noted that sexuality in the schools or public displays of gay pride first generated discussion of homosexuality in their church (1.4 percent and 0.7 percent, respectively). Interestingly, just under a tenth suggested that members' own sexuality generated discussion, either through a member coming out or struggling with questions of sexuality (5 percent and 3.6 percent, respectively); these instances are spread evenly across religious traditions. Evidently, some congregations avoided these issues until 2004, as 7.9 percent indicated that Issue 1 was the source of their first discussion of homosexuality.

Table 4.1
The Initial and Ongoing Sources of Discussions of Gay Rights and Homosexuality in Columbus Churches

Discussion Sources	How did gay rights and homosexuality *first* come up in your congregation?	What has motivated the discussion of gay rights and homosexuality since?
Denominational conflict	22.3	32.8
I preached about it	16.5	41.0
Has not come up before	14.4	—
Political events in the nation	8.6	41.0
Issue 1 in Ohio	*7.9*	*53.3*
A church study group	6.5	13.9
Denomination encouraged study	6.5	21.3
A member came out as gay	5.0	10.7
Member struggling with own sexuality	3.6	13.1
Homosexuality in the mass media	3.6	36.9
I encouraged study of the issue	2.9	19.7
Sexuality and the schools	1.4	10.7
Public displays of gay pride	0.7	20.5

Source: 2004 Columbus Clergy Issue 1 Study.
Note: Answers in the first column sum to 100, while responses in the second column do not since clergy were allowed to circle more than one category. The percentages in column 2 exclude the 14.4 percent that report homosexuality has not been discussed in their church.

The distribution of the source of the first discussion looks quite different from the fonts of continuing discussion (see the second column of Table 4.1), though they are also mostly driven by external sources. Denominations continue to encourage discussion of homosexuality, as a third of the sample clergy mentioned denominational conflict or encouragement of study (again, however, almost all of these are mainline Protestants). Clergy remain significant motivators of the church's agenda (Djupe and Gilbert 2003), as 41 percent said they preached about homosexuality-related issues; that figure remains high across religious traditions (results not shown).

Issue 1, however, is the most commonly cited source of church discussions of homosexuality (53.3 percent), edging out preaching, "political events in the nation" (41.0 percent), and "homosexuality in the mass media" (36.9 percent). "Public displays of gay pride" (20.5 percent) and "sexuality and the schools" (10.7 percent) also have fueled discussions in church. There is no doubt that clergy are interested in Issue 1 and that it has engaged a large number of congregations.

There are, however, at least preliminary indications that this interest did not translate into a tremendous amount of political activity. In results also shown in Figure 4.1, a plurality of clergy indicated they were only moderately engaged in "promoting, opposing, or discussing" Issue 1, although one-third said they were "quite a bit" or a "great deal" involved. Religious traditions do not largely differ in this regard (see Figure 4.2), although we sense that the issue is not engaging all clergy equally. In particular, and in a switch from historical patterns (Guth, Green, Smidt, Kellstedt, and Poloma 1997), white evangelical Protestants report the highest mean engagement score (3.5), while every other tradition is about one-half point or more lower on the scale. Mainline Protestants have the lowest self-reported score, and they are just the constituency that is, according to conventional wisdom, most likely to oppose Issue 1. At the same time, mainline Protestants may suffer from fatigue on issues related

Figure 4.2

Mean Clergy Involvement with Issue 1 by Religious Tradition

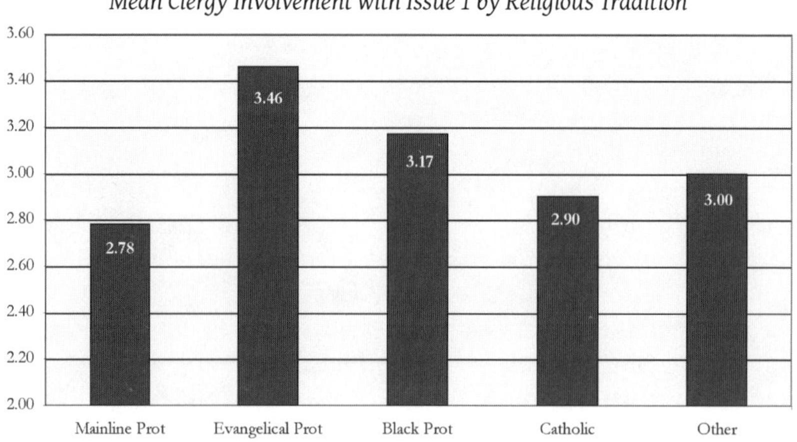

Source: 2004 Columbus Clergy Issue 1 Study.

Figure 4.3
Mean Clergy Involvement with Issue 1 by Partisanship

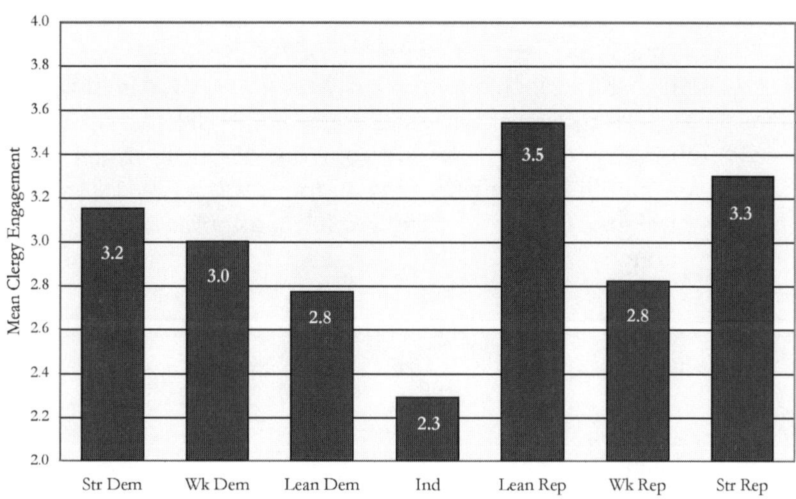

Source: 2004 Columbus Clergy Issue 1 Study.

to homosexuality, stemming from protracted and divisive denominational battles (see Cadge 2002).

Typically we expect strong partisans to be most active in politics, and Issue 1 proves to be no exception. Partisans, routinely the most politically interested and knowledgeable, are most often targets of mobilization from political parties and other groups with an electoral agenda (Layman and Carsey 1998; Flanigan and Zingale 2002). Figure 4.3 shows this familiar pattern, with strong Democrats and Republicans registering higher on the Issue 1 engagement scale (the same scale used in figures 4.1 and 4.2); Independents report the lowest level. Clergy who identify as Republican-leaning Independents stand out as the notable exception. Why these clergy are so heavily engaged is unclear. They are highly evangelical, but so are weak and strong Republicans; clergy in the other traditions are heavily Democratic.

The Interest Group Connection

Many interest groups were active on Issue 1, including some easily recognizable players such as the Christian Coalition of Ohio, the Human Rights Campaign (and their affiliated PAC, Ohioans for

Growth and Equality), and the Catholic Conference of Ohio, as well as some homegrown groups formed just to campaign for this ballot measure, such as the Ohio Campaign to Protect Marriage (for Issue 1) and Ohioans Protecting the Constitution (against).

We find that Columbus-area clergy did have significant connections to these groups, substantiating many of the claims made in the media. Table 4.2 presents the results of a question asking clergy (1) if they were familiar with each of the groups listed, (2) if they had contacted the groups, and (3) if the groups had contacted them.

Even though the sample over-represents mainline Protestants, it is clear from these results that conservative groups out-mobilized groups opposed to Issue 1. Most of the respondents (about two-thirds) were familiar with the Ohio Campaign to Protect Marriage and the Christian Coalition. It is not surprising that although many (approximately 42 percent) were familiar with the Catholic Conference, much smaller portions of the sample (a quarter or less) recognized the remaining groups, *including all of the groups opposed.*

Clergy initiated very little group-clergy interaction, as the second column of Table 4.2 attests. Instead, if there was direct contact, the groups were responsible (as the last column shows). A majority of the sample indicated that they were contacted by the Ohio Campaign to Protect Marriage, two-fifths by the Christian Coalition of Ohio, and

Table 4.2
Engagement of Columbus Clergy with Groups Active on Issue 1

Groups Active on Issue 1	Familiar With	Contacted Group	Contacted Me
Ohio Campaign to Protect Marriage	67.2	4.5	54.6
Christian Coalition of Ohio	69.5	4.6	42.1
Citizens for Community Values	25.0	3.7	21.1
Catholic Conference of Ohio	41.9	4.5	13.1
Ohioans Protecting the Constitution	25.0	1.8	12.3
Human Rights Campaign	20.2	2.7	9.0
Alliance Defense Fund	21.7	0.9	8.1
Columbus Partnership	18.6	0.0	4.6
Ohioans For Growth and Equality	12.4	0.0	3.6

Source: 2004 Columbus Clergy Issue 1 Study.

a fifth by Citizens for Community Values. Far fewer of the remaining groups, especially the groups opposed to Issue 1, targeted clergy.

There are differences among religious traditions, of course (see Table 4.3); but it is noteworthy that most of the clergy contacted by these interest groups were Protestants. By one yardstick, non-Protestant clergy received far fewer contacts across the board. Not counting contacts from the Catholic Conference, Protestant clergy were at least twice as likely to be contacted as non-Protestants. Non-Catholic, non-Protestant clergy received even fewer contacts. Evangelical Protestants received the most contacts from conservative groups, followed by African-American Protestant clergy and then mainline Protestant clergy.

Importantly, it appears that all groups made a major push for the backing of black Protestant clergy, a potential swing vote in a tight partisan battle. African Americans are longtime stalwarts in the Democratic coalition, and sample black clergy overwhelmingly identify with that party. However, African Americans are more

Table 4.3

The Distribution of Group Contacts within Religious Traditions

Groups Active on Issue 1	Mainline	Evangelical	Black	Catholic
Ohio Campaign to Protect Marriage	62.2	57.1	70.0	44.4
Ohioans Protecting the Constitution	15.0	13.5	11.1	0.0
Citizens for Community Values	14.6	32.4	22.2	11.1
Christian Coalition of Ohio	29.3	60.5	55.6	25.0
Catholic Conference of Ohio	2.4	10.8	0.0	100.0
Human Rights Campaign	7.3	5.3	18.2	11.1
Ohioans For Growth and Equality	2.4	5.3	0.0	0.0
Columbus Partnership	2.4	8.1	10.0	0.0
Alliance Defense Fund	2.4	18.4	9.1	0.0
N=	~41	~38	~10	~9

Source: 2004 Columbus Clergy Issue 1 Study.

Table 4.4

Mean Number of Group Contacts, Group Activity, and Issue 1 Politicking in Church by the Partisan Match of the Clergy and the Congregation and by Religious Tradition

	Group Contacts	Group Activity	Church Politicking
Clergy-Church Vote Match			
Kerry-Kerry	1.26	0.55	2.03
Kerry-Bush	1.28	0.31	1.67
Bush-Bush	1.45	0.23	2.10
Religious Tradition			
Mainline Protestant	1.00	0.41	1.71
Evangelical Protestant	1.77	0.21	2.25
Black Protestant	1.58	0.17	1.83
Catholic	1.70	0.20	1.50

Source: 2004 Columbus Clergy Issue 1 Study.

socially conservative than the Democratic Party at large (Calhoun-Brown 1997). Therefore, Republicans have tried to drive a wedge in this lasting partisan coalition, making the stakes of Issue 1 potentially far greater. The Ohio Campaign to Protect Marriage and the Ohio Christian Coalition contacted black clergy at the same rate as white evangelical clergy, and the Human Rights Campaign, a group opposed to Issue 1, contacted black clergy at two to three times the rate of other Protestant clergy (that is, 18 percent compared to 7 for mainline and 5 for evangelical clergy: see Table 4.3).

How strategic was this group mobilization? By targeting clergy, interest groups hope that their information will travel to the clergy's congregation. Interest groups should target clergy who will both be receptive to their message and then pass along the information to an agreeable audience. We try to assess this transmission in Table 4.4, which shows whether groups contacted clergy who agree with their congregation's politics. "D-D" churches (in which both clergy and congregations are Democratic) received the fewest contacts, and churches with Republican memberships received more contacts than congregations with Democratic memberships. Yet none of these differences are close to statistically significant; the difference between R-R and D-D congregations is not quite two-tenths of a contact. Clearly, groups blanketed Columbus-area churches instead of apportioning their resources more strategically.

Interestingly, while mainline Protestant clergy have the lowest levels of self-reported engagement, they display the highest levels of Issue 1 group activity; Black Protestants show the lowest levels (see Table 4.4). Mainline clergy show much lower levels of Issue 1 activity within the church compared to evangelicals, who are by far the most active in their churches concerning Issue 1.

The difference is not solely attributable to mainline clergy being more liberal than their congregations, although that does play a role. Liberal clergy in liberal churches (both voted for Democrats: "D-D") participate quite a bit more in Issue 1 groups than clergy in other political contexts, especially conservative clergy in agreeable churches (there were too few conservative clergy in liberal churches to analyze). But, clergy in D-D congregations were just as active in church on Issue 1 as R-R clergy. Only Democratic clergy in Republican congregations (D-R) engaged their congregations at reduced levels (these clergy are much more likely to be mainline Protestants).

Black clergy were the recipients of many interest group contacts, as noted above. Although most did not participate in the groups advocating on Issue 1 (see Table 4.4), black clergy did engage the issue in their congregations at the second highest rate—behind only white evangelicals. The typical Catholic priest heard from the Catholic Conference and one other group. But, for the most part, priests were not engaged in Issue 1 groups. They were also the least likely to engage the issue in their parishes, averaging 1.5 activities out of three possible.

Table 4.5 gives us further evidence to assess the efficacy of group contacts, which should concentrate on active sympathizers. It shows the correlation between being contacted by each group and levels of opinion and action of clergy. Several groups were able to hit the portion of the population most likely to be receptive to their message, especially the groups opposed to Issue 1. Of course, these groups had smaller war chests and needed to choose their contacts strategically. OPC, HRC, and the Catholic Conference contacted more Democrats, while the Christian Coalition and Alliance Defense Fund reached more Republicans. The Ohio Campaign to Protect Marriage, it seems, targeted everyone; so with our small sample we cannot confirm a trend in either direction.

Table 4.5

The Efficacy of Issue 1 Group Contacts: Correlations between Group Contacts and Clergy Partisanship and Political Behaviors

Group Active on Issue 1	Clergy Partisan Affiliation	Active in Issue 1 Groups, Past Year	Speaking on Issue 1 in Oct.	General Frequency of Issue 1 Speech
Ohio Campaign to Protect Marriage	-0.118	0.251***	0.126	0.067
Ohioans Protecting the Constitution	-0.204**	0.183*	0.026	0.076
Citizens for Community Values	0.018	0.380***	0.136	0.244**
Christian Coalition of Ohio	0.254***	-0.038	0.233**	0.224**
Catholic Conference of Ohio	-0.212**	-0.004	-0.242**	-0.106
Human Rights Campaign	-0.243**	0.351***	0.099	0.184*
Ohioans for Growth and Equality	-0.032	0.163*	0.099	0.151
Columbus Partnership	0.015	-0.033	0.044	0.040
Alliance Defense Fund	0.207**	-0.155	-0.004	0.143

Source: 2004 Columbus Clergy Issue 1 Study. *** p<0.01, ** p<0.05, * p<0.10

The relationships are clear with the other measures of clergy activity and interest group contacts. It is important to note that column 2 of Table 4.5 does not tell us whether the clergy were members of the listed groups, but instead shows the relationship between being contacted by the listed group and indicating activity in "local or statewide groups concerned with Issue 1." The results stress the importance of organizational memberships and issue salience when it comes to taking action (Rosenstone and Hansen 1993). However, the results also suggest that organizational action is different from going public with an issue of concern to a group. Although receiving a contact from the Christian Coalition is not related to being active in an Issue 1 group, it is significantly related to speaking about Issue 1 publicly in the all-important month of October as well as throughout the election year (see the last two columns of Table 4.5). OCPM and OPC do not share that pattern, however. Contacts are related to organizational activity, but not to public speech on Issue 1.

Of course, clergy and their congregations were concerned with more than just Issue 1 in 2004; they also desired to boost civic participation. Table 4.6 shows the extent of church participation in the electoral activities of helping to register and inform potential voters. The results are a bit surprising, showing that mainline churches were the least involved in voter registration. A majority of the other traditions were involved to some extent, and evangelicals and Catholics were the most involved. Church participation in voter registration drives was the most common in congregations with Republican clergy and congregants.

Table 4.6

Church Involvement in Voter Registration and the Availability of Election-Related Materials by Religious Tradition, Clergy-Church Vote Match, and Whether Issue 1 was Discussed (row percents)

Variables	Percent of Churches Involved in Voter Registration	Election Materials Available in Church from: Interest Group	Denom. Org.	Church Source
Religious Tradition				
Mainline Protestant	27.3	7.3	23.6	20.0
Evangelical Protestant	59.6	67.4	17.4	24.4
Black Protestant	50.0	50.0	41.7	33.3
Roman Catholic	80.0	30.0	70.0	60.0
Clergy-Church Vote Match				
Kerry-Kerry	50.0	24.1	41.4	27.6
Kerry-Bush	26.3	10.5	23.7	15.8
Bush-Bush	55.9	59.6	19.3	24.6
Issue 1 was discussed				
Yes	42.6	27.8	22.2	20.4
No	51.6	43.1	27.7	21.9

Source: 2004 Columbus Clergy Issue 1 Study.

According to the results in Table 4.6, electoral information is readily available in Columbus congregations, especially in those where the clergy and congregation agree politically. The coordination across religious interests is striking: most evangelical churches (67 percent) made election-related materials from interest groups available (and surely not those from groups opposed to Issue 1). Also, we only find interest group materials available in significant numbers of churches with Republican clergy and congregants (60 percent).

While we would suspect that mainline Protestant churches would have a heavier denominational presence in information provision, they rank quite low: only 24 percent made materials from the denomination available, which is just ahead of evangelical churches (17 percent) which typically have little denominational infrastructure. Black Protestants and Catholics report far higher rates (42 and 70 percent, respectively) of denominational involvement, which is not surprising for Catholics, but surely is for black Protestants. It is interesting to note how many local churches provided their own election-related materials to their members. In all traditions, the church rivals the denomination as a source providing information. Generally, churches avoid getting involved when the clergy and congregation disagree politically, perhaps to avoid further disagreement in the church or because clergy might not enthusiastically promote such an endeavor. Accordingly, homegrown electoral information is more commonly seen in politically united churches.

While church and denominational sources of information may be important to the political choices of church members, they may not help to build and sustain a wider movement to the extent that interest group-provided information might. Support for this notion is perhaps clearest in Catholic churches, which resisted becoming a part of broader political coalitions. Aside from the hierarchy and the pro-life movement, Catholic churches make much more use of local religious sources than external political ones (Ammerman 2005).

Discussion and Conclusion

This chapter has examined the intersection of religious interests in an important, highly charged issue campaign. We find that clergy are perfectly positioned to provide a glimpse of these intersections, as they are poised atop the most significant collections of religious interests: local congregations. They serve as an important node in the flow of political information to church members, but they are also targets of political campaigns themselves. Many clergy are highly engaged in public affairs and are keen and sensitive observers of their communities.

Addressing Gay Rights and Homosexuality

Overall, a sizable portion of clergy across religious traditions reported talking about Issue 1 both inside and outside their churches. Moreover, many clergy noted that groups involved in the Issue 1 debate contacted them. Thus, in some ways, our survey substantiates many of the anecdotal reports offered by the media about the involvement of religious interests in the debate over Issue 1.

Previous literature has established that clergy of varying traditions differ when it comes to addressing homosexuality. For example, James Guth and colleagues (1997) note that a high percentage of clergy in evangelical denominations (approximately 42 percent) report addressing issues involving gay rights or homosexuality either "often" or "very often" compared to the percentage of clergy in mainline Protestant denominations (approximately 23 percent).[4] A national study of mainline Protestant clergy by Paul Djupe and Christopher Gilbert (2003) lends some support to these earlier findings. They note that a sizable, though small, number of Lutheran (approximately 20 percent) and Episcopal (approximately 35 percent) clergy report addressing gay rights either "often" or "very often"; approximately the same percentages report addressing homosexuality. Our results for Columbus-area clergy confirm these findings. We discover higher levels of clergy engagement surrounding Issue 1 among evangelical clergy than we find among mainline Protestant clergy.

Clearly, however, the approach of asking clergy about their engagement on topics as broad and vague as "gay rights" or "homosexuality" has limited value, though it is a common and accepted practice in the literature (Guth et al. 1997; Djupe and Gilbert 2002a, 2003). Homosexuality may come up for discussion for a variety of reasons, each with its own distinct discussion dynamic. Essentially, the suggestion that speaking about homosexuality in general is a reasonable substitute for discussing something as specific as Issue 1 is off base, since discussing homosexuality could mean addressing either a private or a public matter.

General Lessons

The variety of religious interests involved in the debate over Issue 1, as well as the tight focus on a single policy question, allow us to contribute to several literatures, including those on clergy political behavior, political participation, interest group dynamics, and the church's place in the local community.

The literature examining the political behavior of clergy has evaded unity thus far, but seems to be approaching a consensus around three themes: clergy are directed by (1) their own goals, (2) the needs and opinions of the congregation, and (3) the place of the congregation in the community. Clergy clearly do engage in public affairs inspired by their own political goals and social theology (Guth et al. 1997). However, their actions are not solely, or even mostly, self-interested or self-directed. Instead, clergy engage in public affairs to represent the values and interests of their faith tradition and congregation (Djupe and Gilbert 2003), especially when their congregation is underrepresented in the community (Djupe and Gilbert 2002a, 2003; Olson 2000). As the representative framework would suggest, clergy can be limited in their public expressions by the political opinions of the congregation, as well as their sense of propriety in mixing religion and politics (Campbell and Pettigrew 1959; Djupe and Gilbert 2003; Guth et al. 1997; Hadden 1969; Quinley 1974; Wolcott 1982).

In previous studies, the fonts of clergy's engagement in public affairs have tended to be abstract. Scholars have emphasized principles underlying an agenda, relations between clergy and congregation, or the place of the congregation in the broader community. Here, we asked how issues of homosexuality first arose, and our results suggest that broad sets of factors drive the agenda of a church. Some are congregational; some come from the clergy; and most emanate from outside the church. Only occasionally are clergy able to control the congregational agenda, and external events usually dictate the discussion of issues in the congregation. Moreover, we suspect that the way in which the issue is raised will significantly affect how it ultimately is discussed and the results that the discussion can have (see Neiheisel, Djupe, Sokhey, and Niles 2005). We also observe that most church activity involves reacting to events, but, of course, a church that wanted to be relevant would react to and comment on most, or at least many, events in the world.

As noted above, it is a longstanding finding that clergy in politically diverse and divided churches sometimes downplay their own politics, which we ratify and expand here. Not only are they less likely to engage Issue 1 and issues related to homosexuality in church, but they also experience attempts by groups to recruit them (though this is partly a function of the interest group population), involve their church less frequently in voter registration efforts, and make relatively little information about the election available in church. Clergy-laity political disagreement is a significant barrier to congregational political engagement, which for members can translate into a weak tether between church-gained civic skills and the political process.

The picture that has emerged from analyses of religious interest groups such as the Moral Majority is paradoxical. On the one hand, better links could be established between such groups and clergy, who are assumed to exercise a sort of horizontal control over their congregations. At the same time, clergy's influence and their interest in politicking may stop at the sanctuary door. To rouse the public effectively, therefore, interest group leaders typically have gone straight to the people, bypassing both clergy and church institutional structures. The assumption is that clergy, particularly white evangelicals, have been unwilling to politick in their churches, though they could be considered fellow travelers with, or even members of, interest groups (Guth, Kellstedt, and Smidt 1998).

The results of our analysis suggest that clergy and their churches, especially in evangelical contexts, do indeed have sufficient connections to mobilization efforts by interest groups. Explicit political activities often occur in evangelical churches, including the close to the highest rates of hosting voter registration efforts. Interestingly, almost the only consistent predictor of clergy discourse about Issue 1 in church is interest group contact (regardless of religious tradition; results not shown). Many clergy talk about Issue 1 (or other issues involving homosexuality) in and out of the pulpit, and some clergy reported displaying buttons, stickers, or yard signs concerning Issue 1. Other Columbus-area religious leaders reported being involved in local or statewide groups dedicated to dealing with the controversy, and some even organized groups within their churches to discuss issues involving homosexuality, gay rights, or Issue 1.

The survey revealed other explicit connections among clergy, their religious institutions, and the 2004 campaigns. Many clergy reported that their churches were involved in voter registration drives. Among churches in which Issue 1 was discussed, 43 percent participated in such efforts. Likewise, other connections appear to exist between these local religious institutions and broader political movements. For example, 30 percent of Roman Catholic priests reported that election materials from interest groups were available in their churches in the fall of 2004 (50 percent of black Protestant clergy, and nearly 70 percent of evangelical clergy reported the same). Among the churches in which Issue 1 was reportedly discussed, nearly 30 percent provided election materials from interest groups, and approximately 20 percent provided materials that came from either the denomination or another church source.

Our results suggest that these clerical connections to outside political forces cut in two ways. While some clergy showed initiative by contacting and involving themselves in groups taking positions in the Issue 1 debate, most were contacted by groups (see also Crawford, Olson, and Deckman 2001). Among both clergy and the groups that contacted clergy, a pattern of knowing your audience emerges. Clergy reported politicking on Issue 1 in October 2004 at higher rates when they felt that they and their congregation shared the same presidential preference, a finding that gels with the previous work showing that clergy are sensitive to the constraints that the norms of their congregations and their communities impose on them (Djupe and Gilbert 2003; Jelen 2001). On the other hand, the interest groups involved in promoting or blocking Issue 1 appeared, depending on the extent of their resources, to adhere to a sort of rational recruitment strategy (Brady, Schlozman, and Verba 1999). These interest groups contacted clergy who were more likely to be receptive to their messages so that a higher percentage of evangelical clergy and clergy serving solidly Republican churches were contacted by pro-Issue 1 groups.

We should not assume that connections with an interest group necessarily translate into a coordinated campaign in the congregation. Interest group contacts may help mobilize such an effort, but apparently group membership can sometimes substitute for congregational efforts. When clergy are unwilling to pursue their political agenda through the church, they may direct their energies elsewhere. The finding that mainline clergy join groups at high rates seems to confirm this notion. This stands in contrast to Djupe and Gilbert (2003: 182–83) finding no evidence to suggest that contacting government directly through writing a letter to an elected official or an op-ed column is a substitute for church politicking (in fact, the reverse is true). On the other hand, Jacob Neiheisel and colleagues (2005) find more discussion of politics in ministerial organizations when clergy members report political disagreement with their congregations. Evidently, the ministerial organization provides an outlet for them to express their views.

The same basic dynamic can be found in the work of Djupe and Gilbert (2006), who emphasize the importance of the status of the individual in the community for understanding church influence. Individuals have choices concerning with whom they spend time and the organizations to which they devote resources. Djupe and Gilbert find that individuals whose neighbors are unlike themselves in important ways tend to spend more time in church and develop more civic skills. The implication is the same for interest groups: individuals choose an organization because it gives them a social or political outlet that they would otherwise not have. That logic means that the influence of the group is limited because the member may have a more closed social network (Huckfeldt, Beck, Dalton, and Levine 1995; see also Granovetter 1973).

Altering the view of the role of interest groups for clergy in the religion and politics literature is not difficult; it merely requires accepting at least some shade of an Olsonian (1965) conception of joining groups rather than the implicit, dominant pluralist view. Individuals' motivations for joining groups are varied and may be divorced from the public agenda of a group, although that separation is seldom true to a great extent in practice (Moe 1980), especially in the decision to join (Rothenberg 1988). Here, we add to the literature that individuals join not just because they share the same goals and want to advance them, but because the group gives some a social and expressive outlet when others are closed.

While our study of religious elites in Columbus, Ohio cannot directly answer the question of whether Issue 1 handed George W. Bush the White House, it does substantiate many of the claims heard in the mass media that the mobilization of religious people was an important factor in the election (as but one example, see Cooperman and Edsall 2004). We have provided a tangible mechanism for understanding the turnout of religiously conservative people. It was not simply the case that religious people cared about and were motivated by Issue 1. Instead, they were deluged with information aimed to persuade and mobilize people of faith, especially conservative ones. Moreover, many churches, especially evangelical churches, attempted to mobilize their congregation to participate in the election. Taken together, this also suggests that the church-based forces that shape members' opinions are essentially the same as those that promote political participation.

Appendix

We used the Columbus Area Yellow Pages as our sampling frame because it lists addresses of churches in a wide range of faith traditions. The Yellow Pages seems a reasonable representation of the religious community, especially since there is no reliable alternative. There were 921 churches in the sampling frame.

We sent two waves of surveys to all churches in the sampling frame. The first was sent in late November; the second, follow-up wave was sent to non-respondents in mid-January. Because our survey was administered during the busy holiday season, but also because of the sensitive nature of the subject matter, our response rate was low. In all, 148 clergy responded (for a response rate of 16.1 percent), though several were not usable (typically with unusually large print telling us they had no interest in the survey instrument).

We chose Columbus for several reasons. The authors live there; the city contains a wide range of churches; and Columbus has a sizable gay population. The survey also was designed to gather data for an additional project: a community case study of clergy participation in and evaluations of their ministerial organizations.

The sample, therefore, is not representative of Ohio, and probably not even of the information church members are hearing in Columbus (since the unit of analysis for the sample is the church, which is not weighted by church size). It does, however, give us a sense of what arguments were being presented in churches and the degree to which other religious interests are linked to clergy and churches.

Table 4.7 tests for the degree of response (and sample) bias. Of course, the sampling frame contains its own bias, since it does not list all churches, and probably excludes more conservative religious groups. We compare our results to the county-level census conducted by the Glenmary Research Center (Jones et al., 2002), which has its

Table 4.7
A Test of Sample Bias: Comparison of Selected Denominational Affiliations of Sample Congregations to the Yellow Pages (sampling frame) and the 2000 NCCC sample (percents)

Denominations	Respondent Sample	2005 Columbus Area Yellow Pages	2000 NCCC Sample Churches
American Baptist Churches	1.4	1.7	5.4
Roman Catholic	7.0	4.8	9.3
Nazarene	2.8	2.3	4.6
Disciples of Christ	2.8	1.0	2.1
Episcopal Church	3.4	1.6	2.5
Lutheran (ELCA and LCMS)	6.2	5.9	9.6
Presbyterian (USA)	11.7	3.8	6.3
UCC	3.4	1.3	2.0
UMC	15.9	9.9	14.8
Baptist	6.9	17.7	—

Note: All churches listed in the 2005 Columbus Area Yellow Pages were sent surveys (921 in all).

own problems, as more conservative than liberal religious groups did not participate. These 2000 census figures are Franklin County reports, while the Yellow Pages also include portions of neighboring counties.

As we would suspect, the biases inherent in the sampling frame are magnified in the survey responses. The sample overrepresents mainline Protestants and underrepresents evangelicals. The respondents are about three times more likely to represent either the Christian Church (Disciples of Christ), the Presbyterian Church (U.S.A.), or the United Church of Christ, and twice as likely to be Episcopalians (compared to the Glenmary data). Baptists are heavily underrepresented compared to what we would expect from the sampling frame.

The sample does not represent Columbus-area churches perfectly (though, of course, no sample reflects its population perfectly). The best sampling method would weight inclusion in the sample by church size (and perhaps be further modified by attendance). In the end, it is important to note that the sample contains a wide selection of traditions and views, and we feel comfortable testing relationships and presenting descriptive statistics for the data we collected. At the same time, we present and receive the results with caution and make no claim that they are definitive.

Part II

SOCIAL JUSTICE

Chapter 5

Religious Interests in Community Collaboration

The Quiet Fight for Health Care in South Omaha

Sue E. S. Crawford

This chapter tells the story of how a coalition of religious interests responded to growing health care crises in an urban neighborhood in Omaha, Nebraska. Two Lutheran (Evangelical Lutheran Church of America [ELCA]) ministers began a process that brought various religious interests, including congregations, nonprofit organizations, religiously based health systems, and a religiously affiliated college—into a coalition now called Interfaith Health Services (IHS). Similar to other cases in this volume, the IHS story features religious leaders who stepped up to mobilize a collective response to a specific community concern. Unlike other cases presented in this volume, however, the community concern in this case did not appear as quickly or dramatically as it did in episodes such as a race riot or the opening of a casino. Instead, the IHS case tells the story of mostly mainline clergy leadership in a slow and steady fight to improve the health of an urban community in the face of shifting demographics, rising health risks, limited political influence, and institutional divestment. As such, the case of IHS offers an example of what Robert Wuthnow has described as the typical, behind-the-scenes, quiet influence of mainline Protestants (Wuthnow 2000; Wuthnow and Evans 2002)—in this case, organized to address a serious community concern. Despite greater scholarly attention to protest and community organizing, this quieter collaborative community work is the most common means through which clergy, and perhaps most religious interests, engage in politics in an ongoing basis, especially at the local level and particularly with regard to human service policy deliberations.

Research Design and Data

The account of the development of IHS presented in this chapter draws upon qualitative data gathered from observations at IHS meetings and interviews with twelve key informants between May 2003 and July 2004. The informants ranged in their level of participation in IHS, but all except one participated in at least some IHS meetings during the research period. The research consequently focuses primarily on why certain religious interests chose to get involved and stay involved in IHS and can only indirectly speak to reasons why other religious interests did not choose to become involved.

The core clergy actors in the coalition serve congregations situated quite closely together in South Omaha. Some service-provider professionals in South Omaha also participate. Other individuals representing various religious interests, however, come from religiously based institutions located elsewhere in Omaha and the state of Nebraska. Many of these individuals have current or past ties to some religious health system. Individuals from all of these groups, as well as a government public health professional, agreed to discuss their involvement in IHS in interviews. The identity of the informants remains confidential except for the two main characters, each of whom granted written permission for their identities to be revealed and who approved all quotes used herein. Both of these key informants expressed a preference for this chapter to identify IHS by name. At one coalition meeting during my research process, the group was asked by another person writing about their efforts whether they wanted her to identify IHS by name or use a pseudonym. Several other members of the group also expressed a strong preference for having the identity of the coalition known. The identity and quotations of all other informants remain confidential. I do mention other individuals by name, some of whom may have been study participants, but the chapter only reveals information about these actors that would be considered public information (such as the names of people in official positions) or information from stories frequently shared in open public settings.

The IHS data collection occurred as part of a larger project analyzing religious involvement in local public health coalitions in three midwestern cities. All three locations face health crises prominently found throughout the United States, namely, large numbers of individuals without access to care, seniors with high health risks combined with limited mobility and limited support systems, and individual behaviors that lead to obesity, cardiovascular disease, and diabetes. Two of the sites, including the IHS site, have experienced dramatic increases in their Hispanic populations over the past decade as well. Thus, the health crises in these communities include the added challenges of providing access to undocumented individuals, overcoming language barriers, and tackling problems associated with prejudice and resentment over cultural change in these communities.

Interviews in all three cities followed a similar semi-structured format and similar observation strategies. The interview questions and observations in all three cases were structured to elicit ways in which external government and nonprofit policies and internal religious institution practices shape religious participation in health coalitions, particularly those with a focus on underserved populations. So, although the case itself focuses on South Omaha, the discussion occasionally brings in comparisons to cases in different local contexts.

The IHS Story

In the early stages of my research, it quickly became apparent that the IHS story was not just a South Omaha story. Repeatedly, responses to my questions about the coalition led to discussions of institutions and events outside the local area. A strikingly similar pattern emerged in my research on the other two health collaboration cases. Broader religious interests shape and empower local responses to health crises. This version of the IHS story focuses on the ways in which these broader structures of mainline Protestant religious institutions inform and facilitate religious interest engagement in health crises in South Omaha.

The South Omaha setting of IHS is a familiar one for scholars of urban politics and urban religion. The Missouri River bounds the city of Omaha on the east, and over the years the city increasingly has grown westward. Urban migration patterns in Omaha mirror those in other urban areas in the United States, with heavy growth and development in suburban areas (in this case, situated west of Omaha) leaving older urban areas with older, lower-income populations with access to fewer jobs, goods, and services. One of the founding pastors of IHS, Rev. Robert Johnson, described the flight of institutions, including religious and health institutions, as a key reason for developing Interfaith Health Services.

> When you start dealing with central cities, the services start abandoning . . . you just watch the health facilities move further west, and then you start watching clinics and availability of clinics [erode], and then you throw on in South Omaha, a lot of illegal people, and you start saying, "Oh, my goodness, we better start putting some kind of structures in place where we can care for people even if we can't help them much." So, [Interfaith Health Services] grew out of that kind of discussion (Johnson 2003).

Rev. Johnson noted that his ELCA synod office had also moved, which created some tension and concern on the part of clergy concerned about the vitality of older parts of the city. As he explained, the initial discussions and networks that the ELCA clergy established here became important in the eventual founding of IHS:

> The synod had its offices downtown originally and then they moved it out, way to hundredth and wherever out there and there was still lots of feelings about abandoning the core of the city and we tried to take and build on that through our cluster, called the metro urban cluster, together and through any other organizations we could try to work it so that we would begin to converse and talk (Johnson 2003).

South Omaha, the setting for this case, was earlier an Eastern European immigrant community and now houses a rapidly growing Hispanic population that nears or exceeds majority status in the area. Although the city has district representation on the council, which gives the area a representative in city politics, the realities of citywide mayoral politics and Republican dominance in the state limit the political leverage that leaders can exert in the area. The dynamics of electoral politics in South Omaha and the state at large render all the more strategically reasonable investment by religious actors who have more progressive interests in implementing coalitional policy with human service allies (in government and nonprofit agencies), even if they continue to fight larger social justice battles. If current funding and policies are insufficient, they can at least work with these allies to try to make the existing policy work as well as possible on the ground.

Most of the clergy who work in the IHS coalition come from congregations founded by whites prior to recent major demographic shifts. Most continue to draw mostly white members, many of whom either have or had ties to the South Omaha area and many of whom are elderly. The strong possibility of festering resentment by older power brokers in congregations would seem to be another important backdrop to the stories of clergy deciding how to deal with health crises in this changing community. None of the clergy, however, specifically mentioned dealing with this resentment when I asked them about constraints to their participation or constraints on IHS. Resentment may have been a more relevant force if IHS had chosen a strong Hispanic health focus, but this too may have been defused by IHS's strong focus on serving all congregations.

The population that traditionally would be most likely to join these congregations in these neighborhoods is aging and shrinking. One mainline congregation active in IHS is an exception on this front. It now employs a Hispanic minister, has a Spanish name and signage, and offers all services in Spanish. In this setting—an urban area that is increasingly Hispanic—health ministry provides a way for the mainline congregations to address the health needs of their aging populations as well as to become a partner in community efforts to address the needs of the growing Hispanic population in the area. As one nurse observed, all the congregations in the area, even those without Hispanic members, serve vulnerable health populations.

Area Catholic parishes, on the other hand, are growing rapidly. One informant noted that one of the parishes had recorded over four hundred baptisms in 2003, while another noted the difficulty of Catholic clergy being involved in IHS because of the other demands had created the need to build the capacity to minister to a rapid growth of Hispanic members. IHS, however, does have a Catholic presence. The logo for the coalition that lists the founding congregations includes a Catholic parish. A nurse from that particular parish was involved early on, and both a volunteer parish nurse and a priest attended various IHS meetings that I attended.

The Catholic response to health crises in South Omaha has been especially visible in direct services to Hispanic families and in community organizing efforts. Not far from the immediate neighborhood of the IHS churches sits a large Hispanic Catholic version of a megachurch (Our Lady of Guadeloupe). The parish supports a school and offers multiple direct services to Hispanic families. The dynamic priest credited with building up this ministry also helped build the South Omaha arm of the local Industrial Areas Foundation community organizing organization, Omaha Together One Community (OTOC). The key health issue for OTOC in South Omaha has been working conditions at the local meatpacking plants that employ many of the Hispanic residents of South Omaha. Although the smaller Catholic parishes in South Omaha do not offer services (or support priestly activism) to rival those of Our Lady of Guadeloupe, there are signs of investment in building on that model. At least one of the priests assigned to a smaller Catholic parish in South Omaha spent time training at Our Lady of Guadeloupe before moving to his new parish post, and others spoke of parishes bringing in clergy and staff with experience in Hispanic churches. One of the local parishes has a parish nurse who speaks Spanish and a nun who work with Hispanic parishioners on health issues such as infant care. The fact that IHS began by pooling congregational resources to hire a community parish nurse who would serve multiple congregations also helps to explain the somewhat weaker involvement of Catholic interests in this coalition. The heavy demand for health care support in these growing churches may have made a sharing scheme seem much less workable for the health needs in their own rapidly growing Hispanic congregations.

In the other two cities I studied, a Catholic hospital (founded by a religious order of sisters) served as a dominant health provider and a chief investor in coalitional efforts like IHS. The Catholic health care system in Omaha (Creighton University Medical Center [CUMC]) does not fit that mold. CUMC has strong private ownership and a dominant teaching mission. It also serves a city with multiple health systems. CUMC has most visibly addressed South Omaha's health crises through designing clinics to increase access and encourage healthy lifestyles among students. While health crises in South Omaha do engage Catholic religious interests, and while IHS includes a Catholic voice, the IHS story is primarily a mainline Protestant response to growing health problems and demographic shifts in South Omaha.

The most straightforward account of the founding of IHS relates that two ELCA clergy in the area shared an interest in health ministry and decided to invite other clergy from the local ministerial association to join them in developing a shared parish nurse ministry for area congregations. While this version is technically true, it leaves out several elements of interest here, especially the key roles played by larger institutions in the shaping of this grassroots effort. Both of the ministers who are widely cited as the key instigators of IHS (Rev. Damon Laaker and Rev. Robert Johnson) serve in ELCA congregations. Their experiences in Lutheran settings play important roles in the framing of IHS as a collective ministry and the eventual focus on health as the substance of the collaboration. Both ministers had been involved in ELCA Cluster activities that brought together Lutheran clergy, and both had been working to revive a sense of shared urban ministry among ELCA ministers in the city. Both also learned about health ministry, at least in part, through ELCA-sponsored activities.

According to Rev. Johnson, ELCA Cluster efforts were not being sustained; he and Rev. Laaker were left searching for ways to develop greater collaboration among clergy. "We would . . . spend a lot of time after meetings, standing in the parking lot, talking and thinking about how we operated and how the city operated" (Johnson 2003). Their experiences in the ELCA denomination gave them practice with collaboration among clergy, even if the system in Omaha at the time was not working as well as they would have liked.

Their setting within the ELCA also provided models of clergy collaboration in other cities. One model that Rev. Laaker found particularly important was the Monday Urban Strategy coalition work that ELCA clergy and congregations in Milwaukee undertook cooperatively. Laaker visited the group during a sabbatical from his congregational work. The Monday Urban Strategy coalition brings together clergy from ELCA congregations and ministries for the sharing of prayer and discussion of common ministry concerns. This group meets as part of a larger collective network of ELCA congregations and ministries throughout the metropolitan area (Waldkoening and Avery 1999). It includes a parish nurse component, which Rev. Laaker saw as one of its key strengths. Laaker (and others speaking about Laaker) often describe this sabbatical experience as the key spark for his work to develop a parish nurse response to the health care crisis in South Omaha. In his own words, "We began with a focus on parish nursing, primarily because the parish nursing was so strong in Milwaukee" (Laaker 2003). Upon returning from Milwaukee, Laaker contacted Ronnette Sailors, who at the time worked with Project LIFE, a project of the Lutheran health-care system designed to assist with health ministry in Lutheran congregations. This program was later phased out and Sailors moved on to head the Nebraska Health Ministry Network (NHMN), a partnership of the Nebraska Interchurch Ministries. Nebraska Interchurch Ministries is a coalition of the mainline Protestant bodies in the state, whereas the NHMN works to support other partnerships and collaborations around the state. Sailors' work with Project LIFE and later with the NHMN involved assisting the IHS leaders as they developed the coalition.

The ELCA background of Johnson and Laaker also matters when considering how these two clergy became interested in health ministry because the ELCA has been a leader in developing and supporting health ministry innovations. The effort often touted as the "beginning of parish nursing" occurred in a Lutheran hospital. Granger Westberg, often cited as the founder of parish nursing, worked in this Lutheran setting, regularly speaking to Lutheran gatherings and developing material to be disseminated through Lutheran networks. Reverend Laaker began attending parish nurse meetings before he decided to encourage parish nursing in South Omaha. Reverend Johnson was also inspired to try to implement parish nursing through his links to ELCA resources. He heard Westberg speak in 1975 at a denominational meeting and also observed strong ELCA parish nursing programs as a pastor in Minnesota and Iowa before moving to the Omaha area.

A few years after the first IHS meetings, a denominationally sponsored health ministry conference (which was organized as a joint clergy and parish nurse event) provided additional information and inspiration for Rev. Johnson's work with IHS. He returned from this meeting with tapes and other resources that led him to believe that it would be possible to implement health ministry in South Omaha. He recalls his confidence upon returning from that meeting: "I think having that meeting and coming back and having the tapes, I just felt, 'We could do it now'" (Johnson 2003).

Lutheran investment in IHS also exists in the form of Lutheran grant monies and gained due to the grant-writing abilities of Bob Prucha, a community development specialist working at the time for Immanuel Lutheran Health Services, which focuses largely on long-term health care and senior services, and which has no visible presence in the immediate IHS South Omaha area. Prucha, however, regularly attends IHS meetings and offers advice. Several participants credit the ability of IHS to garner grants for staff salaries and computers to Prucha's contributions and abilities.

Lutheran leadership in health ministry nationwide is documented in recent research on clergy in which more ELCA and Catholic clergy report congregational health ministry activities than do clergy from any of the other religious traditions, with the Lutheran Church-Missouri Synod topping the second tier. Table 5.1 reports the percentages of clergy in various religious traditions who report the highest levels of congregational health ministry activities based on data from the 2000 Cooperative Clergy Survey, a national survey of clergy from twenty different denominations. ELCA and Catholic congregations tie for the highest levels of involvement—roughly 30 percent of their congregations are involved in some form of health ministry (see also Ammerman 2005; Chaves 2004).

Although Lutherans and Catholics top Table 5.1, other mainline Protestant denominations also report a sizable commitment to health ministry and as a result have sizable numbers of congregations with health ministry programs. The same is true in the Omaha area. IHS includes Catholic, Presbyterian, and United Methodist congregations. A pastor from a nearby Disciples of Christ congregation attends the meetings as well.

IHS congregations and others in the area benefit from resources and networking through the interfaith NHMN and from technical assistance and biannual health ministry meetings sponsored by the

Table 5.1

Congregations with Health Ministry Programs

Religious Tradition	Percentage of Congregations
Evangelical Lutheran Church in America (ELCA)	30
Roman Catholic Church	30
Lutheran Church-Missouri Synod	21
Willow Creek Association	21
Presbyterian Church, U.S.A.	19
United Methodist Church	17
Christian Church, Disciples of Christ	14
Reformed Church in America	14
Assemblies of God	8
Southern Baptist Convention	7

Source: 2000 Cooperative Clergy Data.

area Methodist health-care system. The Methodist system hired Rev. Dan Johnston to provide assistance to health ministry efforts in the city. Johnston organizes meetings with informative programs and networking opportunities about twice a year and sends out monthly e-mail newsletters that contain information and inspiration for people working in health ministry. He also spends a great deal of time providing one-on-one advice and support to those working in health ministry in the area, including IHS. Consequently, his work goes beyond the technical assistance of the "here's what you should do when you get back home" variety often dispensed at workshops, and instead works with people in their own settings and for longer periods as they determine how to develop health ministries that fit their organizational strengths and theologies. Johnston was not only working with existing IHS partners around the table, but that he was also working hard to get new partners to the table. In some ways, Johnston was in a unique position because building IHS and other collaborative projects is his core job expectation.

United Methodist investment in IHS also came in the form a donation of a portion of Dr. Susan Ward's time to coalition development. Dr. Ward, a faculty member of Nebraska Methodist College, was provided an arrangement that allowed her to work part-time for the coalition to help move them through the critical and time-consuming tasks of formalizing IHS's mission and organizational structure.

Although the IHS coalition began initially with a fairly narrow vision of health ministry and a goal of bringing parish nursing resources to South Omaha congregations, as more people came to the table and as deliberations continued, the broader vision of health ministry became increasingly important to many members. Although this broader vision made initial recruitment more difficult because recruits had to be educated about what health ministry meant and what the coalition itself was doing, the vision also proved useful as it helped the coalition define various activities and successes as health ministry successes. This flexibility allowed IHS to take advantage of various opportunities and partnerships that emerged over the years. This flexibility was particularly useful, since the initial goal of placing a health resource person in various South Omaha congregations took a long time to materialize and is heavily dependent on external grant funding.

The structure of IHS meetings has also changed over time. Initially, all business and relationship building took place at the large coalition meeting. These meetings began when Rev. Damon Laaker invited others in the area to join IHS, and continued to expand as new participants invited others to join in the discussion. While the vision of a shared health ministry was the underlying business of the group, discussion at coalition meetings often turned to immediate opportunities and pressing concerns related to health in the community. One participant recalls that discussion often centered on some specific health problem that had come to a minister's attention when discussion would ensue about whether others had encountered the same problem, and sometimes group members would offer ideas about addressing the problem.

On the positive side, this networking allowed IHS to foster partnerships between nonprofits and congregations and celebrate accomplishments along the way. Nebraska Methodist College nursing students administered flu shots and taught health programs in various congregations, and a physical therapy student partnered with another congregation to offer Tai Chi classes. The coalition also partnered with the local public health department on a safe walking program, and now IHS sponsors walking clubs of its own, including one that draws Hispanic women from the area. These programs resulted from those problem-solving discussions at IHS meetings, illustrating how specific partnerships developed out of the coalition to improve the health of community and congregation members.

On the other hand, because IHS coalition meetings included significant amounts of time spent on building relationships and short-term problem solving, little time was left for the business of developing the organizational structure necessary for defining and meeting the larger goal of a shared health ministry program, or even deciding what that shared program would be. Undoubtedly, this use of time contributed to the perception of some IHS participants that the group got stuck at different points in time and needed a push to get back to its initial goal.

IHS retained its basic single-coalition structure for about five years. Initial decisions concerning the mission and bylaws were ironed out under this organizational rubric. Once the larger group made the decision to apply for 501(c)3 tax-exempt status, it became necessary to develop a formal board structure. Today, board meetings occur prior to the larger, open coalition meetings. Currently, the board and the larger group meet once a month in a partner church building, with the board meeting from 9:00 to 10:00 a.m. and the larger coalition meeting following immediately. The board meets to discuss core organizational issues such as funding and personnel issues. The larger group continues to serve as the core community-building group, which is the main networking function of IHS, and as the avenue through which the IHS director can communicate with all coalition partners.

The board has official members, but there is no set definition of who qualifies as an IHS partner or as a member in the larger coalition. Although the logo of the coalition lists the initial churches that founded the coalition, anyone can come to the larger coalition meetings, and anyone who attends the meetings is placed on the mailing list and is treated as a coalition member. Anyone can join in the discussion and anyone can offer information about partnership opportunities. When asked about core norms or rules of the coalition, members often discuss norms that reinforce the value of inclusiveness in these meetings. Examples of such norms include the expectation that anyone can voice an opinion; that all views are valued (as opposed to the preference for professional expertise); and the absence of rules that set boundaries on becoming a coalition member. One person who attended many IHS meetings early in the coalition's existence expressed some concern that the prevalence of new faces at each meeting made keeping the "ministry" in health ministry more difficult. That person noted that the group was attractive to agencies seeking new populations for programs. It took considerable effort to help members of the coalition understand that health concerned more than access to the services that these agencies might offer, and that congregations had more to offer to health agencies than just easy access to a population.

A few other longtime participants in the coalition expressed concern that such open membership made motivating congregations and other nonprofits to contribute financially to the coalition more difficult. The group discussed asking all member congregations to commit to a health ministry line item in their budgets, but this idea was left as a goal rather than a condition for continued membership in the coalition. Some expressed special concern about expecting individual congregations to contribute substantially to financing IHS given the financial stress and small size of most of the congregations in the coalition.

However, it is critical to recognize the value of the community building, health networking, problem solving, and small health programs that have come along the way. More than one participant in the study argued that the community building and commitment of partners to continue working together month after month was the group's biggest success. This community building and networking establish a capacity for congregations and groups in the area to tackle new health problems (or opportunities) as they arise.

While the story of IHS thus far places the work in South Omaha within the larger context of national denominational structures, it is also important to place the story within the context of important national shifts in government policy approaches to social needs, including health needs. The U.S. government is increasingly employing a partnership model of policy implementation, in which policymakers focus more on facilitating and funding programs than on running the programs directly. Thus, the roles of religious nonprofit organizations in the quiet work of negotiating collaborative efforts that leverage private and government funds to address the needs of those with little political power become even more important. Government and foundation grants now require potential grantees (including local government applicants) to develop an inter-organizational coalition in order to compete for funds. Recently many such programs have explicitly encouraged coalitions to include religious institutions as partners, which open the doors for even greater civic involvement of this kind by religious interests.

In the area of public health, multiple foundations, including the Robert Wood Johnson Foundation, fund health programs with which religious institutions have partnered. The Centers for Disease Control funds projects that give attention to faith and health partnerships and building leadership, both of which facilitate community collaborations for health ministry. The Department of Health and Human Services, like other departments in the Bush administration (Black, Koopman, and Ryden 2004; Cnaan 1999, 2002), has an office assigned the task of working with faith-based and community initiatives. The Healthy People Initiative and the Health Foundation encourage hospital administrators, public health departments, and other health professionals to develop community coalitions that include religious partners. The American Heart Association, the American Cancer Society, and similar groups also fund and facilitate program development with and for religious institutions. Moreover, tobacco settlement money in states (prior to state budget crises in the early 2000s) also provided money for public health initiatives, which often included religious congregations and religiously based hospitals. IHS benefited from some of these efforts. They received money for computers from a Nebraska program funded through the White House Office of Faith-based and Community Initiatives' Compassionate Capital Campaign. They also benefited from technical assistance from a person who was working on health issues through a Robert Wood Johnson public health grant and from Nebraska tobacco settlement fund monies.

The setting for this story means that the demand for collaboration, and health-care collaboration more specifically, does exist; although in fairness to those blazing the trail, less demand and fewer opportunities for a health-care coalition existed when IHS was first formed. However, the setting is also one of fragmentation and risk. The shift in community politics created by increased government attention to funding coalitions as a key tool for policy implementation has led national and state policies in many nation-states, including the United States, to push risk to the bottom levels (Taylor 2003). Both governments and private foundations increasingly direct funding for health and other social needs through competitive grant processes that require local coalitions to compete for funding. It is left to local leaders to develop program ideas and to form and maintain collaborative coalitions to compete for funds. These programs often also require the local coalition to demonstrate effective results on a relatively short timeline to justify continued funds. These grant programs quite often also expect the local coalition to demonstrate "sustainability," which means that the coalition must demonstrate how they will take over the financial responsibility for the coalition's work. The underlying assumption tends to be that if the coalition work cannot become self-sustaining, then the coalition does not serve a public need of sufficient importance to remain in existence. The emphasis on payment for performance and demonstrating sustainability in these social programs shifts the risk of successfully addressing community social needs to local leaders who must piece together coalitions and grants to deal with local crises.

Although there has undoubtedly been some shift of risk in current social policy processes (Taylor 2003), Dr. Gary Gunderson emphasizes that health care in the United States has grown fragmented as a critical element of the environment in which religious interests and health professionals might work to address local health needs. At a national level, Gunderson heads the Interfaith Health Partnership, which includes initiatives in partnership with the Centers for Disease Control, foundations, and public health departments. In workshops and training material, Gunderson stresses that the health safety net is fragmented and that health ministry often requires faithful leaders to be "boundary-spanners," working between organizational boundaries to bring together holistic packages of resources and build bridges between providers and those needing health services (Gunderson 1995, 2004).

Prophetic and Patron Engagement in Quiet Fights

Although the details of the story presented here are particular to the work of IHS in South Omaha, the basic plot—mainline religious leaders collaborating to develop local capacity to address social needs—is a familiar one. Recent work on congregational programs (Ammerman 2002; Cavendish 2000; Chaves 2001; Cnaan 2002; Cnaan and Yancey 2000) and faith-based initiatives underscores the centrality of collaborative work in the public engagement of religious interests. If we include activities undertaken by congregations or clergy as part of informal coalitions, (like IHS was at the beginning), the prominence of this expression of religious interests in the public square is all the more striking. In a recent study, slightly over 70 percent of mainline Protestant congregations reported working with at least one such informal coalition, as did over half the congregations from other Christian traditions (Ammerman 2002: 145). Studies of the political activities of clergy repeatedly show heavy involvement of clergy in local coalitions. This work spans both coalitions that focus on advocacy for policy change and coalitions (like IHS) that coordinate and negotiate local implementation of government and foundation programs (Crawford 1995; Crawford, Olson, and Deckman 2001; Djupe and Gilbert 2003; Olson, Crawford, and Deckman 2005).

As the IHS story shows, studies of congregation and clergy engagement in local coalition politics only partially reveal the participation of religious interests at the local level. One finds a diverse array of actors from religious institutions in these coalitions, including ministerial associations, religiously based universities, and religiously based hospitals and hospital foundations.

Addressing the core questions that motivate this volume means asking what religious interests contribute to these collaborative efforts and what makes them different from other nonprofit institutions that engage in such activities. More specifically in this case, how do mainline Protestant religious interests shape the nature and ability of coalitions to address health needs in communities with high-risk populations?

Studies of clergy political engagement tend to emphasize clergy's high levels of political engagement in circumstances where their political views stand in contrast to those of the majority in their congregation, city, or neighborhood (Crawford 1995; Djupe and Gilbert 2003; Olson 2000; Olson and Crawford 2001; Olson, Crawford, and Deckman 2005). We see such prophetic engagement by mainline Protestant religious interests in quiet coalitional work as well.

Brian Steensland notes that mainline Protestant involvement in political debates about social welfare involves the struggle to inject their distinctive "moral and holistic values" into those debates (2002: 232). A similar fight to inject moral and holistic values into public discussions of health and community life occurs on many fronts through involvement in coalitions such as IHS.

Religious partners draw upon a rich array of images, traditions, and stories linking health to religious and normative values that offer a vision of health that contrasts with dominant medical perspectives. Those from Christian traditions (including all of the partners in IHS) can turn to any of the gospels and find many stories of Jesus healing others. A presenter at the 2002 NHMN meeting argued that health was the "original Christian ministry" since Jesus and his early disciples made it a top priority. The presenter argued that the current emphasis on health in religious institutions marked a return to an original vision or ministry that people should be healed and whole. The notion of helping people and communities become whole resonates well with the emphasis on holistic values in Christian and Jewish traditions. Attention to healthy behaviors also draws upon a longstanding emphasis on stewardship in many of these religious traditions. This approach contrasts with the prevailing secular emphasis on improving health by gaining access to medical services.

Emphases in health ministry circles, including many in IHS, involve developing healthy behaviors and attitudes within congregations. These efforts seek to build on the healthy congregational practices such as visiting those who are homebound and caring for one another, as well as making other congregational habits (such as the food choices at congregation activities) healthier. This position is not terribly controversial and thus might not be seen as clearly prophetic. It, nevertheless, exemplifies religious interests that intentionally hold up holistic health norms.

At an even broader level, seminars and workshops sponsored by various mainline Protestant interests train ministers and other leaders to run meetings in ways that emphasize holistic community building. Training in this "systems" model teaches strategies for resolving conflict and running meetings in ways that encourage everyone to participate, build relationships, and value all input. This training emphasizes the need for holistic approaches in meetings and the encouragement of humane, diverse discussion. This emphasis appears quite clearly in programs and meetings geared to those with health ministry interests. For example, the 2003 state meeting of the NHMN featured two national experts in such processes. In this way, mainline religious interests seek to insert holistic values into collaborative ventures despite the increasing reliance on business values and market models throughout the nonprofit sector.

Rev. Damon Laaker, one of IHS's key religious leaders, notes that the systems model significantly influenced him. He argues that building relationships is the most important part of IHS meetings. He argues that people need relationships and that the feeling of relationship from IHS meetings brings people back, time after time. In this way participants receive solidary benefits from their participation (Clark and Wilson 1961). Laaker contrasts this emphasis with that of the business model that dominates in most other government and nonprofit enterprises. For him, attention to relationships in community building efforts is a form of prophetic witness.

> We all want to see something happen tomorrow, and would really like to see it happen today. This is another problem with the business model that drives so much. It expects to be able to measure change right away. If there aren't changes that you can measure, then it assumes that we should not have bothered with you in the first place (Laaker 2003).

Laaker begins each meeting with a few jokes and then segues into a question for all to answer during introductions around the table. The questions range from "what is your favorite part of summer?" to "who has changed your life?" or "what scares you most?" The questions are designed to allow people to talk about spirituality should they choose to do while still leaving them free to answer without any religious or spiritual reference. The responses generally include some short and simple answers, some humorous answers, and some emotional answers. This part of the meeting, which easily takes thirty to forty-five minutes, injects the holistic perspective emphasized by the systems method. It also reinforces the mainline Protestant values that people's personal lives are more important than efficiency and productivity.

A few members express frustration at the amount of time that relationship-building efforts take, and several who work in multiple coalition settings in the community confirm that this relationship-building emphasis is not standard practice in their other coalitions. Some participants admitted impatience at times, noting that the coalition was easily stuck in a sharing and networking mode. Participants also expressed frustration that often a key leader had to push the coalition to focus on tasks to move the work along. However, even many who were at times impatient discussed the value of the investment in these relationships. One woman admitted that when she first came to an IHS meeting, she wondered "How do they ever get anything done?" but acknowledged that she later found this leadership strategy to be "perhaps the biggest success of the group." She said the relational approach helped the group last because "people feel cared for and nurtured."

Analysis of the prophetic role of religious interests stresses the ways in which such interests can offer a strong voice that challenges existing assumptions, particularly when those messages might be needed urgently. The IHS story reveals another important role for religious interests: investing critical resources that allow the quiet fights to continue. In this sense, the religious coalitions play a patron role. Although this chapter stresses the patron role of religious interests for collaborative responses to community crises, the investment of religious interests in civic capacity is not limited to quiet fights, as stories in other chapters reveal. Clearly the institutional resources of religious interests (buildings, staff, volunteers, computers) provide important support for many community civic activities (Wuthnow 2003). In past work on clergy engagement, I found that Indianapolis clergy appeared to step up to higher levels of activity in neighborhoods where few other professionals were around (Crawford 1995; see also Crawford and Olson 2001b; Olson 2000). In such instances, clergy stepped up to fill in a professional vacuum in these neighborhoods. The IHS case demonstrates similar dynamics in coalitional politics, with religious interests providing much-needed resources to compensate for gaps that grant-driven policy dynamics tend to exacerbate. The gaps of particular concern for coalitional politics result from the fragmentation of social services and the burden of risk placed upon communities to develop ideas and make collaborative processes work with limited technical assistance and support services. In this environment, religious interests can serve as patrons by nurturing innovation and diffusing knowledge of successful coalition strategies. Religious interests also absorb risk by investing funds and concentrated technical assistance to assist collaborative efforts in making it through the long process of competing for grant funds, sustaining coalitions in the absence of grant funding, and supporting coalition activities that are not easily covered by grants.

The multilayered, multifaceted nature of mainline Protestant organizations provides enormous assets for this kind of patronage in community after community. The polycentric nature of mainline institutions creates laboratories for innovation in much the same way as states operate as policy laboratories in the United States. Information about experiments (in this case, public health care experiments) is spread through denominational and interdenominational meetings and seminars. Program experiments in Milwaukee, Iowa, and Minnesota clearly informed and inspired IHS work. Similarly, the professional positions of Ronnette Sailors and Rev. Robert Johnston allowed them to learn from multiple programs—and subsequently to share that knowledge with others.

This institutional learning fits well into the day-to-day preaching, teaching, and program needs of religious organizations. Both national and regional bodies can invest in this kind of institutional design. Information about innovations at the local level can be shared with others, and new institutional ideas can be debated and taught.

The IHS story demonstrates the long process that is often required to establish a meaningful collaborative effort. It took about five years for the group to reach the point where they were able to compete for grants and hire staff. The story also demonstrates the importance of sustained technical assistance, especially for coalitions like IHS that seek to include a broad range of grassroots organizations. IHS was fortunate to have technical assistance resources from ELCA health systems, United Methodist health systems, a

United Methodist college, and a coalition of mainline denominations. Moreover, religious interests offered technical assistance and training for the two ELCA leaders of the coalition.

The level of investment in IHS activities on the part of religious institutions over the years has been remarkable. One observer commenting on the community-building results of the coalition notes that IHS brought large competing health systems knee to knee around the table. When the coalition brought more people to the table, it allowed them to develop a formal organizational structure and mission and to obtain needed grant monies. To assume that coalitions such as IHS would spring up, survive, or operate in the same way without being nested in larger religious institutional structures would be a mistake.

One hospital administrator who works in a coalition in a different city notes the similarity between the need for religious interests to invest in coalitional public health efforts now and their legacy of investing in building hospitals in the past. She notes that in the past, religious hospitals stepped up to provide a health service that others were not providing adequately. Now they are stepping forward to provide a different kind of health service (community public health) that others are not providing adequately. While in the past the religious institutions stepped into the risky frontier and urban immigrant centers to build hospitals to care for those who were neglected, today religious institutions may be called to invest in community ventures that bring new partners, ideas, and values into health ventures that would seem too slow and risky for many other nonprofit entities.

The IHS story illustrates the importance of interactions between diverse religious institutions (congregations, health systems, hospitals, seminaries, and denominational organizations) that allow prophetic voices to be nurtured and patron resources to be distributed. As grant-driven politics increasingly stresses investment in fragmented and short-term human services programming, the prophetic voice and patron resources of mainline Protestant religious interests provide critical capacity for continued quiet fights for social justice in community after community.

Chapter 6

Homelessness, Ecumenism, and Politics in Racine, Wisconsin

Laura R. Olson

From 1993 until 2005, a faith-based organization almost single-handedly sheltered the burgeoning homeless population of Racine, Wisconsin, a small city south of Milwaukee. Each year, a network of seven churches—some longtime participants in the program and other short-term volunteers—agreed to offer shelter to the homeless each night during the cold-weather months of October through April. These churches, organized under the auspices of the Racine Emergency Sheltering Taskforce (REST), donated resources ranging from the use of their facilities to thousands of volunteer hours—all for no tangible reward. The REST program comprised congregations from a wide range of religious perspectives, including the dominant faiths of the Upper Midwest (Lutheranism and Catholicism) and other mainline, African-American, and evangelical Protestant denominations. REST congregations agreed to put aside theological differences and work ecumenically to address the visible and growing signs of the encroachment of poverty into their city. What factors motivated these congregations to work together toward the amelioration of poverty? To what extent did the faith-based roots of this sheltering program facilitate its work?

Religious communities have long been active in programs designed to alleviate poverty, and their efforts are frequently collaborative in nature (Ammerman 1997; Chaves 2004; Roozen, McKinney, and Carroll 1984). The Social Gospel movement within early twentieth-century Protestantism emphasized the Christian obligation to serve the disadvantaged, and mainline Protestants remain especially dedicated to antipoverty initiatives (Wuthnow 1988; Wuthnow and Evans 2002). Catholic social teaching has long embraced the moral imperative of assisting the impoverished (Himes 2005), and the Jewish and Muslim traditions also place great value on coming to the aid of people in need (Maisel and Forman 2001; Smith 1999). In recent years, the emphasis of the federal government upon faith-based initiatives has spotlighted the antipoverty work that faith-based organizations undertake and has allowed them to compete with secular groups for federal funding for welfare service delivery (Black, Koopman, and Ryden 2004; Chaves 1999, 2004; Cnaan 2002; Wuthnow 2004). Using data from his National Congregations Study, Mark Chaves (2004) reports that most American congregations actually do not engage in comprehensive antipoverty programs. In fact, only 8 percent of the congregations in Chaves' nationwide study participated in programs to combat homelessness. "For the vast majority of congregations, social services constitute a minor and peripheral aspect of their organizational activities, taking up only small amounts of their resources and involving only small numbers of people" (Chaves 2004: 93). As such, congregations that volunteer their houses of worship as homeless shelters on a weekly basis would appear to be rather unusual.

Data and Method

This study is intentionally ethnographic in its approach. No survey data are available to aid in the analysis of the REST program, nor does any authoritative written record of its efforts exist. I rely on an ethnographic research strategy combining personal interviews and archival materials to explore the life course of the REST program. Because REST no longer exists and has been replaced by a centralized (and secular) single-site homeless shelter in Racine, its story has now been played out in its entirety. The history presented here marks the first effort to codify REST's work to any extent. I conducted in-depth personal interviews with REST's longtime executive director, Donna Bumpus (Bumpus 2003), and a former president of its board of directors, Ron Thomas (Thomas 2003), for basic threads of oral history and background information. I also rely on newspaper accounts of REST's work and its implications for the community as reported from 1996 to 2005 in the *Racine Journal Times* and (to a lesser extent) the *Milwaukee Journal Sentinel*. Moreover, to analyze the motivations and goals of participating congregations, I conducted in-depth telephone interviews with the clergy of five REST shelter congregations in December 2003.

The Challenges of Poverty and Homelessness in Racine, Wisconsin

Racine, Wisconsin is situated on the banks of Lake Michigan, thirty miles south of Milwaukee and sixty miles north of Chicago. The "Belle City" was incorporated in 1848, the same year in which Wisconsin became the thirtieth state in the Union. Its settlers included many immigrants from Denmark and Germany, and the city retains a distinctly Danish flavor to this day. Racine also has a long history of concern for social justice; it was a hotbed of abolitionist sentiment in the nineteenth century and served as a prominent stop in the Underground Railroad. Thanks to its close proximity to Milwaukee and Chicago, as well as its ability to serve as a port city, Racine underwent steady industrial growth beginning in the mid-nineteenth century and remained a thriving factory town until the recent past. Both malted milk and the kitchen sink garbage disposer were invented in Racine. The city's best-known business is the SC Johnson Company, which was founded in 1886 as a parquet flooring dealership. It grew into a successful household wax company in the early twentieth century and is today a highly diversified, privately held Forbes 500 multinational corporation whose brands include Drano, Glade, Pledge, Raid, Windex, and Ziploc. According to the 2000 United States Census, Racine has a population of 81,855. The city is 69 percent white and 20 percent African American. Fourteen percent of Racine's population, as compared to eleven percent of the U.S. population at large (United States Census Bureau 2001), lives below the poverty line.[1]

A recent study undertaken by advocates for the homeless in Racine County revealed the magnitude of the crisis of homelessness facing the area (Tunkieicz 2005b). On the basis of a one-day census taken on January 28, 2005, at least 276 people were homeless in Racine County. Of that number, sixty-six people were classified as chronically homeless. And these figures may be low estimates, according to Dave Maurer, executive director of the United Way of Racine County, who told the *Racine Journal Times* that he "estimated there were more than 1,200 homeless people in the county on a regular basis" (Block 2005a). When asked in the 2005 survey to identify their most pressing needs, Racine's homeless prioritized basic requirements such as "meals, access to mainstream resources, bus tokens/program transportation, emergency medical care (including life-saving prescriptions), employment, transitional housing, emergency shelter, bathing facilities, and utility assistance" (Tunkieicz 2005d).

Despite its reputation for a good standard of living and excellent public schools, both urban and rural poverty are endemic in the State of Wisconsin. According to the United States Census Bureau, no other state saw its poverty rates increase more steeply between 2003 and 2004, and by 2004, Milwaukee was listed as the seventh poorest city in the United States (Held 2005). Poverty in the Upper Midwest, and in southeastern Wisconsin in particular, has resulted from business trends such as the transition to a service-based economy and the relocation of firms to warm-weather states with lower tax rates. "The rise in poverty [in southeastern Wisconsin] reflects the decline of a once-strong industrial center that has been unable to turn around its economy and sustain family-supporting jobs" (Held 2005). Because Racine is a small city in the shadow of Milwaukee and Chicago, its problems reflect those of the two larger cities on a smaller scale.

Economic reasons are frequently cited to explain the existence of Racine's homelessness problem. Unemployment rates in Racine County were high throughout REST's existence, and REST board members, such as former alderman and mayoral candidate Ron Thomas, usually blamed unemployment for homelessness (Tunkieicz 2004a). REST executive director Donna Bumpus explained in the *Racine Journal Times* that homelessness results when "there are [not] enough jobs that pay good wages; some men find it hard to survive economically" (Parks 1999). At root, REST officials argued, "the problem is that the manufacturing jobs are gone, the ones that would pay twenty dollars an hour" (Thomas 2003). As Adrian Ortega, a homeless man who frequently relied on the REST program for shelter, explained, "We do what we can to survive in the city with a lack of shelters and a lack of jobs" (Drummond 2003).

In 1995 the Wisconsin State Legislature passed a comprehensive, cutting-edge welfare reform program.[2] Building upon earlier state-level reform programs implemented in the early 1990s, Wisconsin's new welfare program was called Wisconsin Works, which was abbreviated W-2. The program, which required welfare recipients to work in order to receive state benefits, dramatically reduced the size of the state's welfare rolls (Mead 2005). Whereas 719 people in Racine County were receiving welfare benefits in September 1997, only 155 were on the welfare rolls by September 2000 (Tunkieicz 2001). Not long after W-2 took effect, the number of guests at REST shelters increased noticeably (Bumpus 2003). Donna Bumpus told the *Racine Journal Times* that W-2 "was a factor in the greater demand. 'Thirty [guests] is a lot, but 50? Oh my God, W-2 is here. . . . We knew this [increase in demand] was going to happen'" (Sterling 1997; see also Pfau 1998c). By 2001 a state-commissioned study indicated that relatively few people who left the welfare rolls under W-2 had succeeded in securing jobs that paid more than poverty-level wages. "But those who run the Racine County non-profit agencies that try to help poor people say they didn't need a 221-page state Legislative Audit Bureau report to tell them that. From their perspective, poor people are no better off under W-2, and in many ways, they think the situation is worse" (Tunkieicz 2001).

A History of the Racine Emergency Sheltering Taskforce

Racine residents Donna Bumpus and Pat Liesch founded the REST program in 1993 as an outgrowth of their work with local food pantries (Bumpus 2003; Danielson 2001). They became aware of a network of locally run homeless sheltering programs in southern Wisconsin and northern Illinois known as Public Action to Deliver Shelter (PADS), which operated out of churches in small towns (Gardner 2003). Moreover, Racine's neighboring city, Kenosha, recently had established a faith-based homeless shelter, the Interfaith Network Nightly Shelter (INNS) program. "The food pantry members decided that if there was a need in Kenosha for a shelter, we must need one also" (Bumpus 2003). From the start, REST was intentionally faith-based, a model that was not unprecedented in Racine. For instance, in 1970, Louise Hunter, a woman whose Christian beliefs moved her to work toward the amelioration of poverty, founded the Love and Charity Mission for homeless men (Woods 2005).

Bumpus began informally by talking to people who used local food banks about their living situations to determine whether Racine needed a sheltering program. She consulted with the leaders of Kenosha's INNS program about how they ran their organization through churches. She also sought assistance and support from area congregations and raised a small amount of seed money (Bumpus 2003). She then approached approximately sixty congregations, speaking to pastors and addressing worship services, to gauge their interest in joining a collaborative homeless sheltering project. "I went to all different kinds of churches. I went to every possible church [or synagogue] where I knew a pastor, priest, or a rabbi" (Bumpus 2003). Ultimately Bumpus succeeded in recruiting seven congregations—one for each night of the week—to join her effort. She quickly "began working up a training schedule, picking coordinators, setting times, and figuring out where the food would come from. I spent a lot of time talking to the pastors, priests, and rabbis, hoping we could get something together" (Bumpus 2003). REST churches began opening their doors to homeless guests every night beginning in the fall of 1993.

REST guests were a cross-section of Racine's poor population. Roughly half of all REST guests from 1998–2003 were African American, 5 percent were Hispanic (Bumpus 2003), and the remainder white. A majority of guests over the same time period were between the ages of thirty-one and fifty; very few were under the age of twenty-one or over the age of sixty (Bumpus 2003). Roughly 85 percent of guests, however, were men (Bumpus 2003), in part because separate sheltering programs (Homeward Bound and the Women's Resource Center) were specifically designed to serve Racine's homeless women. Nevertheless, REST prided itself on being the only sheltering program in the city that did not segregate homeless guests by gender. As Bumpus explained, "In the past, families had to split up at the shelters. Men had to go to Love and Charity Mission, while the women and kids had to go to Homeward Bound. Now, we let the families stay together. We also have lots of nonnuclear families and they can stay together, too" (Sterling 1997). Each guest was provided with a light dinner, a continental breakfast, a bag lunch, and personal items including donated toothbrushes, toothpaste, soap, razors, and clean clothing (Danielson 2001; Knuteson 1996). Guests slept on pads on the church floors and were supplied with sheets, pillows, and blankets. Showers and laundry facilities for personal use were available at some of the church sites. A local barber provided free haircuts, and guests were given referrals to doctors and dentists (Danielson 2001). Donna Bumpus even personally ferried guests to a doctor or hospital if they became very ill.

Over the twelve years of REST's existence, its shelters gradually found themselves serving larger numbers of guests. In the 1990s, REST sheltered an average of thirty guests per night (Danielson 2001). After 2000, that number climbed to more than fifty guests per night (Block 2003a), and eventually REST congregations also began hosting an overflow of homeless people from nearby Kenosha (Killackey 2003). In 2005, REST's last year of operation, its shelters were serving an average of seventy guests per night (Tunieicz 2005c).

As early as 1998, REST's executive director and its board of directors began appealing to the City of Racine for assistance in establishing a year-round, single-site homeless shelter. Their aim in establishing a single-site shelter was to remove the burden (which was growing in the era of Wisconsin's W-2 welfare reform policy) from local congregations. The city government, however, was slow to respond. It commissioned an ad hoc committee of its Human Services Board to consider REST's request in 1998, but that committee seems never to have reached a concrete conclusion. For four years, REST advocates continued occasionally to ask for the city's support for a year-round, single-site shelter (Buttweiler 2002). As REST board president Ron Thomas explained, from the program's perspective, "at some point it needs to be a community buy-in. It can't just be the churches" (Thomas 2003).

Many concrete reasons were cited for the need for a single-site shelter. In Thomas's words, "We are a fragile organization, we are a band-aid. We are a pseudo-agency, that's what we've evolved into" (Thomas 2003). One specific concern was the difficulty inherent in asking untrained volunteers to deal with the special needs of the portion of the homeless population living with mental challenges, serious illness, and substance abuse (Thomas 2003). As one REST congregation pastor told me quite bluntly, "We're not equipped to handle schizophrenics." Another REST clergyman asked, "If you've got two retired people down there at 2:00 in the morning and something bad breaks out, what are you going to do?" The program established a policy that guests would not be admitted to the shelters after 10:00 p.m. unless they were accompanied by a police officer, and beginning in the fall of 1998, shelters refused to accept guests under the influence of drugs or alcohol (Pfau 1998a). An additional concern was transportation; for many years, American Red Cross vans picked up homeless people in Monument Square, a visible retail area in the city's downtown district. There were rumblings that

Racine's business community did not favor Monument Square as a transportation hub for the homeless: "there were problems, so you have a stigma, call it what you want to call it" (Thomas 2003). A third concern was that the REST program operated only during the cold-weather months of October through April, leaving the homeless to sleep on the beach or in city parks during the summer. For a time, Bumpus attempted to help homeless people on her own during the summer. She often met informally with homeless men in downtown Racine, bringing them items (at her own expense) such as "a cooler of punch, a tray of chicken wings, and a large bag of tortilla chips . . . [as well as] a pile of supplies, including nonperishable food, clothing, and toiletries" (Pfau 1998b).

Advocates for the homeless redoubled their efforts for the establishment of a single-site shelter in 2003. After years of inaction by the city government, the United Way of Racine County took matters into its own hands by convening a community task force (the Transition Advisory Council) to assess the needs of Racine County's homeless population. The task force was charged with analyzing "needs and social services gaps . . . [and helping] with fund-raising and planning efforts" ("REST Shelter News" 2004). It quickly set a primary goal of identifying tenable solutions to the problem of chronic homelessness and decided that a centralized effort to fight homelessness would be necessary. Transition Advisory Council member Dave Maurer said, "We applaud the incredible work REST and its coalition of churches and volunteers do and have done in providing emergency shelter and sustenance during the cold winter nights for those who had no place to sleep" (Maurer 2003). It had become clear, however, that a permanent, single-site shelter was needed (see also Burke 2003).

By the winter of 2004, the Transition Advisory Council had announced that a prominent Racine family, the Neubauers, had volunteered the use of their factory warehouse building near Lake Michigan as a permanent homeless shelter (Steinkraus 2004). REST aimed to make this permanent shelter available twenty-four hours a day by Christmas 2005. The permanent site is conveniently located adjacent to the Racine County Human Services Department, its Workforce Development Center, and the Racine County Food Bank. Moreover, "this wouldn't have happened without the Neubauer family. . . . [They] are members of . . . one of the first churches to enroll in REST when it began" (Steinkraus 2004).

Around the same time as the announcement of the single-site shelter plan, the formation of a new homelessness assistance organization was also announced. The organization, which would be called the Homeless Assistance Leadership Organization (HALO), would subsume REST and Homeward Bound, a shelter that served homeless women exclusively (Sides 2004; Tunieicz 2004b). Debra Lake, the chairwoman of the United Way's Transition Advisory Council and a HALO board member, said, "As we look to the future, we can say there are ways we can do this better by not duplicating resources and really address the cause of chronic homelessness together, not just as individual groups addressing pieces of it" (Tunieicz 2004b).

HALO envisioned improving service delivery for the homeless and putting them on the path to self-sufficiency. Two separate shelters would be housed in the Neubauer building: one for men and one for women and children. A total of 120 beds and a daytime shelter room would be made available (Sides 2005b). To finance the renovation of the Neubauer building, HALO applied for and received a $750,000 grant from the State Department of Commerce. The funds came from the state's "Brownfields Program," which is designed to clean up and develop contaminated land areas (Sides 2005a; Tunieicz 2005b).

After the single-site shelter and the formation of HALO were announced, several personnel changes also ensued. Although REST agreed to continue for one final year with its seven-church shelter program during the winter of 2004–2005, Donna Bumpus was removed as executive director of REST. She was instead named the organization's "fund-raiser and project coordinator" ("Plan for Single-Site" 2004), while Rev. Kevin Mieczkowski, a labor union chaplain, took over as REST's interim executive director, "because he had more involvement with HALO than Bumpus" ("Plan for Single-Site" 2004). When REST formally disbanded in May 2005, "both Bumpus and [Pat] Liesch [who together founded REST in 1993] . . . [were placed] on paid leave from their jobs until HALO begins. Both were told they had to reapply for their jobs with the new organization" (Block 2005b). Bumpus later criticized HALO in the *Racine Journal Times*, saying that the program "isn't focused on helping the homeless as much as it is giving the United Way . . . major control" (Gutsche 2005b).

The HALO shelter formally opened its doors to homeless men on November 4, 2005 and set December 2005 as its target date for accepting homeless women and children. When the HALO shelter formally opened, the REST program formally became a thing of the past. Even though its story is now complete, it is useful to study the REST model as a means of understanding the resources required to create a successful, sustained ecumenical effort to address an intractable social problem like homelessness.

Resource Mobilization in the REST Program

REST would never have survived for twelve years were it not for the program's ability to marshal and use scarce resources effectively. John McCarthy and Mayer Zald (1977; see also Zald and McCarthy 1979) pioneered the concept of resource mobilization as a means of explaining social movement activism.[3] The REST program itself was certainly not a full-blown social movement; it could, however, be described as a social movement organization. McCarthy and Zald define a social movement organization as "a complex, or formal, organization which identifies its goals with the preferences of a social movement or a countermovement and attempts to implement those goals" (1977: 1218). REST's goal was to shelter the homeless, which makes it (at least in a small way) a part of what Frances Fox Piven and Richard Cloward (1977) have labeled a "poor people's movement," even though the movement was not itself comprised of poor people. Moreover, the REST congregations qualify as "conscience constituents," to use another of McCarthy and Zald's terms, meaning that they were "direct supporters . . . who [did] not stand to benefit directly from [REST's] success in goal accomplishment" (1977: 1222). If we therefore conceptualize REST as a social movement organization, it becomes clear that REST's leaders and member congregations would have been responsible for mobilizing the needed resources to accomplish their "target goal" (McCarthy and Zald 1977), which was to shelter homeless people and raise community awareness about their plight. REST's principal resources included money, political visibility, and above all, the volunteer support of its member congregations.

Financial Resources

From the start, REST's administrative costs were low. Typically just one person was on the payroll: executive director Bumpus, who was largely responsible for the generation of most of REST's resources (both financial and otherwise). Members of REST's board of directors, including its president, were unpaid, as were the volunteers who staffed the shelters each night. Nevertheless, REST faced fundraising concerns. Its budget grew from $25,000 in 1998 (Pfau 1998d) to $54,000 in 2001 (Danielson 2001) to $84,000 in 2002 (Buttweiler 2002). Moreover, REST worked with "the 'general' homeless populations, so it [was] not eligible for funds directed toward more specific [groups, such as homeless veterans]" (Block 2003c).

Over the years the REST program used innovative strategies to pay its bills. It went directly to "authorities and . . . delegated agents of social control" (McCarthy and Zald 1977: 1222) in search of funding and succeeded (at least to some extent). The program received funds from an Emergency Shelter Grant, the Department of City Development, the Federal Emergency Management Agency, and the U.S. Department of Housing and Urban Development. In 2003, Racine County agreed to allow county jail inmates to do REST's substantial daily laundry load as long as REST paid for the electricity and detergent (Block 2003a). The United Way of Racine County also provided assistance in the form of office and storage space (Maurer 2003) and later made a spare room in their offices available for homeless people who needed a place to stay during daytime hours (Drummond 2003). The majority of REST's funding, however, came from private donations, especially from Racine-area congregations. REST board president Ron Thomas explained that the program never would have survived without "the generosity, the in-kind donations; we have never had to pay [for] electricity. . . . These are tremendous things" (Thomas 2003). As Donna Bumpus added, "the churches have been a blessing to us. If we had waited for the city to help us, we would have people all over the street like they do in the City of Milwaukee" (Bumpus 2003). The community at large, or what Ralph Turner (1970) terms "bystander publics," was also generous. For example, in 1998, fundraising jars were placed in churches, and a new Wal-Mart Supercenter matched the amount raised in the churches (Pfau 1998a). Numerous articles in the *Racine Journal Times* also made direct appeals for financial resources on behalf of REST to the community at large, to great effect (Thomas 2003).

Political Resources

The political significance of REST ought not to be underestimated. Ron Thomas was a city alderman before he became affiliated with the program. He was also a candidate for mayor in 2003; he placed second in a five-way nonpartisan primary—ousting the incumbent mayor in the process (Olson 2003)—but ultimately lost in the general election with 40.6 percent of the vote (Kertscher 2003). Thomas told the *Racine Journal Times* that "his campaign for mayor could not be separated from his work with Racine's homeless" (Block 2003b). Thomas's political connections undoubtedly helped REST gain visibility and access to local policy-makers.

REST participants themselves occasionally undertook political action. In 1997, Racine-area homeless people met informally with a state legislator, (now former) Sen. Kim Plache, to voice their concerns. Andre Drane, a frequent guest at REST shelters, said to Plache, "I want to see what you're going to do . . . [about a lack of jobs in Racine]. What job program? I'm tired of going from temp to temp to temp" (Flores 1997). In 2003, homeless people staged a small protest when "about 175 people gathered . . . for the annual National Day of Prayer. . . . The homeless men and women who attended the prayer gathering raised their sleeping bags in the air during the singing of the national anthem" (Drummond 2003). Donna Bumpus described this action as a means of communicating "a silent awareness" (Drummond 2003), which seems to indicate that the homeless REST guests saw themselves at least to some extent as a political constituency.

The REST program even had consequences for local elections. In 2005, a close race for an aldermanic seat was disputed because fifteen homeless people who stayed once a week at a REST shelter housed in a church situated in the aldermanic district in question had voted in the election (Gutsche 2005a). After much debate, a judge finally ruled that they were, in fact, entitled to vote (Tunkieicz 2005e).

Volunteer Resources

By far the most significant resources that the REST program mobilized during its twelve-year existence were the time and talents of hundreds of volunteers. Racine's congregations and the community at large contributed well over ten thousand volunteer hours to REST each year (Bumpus 2003; "REST Shelter News" 2004). Volunteers staffed the church shelter sites from 6:30 p.m. to 7:00 a.m. each night. They worked in three shifts: 6:30 p.m. to 11:00 p.m.; 11:00 p.m. to 3:00 a.m.; and 3:00 a.m. to 7:00 a.m. Volunteers could work as many nights, or as few, as they chose. "Each night, volunteers [were] on hand to maintain a safe, secure environment. At 6 a.m. those in [the church] shelter help clean up [and] have breakfast, and at 7 a.m. they leave the church" (Knuteson 1996). Volunteers also did paperwork cleaned, and offered advice to shelter users about facility rules (Pfau 1998c). To prevent burnout, some churches organized their volunteer corps so that no individual would be asked to work more often than once a month. Each congregation was also required to have a designated lay REST coordinator. Some churches required members of their teenage confirmation classes to volunteer at REST sites as well.

What Led Congregations to Participate in the REST Program?

Why would congregations volunteer to open their doors to homeless people once each week, and why would their members volunteer to staff these shelters? Congregations would not benefit directly from participation in the REST program. In fact, they could lose from it, or at least to be challenged by it. Moreover, it is uncommon for American congregations to provide large numbers of volunteers for any social service initiative (Ammerman 1997; Chaves 2004; Price 2000; Roozen, McKinney, and Carroll 1984). What factors inspire a congregation to volunteer so generously of its resources for a program like REST?

One major theme that emerged from my interviews with Donna Bumpus and Ron Thomas is that clergy played a crucial role in mobilizing their congregations to participate in the REST program. Previous studies have established the important role that clergy can play in mobilizing their congregations for political activism (Crawford and Olson 2001a; Djupe and Gilbert 2003). Said Bumpus, "I think the clergy drive it. . . . The pulpit is where it has to come from. . . . I think if the pastor is for it, then the congregation will be for it" (Bumpus 2003). Thomas agreed: "The leadership has come from the clergy. . . . It was the clergy [who] stepped up and said, 'here we go, this is what we need to do, there's a problem in this community'" (Thomas 2003). One REST congregation minister, however, felt "this is very much a lay-led program and has been since its inception. I've been there to cheerlead, but I've not had to do any of the hands-on work myself." These comments make it sound as if this minister did not play any mobilizing role in stimulating the congregation to participate in REST, but he added that participating in the program "is all part of who we understand we're called to be, and that is to be there for the least, the lost, the lonely, the disenfranchised. They hear a lot of that *from the pulpit*."

Beyond mobilization by their clergy, what other factors may have motivated and sustained REST volunteers? Perhaps more significant than any other motivation, REST volunteers evidently grew close to one another and to the guests. Fourteen-year-old volunteer Mike Pedersen said of his involvement in REST: "It gives me self-esteem to know I'm doing something for the community and I'm not getting paid for it. . . . I'm pleasing God when I help out every Tuesday. It makes me feel special" (Tenuta 2003). REST volunteers were also compelled to participate in the program from their personal desire to help the homeless. As the pastor of one REST congregation explained, "first of all, they knew there was a need, and then I think they felt very strongly that we have been blessed with so much, and the least we can do is let our space be used. . . . This church has always had a fairly strong social ministry background, so it wasn't a real stretch." This pastor's congregation arranged for cable television to be installed in the church for the enjoyment of the homeless guests. One of his congregation's families donated a washer and dryer, and another family paid to remodel the church to accommodate the washer and dryer. This congregation and another REST church also sponsored the addition of shower facilities to their buildings specifically for the use of REST guests. As one REST pastor observed, "When they [volunteer], it's an unambiguous feeling of 'I know I did a good thing. . . . This is what God wants me to do'. . . . When you feed somebody who's patently hungry and they look like crap, and you know you kept them warm . . . and they didn't have to sleep under a bush somewhere. . . . It's just clearly the right thing to do, so there's that sense of reward."

Participation in the REST program seems to have enhanced the identities of its member churches and made its members feel that they were contributing tangibly to a cause, suggesting the significance of both solidary and purposive benefits for its volunteers. Solidary benefits offer participants feelings of social unity with their fellow participants, whereas purposive benefits give participants a pleasurable feeling of having contributed to a normative cause (Clark and Wilson 1961). One REST pastor clearly identifies solidary benefits as a major incentive for his congregation's volunteers: "Some of them enjoy the camaraderie of being together with the other folks who work there." Another REST pastor emphasizes the salience of purposive benefits for his church's volunteers: "They come as a means of honoring God and serving Him. We're really big here . . .

that the Lord has called us all to service . . . and this is certainly an avenue to do this."

Politics and Ecumenism in the REST Program

The REST program had to mobilize a wide range of resources in order to sustain itself for twelve years. Beyond these tangible resources, other factors helped contribute to the program's long-term success. In particular, REST was able to attract congregations that were intrinsically interested not only in ameliorating poverty, but also in working collaboratively to do so. Remarkably, the REST program does not appear to have created much controversy either within the participating congregations or in the city at large. In part this must have been due to the willingness of the REST congregations to make the project intentionally ecumenical.

What factors distinguished REST congregations from other congregations in the Racine area? In the opinion of Ron Thomas, "If there's a general thing, there's a willingness to give, a willingness to learn" (Thomas 2003) on the part of congregations that choose to become REST shelters. Size also matters in this context. Small churches had particular difficulty participating as shelters (Bumpus 2003; Thomas 2003) because they had to worry about the basic survival of their congregations before all else. In recruiting congregations to be shelter sites, REST knew it had to take into account the fact that "churches vary in size, churches vary in location, and churches vary in the politics of the congregations within" (Thomas 2003). Anxiety about the nature of the task also prevented some congregations from participating in REST, according to Bumpus: "With the ones that said no [to her request that they become REST congregations]. . . . I could feel their apprehension; I could feel that they felt there were going to be people of color in their church that they couldn't control" (Bumpus 2003).

REST congregations do not appear to have been motivated primarily by a political agenda to participate in the program. From her perspective as REST's executive director, Donna Bumpus never "believed that the congregations see [homelessness] as a political issue" (Bumpus 2003). One REST congregation pastor was adamant that "Ours was not in any way a political motivation; ours was a spiritual motivation. This was living out the life of Christ; this was representing Christ. . . . When you look at God's heart in the scriptures, he has a heart for the poor. . . . There's nothing political about it." As another REST clergyman explained, "The motivation [here] was purely spiritual. The Gospel of Matthew, chapter 25, [says] 'I was thirsty and you gave me [something] to drink, I was homeless and you took me in.' Absolutely that was the motivating factor." Another clergy member from a REST congregation cited the same passage of scripture, but put a slightly more sociopolitical spin on his interpretation of his congregation's motivations for participating in the program: "I think it's only right that we take care of homeless people, as people who embody the Gospel's message of serving those in need. . . . We feel like we're welcoming Jesus when we welcome the guests. . . . [In] Matthew 25, the people ask Jesus, when did we see you naked or hungry or imprisoned? And Jesus said if you did it to the least of these, my brothers and sisters, you did it to me." According to Ron Thomas, "It's a religious mission, it's a church mission, but it's also a social thing. They grow into realizing that it's a social mission" (Thomas 2003).

Finally, to what extent did a spirit of ecumenism drive REST's success? From the perspective of one clergyman, "I think the [congregation] is very proud of the fact that we're able to do this. . . . It brings us to the table with people of other denominations . . . and we work together in that respect." Another REST pastor disagrees, however: "I don't think [REST] is leading to a great spirit of ecumenism in Racine." In the opinion of a third REST minister, "I can't give it an A grade [for capturing the full range of religious diversity], but I guess I could give it a passing grade, a C+ or B-. It depends on what aspect of the program we're looking at. The ecumenical aspect comes in that the seven churches do acknowledge and see each other as compatriots in a really difficult task." REST did encompass Catholic, mainline Protestant, evangelical Protestant, and African-American Protestant congregations, although it is fair to say that roughly two-thirds of the participating churches were members of mainline Protestant denominations. This is not entirely surprising, as evangelical churches are typically less involved in social service programs, including those to combat homelessness, than are congregations from other religious traditions (Chaves 2004). The pastor of an evangelical REST congregation explained his congregation's view on the ecumenical aspect of the program in detail: "I don't see that we have really linked arms with the other churches. There would be some theological differences that are there. I think we all value the poor and value serving. . . . But in terms of an ecumenical thing, we don't get together with these other churches. There are some pretty diverse religious traditions that are represented here. I don't even know some of the pastors of the other churches." A mainline Protestant REST pastor summarized the extent of the REST program's ecumenism: "In most congregations there is a certain percentage who are big-hearted for missions. . . . In our community, the REST program touches those big-hearted people, but it hasn't been a huge ecumenical gathering point. . . . There's a certain amount of protectionism and parochialism that keeps it from being a truly ecumenical effort."

Donna Bumpus (2003) and Ron Thomas (2003) offered the same illustration of the limitations of REST's ecumenism. One prominent downtown church never became formally involved in REST, even though its congregation was extremely supportive of the program and often sent volunteers to various church sites. According to Bumpus (2003), some of the REST congregations would not have wanted to continue working with the program if this church was formally involved because its pastor and many of its members are openly gay. As Ron Thomas put it, "part of the challenge of the seven different churches [is that] you've got different religions [and dynamics such as] one church, if it knew that this other congregation was there, wouldn't participate" (Thomas 2003). Citing another challenge, one pastor observed that "A certain percentage [in any congregation], and I would classify these as small minority percentages, are not anxious at all to interact with the homeless [because] they have preconceived ideas of who the homeless are and what they are like."

In the end, the REST program disbanded because of the limits to which congregations could sustain such intense activism. Congregations were organizationally too fragile to sustain the workload that the REST program required. On the whole, congregations may not be equipped to undertake the faith-based initiatives that the federal government currently promotes (Black, Koopman, and Ryden 2004). Nevertheless, for twelve years congregations across the religious spectrum did come together to shelter homeless people in Racine. Even though they did not always see eye-to-eye on theological matters, they did share a common concern for the amelioration of poverty and marshaled resources to the best of their ability to help homeless people.

The case of REST illustrates one way in which religious organizations can step in to address a community deficit in service provision (in this regard, see also Sue Crawford's discussion of health care in South Omaha in this volume). Donna Bumpus acted as a visionary policy entrepreneur (Salisbury 1969) in rallying Racine's congregations to action when she perceived a significant deficit in policies designed to assist the homeless. Previous research has illustrated how clergy can act in such an entrepreneurial fashion (see Djupe and Gilbert 2003), but the case of REST reveals that activist lay leaders can be just as effective in resource mobilization to solve community problems.

Beyond the REST Program

A serious concern facing the coordinators of Racine's new single-site shelter is how to retain the faith-based element of the services offered to Racine's homeless. Donna Bumpus shared the fact that a local clergyperson "didn't want us to get a single site, because . . . he feels that [REST] brought his church together" (Bumpus 2003). The new HALO organization is secular and involves prominent local business and community leaders, including Helen Johnson-Leipold, CEO and Chairman of Johnson Outdoors, Inc. (a division of the SC Johnson Company). What HALO adds in organizational resources, it may lose in faith-based resources. As Ron Thomas explained, there were concerns that the single-site shelter would deprive congregations of their power, autonomy, and "turf" by removing their input and therefore their "ownership" (Thomas 2003).

Nevertheless, at least one REST congregation minister feels that in the long run, the move from REST to HALO will be helpful for Racine's homeless population. He said, "I predict that when there's a single site . . . it may lose some of its warm, fuzzy personality, but for the clients, it'll be healthier. . . . Other agencies will be involved. . . . Homelessness is bigger than what can be addressed in churches . . . [because] we don't have the tools to deal with all the systemic issues." Moreover, the last REST board president, Rev. Kevin Mieczkowski, emphasized that HALO representatives "have said all along that faith-based is a key component. . . . Bumpus also said that HALO knows it is important for them to retain their faith-based ties. 'We want to keep the spirituality in it. They promise us it will be'" (Block 2005b). Bumpus had hoped that the single-site shelter would still allow individual congregations to serve as official hosts on specific nights (Bumpus 2003); however, as of this writing, that hope has not come to fruition.

To retain the faith-based component of Racine's programs for the homeless, HALO has made a habit of reaching out to local congregations for their financial support. As a March 2005 letter signed by eight prominent area clergy (including some whose congregations had been REST shelter sites) explained, "To achieve [our capital campaign] goal we need nearly $200,000 from churches around our community. . . . Would your congregation please consider a 3-year pledge totaling $1,000 to $4,000?" A September 2005 letter reminded local congregations that they "have become the very foundation of HALO. And that foundation is made strong by the many people from churches, synagogues, and mosques who have given of themselves in the aid of those without shelter or the means to breakout [sic] of their homelessness." These appeals bore fruit, as twenty-eight Racine churches contributed money to HALO's 2005 fundraising campaign (Tunkieicz 2005a).

Resource mobilization will not likely be as serious a concern for HALO as it was for REST, as HALO is clearly a more organized, professional operation than REST was. HALO does, however, appear to be in danger of losing the faith-based component that sustained REST. Whether HALO will be able to attract and retain community volunteers as effectively as REST did remains to be seen. The single site, while undoubtedly beneficial for the homeless guests themselves, could diminish the program's ability to offer solidary and purposive benefits to volunteers. That congregation members evidently bonded with one another while working in their church-based REST sites suggests that friendship networks sustain volunteer activity as well as motivating it in the first place. According to their clergy, congregational volunteers also gained enormous purposive benefits from their participation in the REST program, as they felt they were doing "the Lord's work," as one pastor put it. Moving away from the faith-based, congregation-centered model removes the basis for both of these benefits. On the whole, the lesson to be gained from the example of REST is that to be successful in social-service delivery, congregation-based programs must find creative ways of marshaling resources and providing an array of benefits to their volunteers. Without these two strategies, the REST program would never have lasted for more than a decade, and the homeless people of Racine, Wisconsin would have had an even more difficult struggle.

Part III

RELIGION IN THE PUBLIC SQUARE

Chapter 7

Religious Interests and the Martin Luther King Jr. Holiday in Greenville, South Carolina

James L. Guth, Lyman A. Kellstedt, Joshua Copeland, & Christine Rowland

Greenville County, South Carolina, is exactly the sort of place to observe "culture wars" first hand. As the state's largest county, Greenville is a big notch in the Bible Belt: one birthplace of the conservative Southern Baptist Convention, the nation's largest Protestant denomination, and home to Bob Jones University, a leading fundamentalist college. The evangelical tradition still dominates Greenville County, especially in the form of the 168 Southern Baptist churches, accounting for about half the religious membership and almost a third of the population (Jones, Doty, Grammich, Horsch, Houseal, Lynn, Marcum, Sanchgrin, and Taylor 2002). Part of the remaining religious population consists of smaller evangelical, fundamentalist, Pentecostal, charismatic, and Holiness churches, many of which are often missed by formal surveys. And like many other burgeoning Sunbelt metropolitan areas, Greenville also boasts several new nondenominational evangelical megachurches.

Although the evangelical tradition dominates Greenville, other Christians are also well represented. United Methodists, with sixty-four congregations, comprise 11 percent of the church members and 6.5 percent of the population. Catholics are the next largest group, with seven churches, 8.1 percent of adherents, and 4.7 percent of the population. Several other mainline Protestant groups are also present, including the Presbyterian Church U.S.A. (6.1 percent of members), Episcopal Church (3.0 percent), and Evangelical Lutheran Church in America (1.6 percent). The social influence of these mainline churches often exceeds their size, given the many community leaders who are active members. About 18 percent of Greenville's population is black, so African-American congregations are also numerous, although poorly counted by religious surveys, with Baptist and black Methodist congregations most common. To round out the mix, Greek Orthodox, Jewish, Muslim, Baha'i, Mormon, and Metropolitan Community Church congregations are also present in the community (Jones et al. 2002).

The challenge that this religious diversity presents to evangelical domination has emerged from three decades of economic transformation, in which Northern and international enterprises have gradually replaced the declining textile industry. Michelin, BMW, and Fuji are just three of the major foreign employers, contributing substantial social diversity in the form of their French, German, and Japanese management personnel. Other migrants have come from the Northeast and Midwest, as domestic corporations seek the friendly environment of a low-tax, nonunion state, close to burgeoning southeastern markets. From Latin America has come a rapidly growing Hispanic population, part Catholic and part Protestant, adding even more diversity to the social and religious mix.

Not surprisingly, Greenville has struggled recently with cultural issues, including battles over gay rights, gambling, Sunday alcohol sales, and restrictions on adult clubs. In each instance, conservative religious forces have mobilized (with mixed success) to defend traditional moral norms embodied in public regulations. In 2003, however, an even broader religious mobilization occurred over an unusual issue: the local observance of the Martin Luther King Jr. national holiday. Although this case involved what some scholars have called symbolic politics (see Edelman 1964), the controversy was no less divisive because it involved competing views of community values. Naturally, religious forces played an important role in the development and resolution of the issue, but not without input from other important business and political interests. Indeed, the intersection of religious and other interests is one of the most fascinating aspects of the story.

Data and Methods

This case study is based on an extensive body of information. First, we have relied heavily on local media. The *Greenville News* covered the Martin Luther King, Jr. Day controversy in depth, reporting not only on County Council meetings, but also on events outside Council chambers. We relied especially on the reporting of Deb Richardson-Moore, an award-winning local religion reporter, and her colleagues, especially Sarah Bonnette, Jeanne Brooks, E. Richard Walton, Jason Zacher, Ron Barnett, and Paul Alongi. As a supplementary source, WYFF-TV, the local NBC affiliate, sometimes focused on aspects of the story neglected by the print media.

For behind-the-scenes developments, we draw on extensive participant observation. We made the controversy the focus of our spring 2003 political analysis class, sending forty students out into the community to observe Council meetings, political rallies, church services, and a host of other venues. In addition, we interviewed several dozen participants, including Rev. Jesse Jackson, Dr. Bob Jones III, Council members, business leaders, and clergy. Unattributed quotations come from interviews and direct observation. Without such confidential interviews, our understanding would be greatly impoverished. Altogether, these ethnographic materials provide us with a rich picture of the politics around the holiday issue.

The Battle Begins

Although President Reagan signed the Martin Luther King, Jr. Day into federal law in 1986, South Carolina was the last state to recognize it as a state holiday, holding out until Democratic Governor Jim Hodges signed authorizing legislation on May 1, 2000. This law—in true Dixie logrolling fashion—simultaneously recognized May 10 as Confederate Memorial Day. Hodges sympathized with bitter complaints from civil rights leaders about this combination but warned that he was not going to wait another "five or ten years before we had a King holiday" (Hammond 2000).

Most local governments quickly followed the state's lead, giving their employees the day off. By 2002 all but a few counties had done so, most with little controversy. Greenville County was one of the holdouts, although the city of Greenville, with its substantial minority population, did recognize the holiday. Quiet moves by African Americans on the County Council failed to muster the votes to create a holiday. By late 2002, however, a new effort began to bring the County into line, as African-American Councilor Xanthene Norris put the issue on the docket for the new Council elected in November 2002 (Bonnette 2002).

This Greenville Council differed substantially from the one that Alan Ehrenhalt described when he studied this body in 1991. White, rural, retired Democratic men dominated the body Ehrenhalt studied. The Greenville Council of 2002, however, was now overwhelmingly Republican (eight to four), racially representative (ten whites, two African Americans), and noticeably younger. It also had four women, including Republican Phyllis Henderson, its chair. Two aspects of Ehrenhalt's description still obtained, however: the Council remained split between its city members, mostly Democratic, and its rural and suburban members, now mostly Republican. It still reflected local religiosity: Republicans attended conservative Baptist or fundamentalist churches, and Democrats belonged to African-American or mainline Protestant congregations. These partisan and religious divisions would prove impediments to a holiday, but they were not the only obstacles.

In January 2003 the holiday issue rose immediately to the top of the Council agenda. In response to prodding by Xanthene Norris and Lottie Gibson (the widow of a former national NAACP chairman), the Council finally considered a resolution officially recognizing Dr. King's birthday, but not creating a new employee holiday—although individual county workers would still be allowed to use a floating holiday to honor Dr. King. Vice-Chair Scott Case, speaking for the Republicans, argued that the county could not afford a new holiday, which would cost $150,000. The Council action thus raised expectations by bringing the issue to the forefront, but then disappointed proponents, paving the way for expanded conflict (Padgett 2003).

Turned away by the Council, holiday proponents opened their public campaign on Dr. King's birthday with numerous commemorative events, some in white churches and others in joint interracial worship services. Participants were invariably told of the county's failure to emulate federal, state, and city governments and were urged to lobby the Council. That most such gatherings were in houses of worship was a harbinger of things to come.

Holiday supporters enjoyed plenty of competition for leadership. County NAACP director Paul Guy, associate pastor at Faith Cathedral, hoped to revive his organization, which in recent years had lost ground to the Urban League, a group Guy viewed as too close to the white power structure. He announced an ambitious new NAACP agenda, including educational and economic development, attacks on inequities in the criminal justice system, and the elimination of racial profiling in law enforcement. Guy quickly perceived that a campaign for the holiday might advance his organizing goals (Bonnette 2003b). Other civil rights leaders latched on to the same possibility. Rev. Al Sharpton hammered on the issue during his frequent stops at Greenville churches as he sought support in the 2004 state Democratic presidential primary. In one stump speech, Sharpton complained: "Greenville County does not acknowledge Dr. King's birthday. The city does, the state does, but the county says it's too expensive. There is no price too high for the American holiday. Dr. King was not for blacks only."

The most prominent leadership role, however, would be played by Rev. Jesse Jackson, a Greenville native and frequent visitor, who was invited by some black ministers to get the ball rolling. Jackson hoped to revive the local unit of his Rainbow Coalition/Operation PUSH, and saw the holiday as a valuable stimulus. He stopped in Greenville in late January 2003 for four days, calling the holiday fight "a patriotic challenge." In a speech, Jackson said: "Greenville is personal to me, Dr. King is personal to me. But beyond the personal, it is a holiday recognized by the state of South Carolina, by the city of Greenville, by the president." Jackson, who had actually given the invocation at the January Council meeting that had rejected the holiday, now vowed to attend each biweekly session until King was recognized (Dykes 2003). He raised the issue's visibility and promoted mobilization, but also created tension with local African-American religious leaders, who felt eclipsed by Jackson, and his appearance "hardened some hearts" among whites.

Initially, though, these events stimulated cooperative organizing by African-American churches, led by black ministers taking a cue from Dr. King (Richardson-Moore 2003a). James Adams, president of the Baptist Ministers Fellowship, noted that King's "movement originated in the church. I believe that's going to make a difference here in Greenville." John Corbitt of Springfield Baptist Church, Greenville's oldest and most prestigious black congregation, told us that the "church is still the meeting place for a lot of black people. It's the one place we can get the announcement out about concerns in the African-American community." Corbitt nostalgically remembered "the old days when all the rallies were held at the local black church." Rev. Ennis Fant, former county NAACP director, led a clergy committee that assigned responsibility for filling Council chambers during specific meetings. Rev. S. C. Cureton of Reedy River Missionary Baptist, a leader of the National Baptist Convention, U.S.A., Inc., joked with us, saying, "I think they're going to get tired of seeing black faces." And Jackson kept his pledge and attended each meeting, accompanied by his own supporters.

Council Chair Henderson professed to be pleased by the rush of citizen activism, "That's great. We love to have people involved in the democratic process." Not all Council members welcomed the black churchgoers filling the chambers, however: Vice-Chair Case pointedly dismissed them as "extremists." Although the Council quickly reaffirmed its earlier decision, harbingers of a possible compromise soon appeared. On February 3, 2003, the Council's Public Safety Committee decided to wait six months before reconsidering the issue to allow a citizens' study committee to canvass solutions. All factions quickly embraced this classic delaying technique. Committee chair Republican Steve Selby, who professed to be "open-minded," argued, "We'd like to get viewpoints and suggestions from the whole spectrum of people, from people who don't support the holiday, people that do support the holiday, people who support a resolution, people who don't support a resolution." Selby offered to work with Norris, the chief holiday proponent, on recruiting the task force. Norris agreed, knowing that an immediate vote would defeat the holiday again and preclude establishment of a broader supporting coalition (Bonnette 2003a).

This action left the Council with no King agenda item for its next meeting. Nevertheless, on February 4 black church members once again packed the Council chambers. The fire marshal had to ask protesters to move to overflow rooms to watch proceedings on TV monitors; even Councilor Gibson encouraged some to go home, thanking them for taking the initiative to "come down and show your support." Chair Henderson observed, "I've been on the Council for two years. I don't ever think I've seen anything like this." Jackson expected to state his case during the public comment period, and after the completion of the Council's agenda. Because of the crowd size, the Council debated extending the period beyond the usual half hour, but opted to adjourn on schedule. Several citizens endorsed the holiday (and one spoke against it), but time had almost expired by the time Jackson's turn to speak arrived. The Council refused to extend his time, producing a large uproar from Jackson's retinue. Ultimately, eighty protesters sat in chambers all night, including Councilor Gibson, accompanied by law officers. "It was not our plan to stay here all night," said Jackson. "This is plan B." Jackson promised an even larger turnout at the next session (Bonnette 2003c).

A bigger crowd did appear on February 18, warmed up by a Baptist Ministers Fellowship civil rights movement-style rally, complete with church choirs, gospel singers, and prayer vigils. The overflow crowd was orderly, with latecomers shuttled to overflow areas where a loudspeaker carried the proceedings. Jackson, true to his word, appeared on time, even shaking hands with his nemesis, Vice-Chair Scott Case. Now he had time to speak (and, in fact, ran three minutes over his allotted five) and led the crowd in the civil rights anthem "Ain't Gonna Let Nobody Turn Me 'Roun'." He also delivered a petition with almost ten thousand names to Councilor Gibson. All this activity did speed up the creation of the citizens' task force, as Henderson directed the Public Safety Committee to propose nine names within two weeks (Bonnette 2003d).

Greenville Religious Communities Mobilize—Or Fail To

As the Council awaited creation of the citizens' study committee, discussion spread beyond the African-American community. The "big steeple" downtown churches, filled with the community's (mostly white) business and professional elites, were the first to act, usually prompted by their clergy. Jeff Rogers, pastor of the historic First Baptist Church, told both his congregation and the media that the holiday "is a question of when, not if. Whether this County Council reverses itself or another County Council reverses it, Greenville County will have a Martin Luther King Jr. holiday. It's only a matter of time." Allen McSween of Fourth Presbyterian, another historic mainline Protestant church, added: "a special holiday honoring the legacy or Dr. Martin Luther King Jr. is very much needed. Without his eloquent leadership and that of many other black clergy who forced us to deal with the racial issue in a nonviolent way, the life of our state and of the nation would be vastly poorer." Ludwig Weaver, pastor of the influential Westminster Presbyterian Church, wrote a Greenville News op-ed piece endorsing the holiday. Even Frank Page of Taylors First Baptist, a prominent evangelical congregation, told his congregation "to stand up for that which is right, whether it's popular or not," showing "sensitivity to a huge segment of our population who were oppressed for many years" (Richardson-Moore 2003b).

Beyond sermons and public pronouncements, mainline leaders also pressured the Council. Baxter Wynn, Rogers' associate at First Baptist, circulated a petition:

> We the undersigned clergy of churches/synagogues in Greenville County, as an expression of personal conviction, do hereby respectfully urge the Greenville County Council to adopt the third Monday in January as a holiday honoring the legacy of the Reverend Dr. Martin Luther King, Jr., through whose courageous, nonviolent leadership our country and state were enabled to face our history of racial injustice which was both a denial of the faith we profess and the ideals of our nation.

Wynn told us that he hoped "to encourage clergy in the majority community to express their opinions and let their voices be heard with two thoughts in mind. One is we want County Council to hear how strongly many of us feel about the issue. Secondly, we want to send a clear message to the African-American community, particularly clergy, to know they're not in this by themselves." Ultimately the petition boasted 130 names, reading like a "Who's Who" of the mainline Protestant establishment, including Taylors and the pastoral staffs of the First Baptist Churches of Greenville; several Presbyterian Church (U.S.A.) congregations, including both the evangelical First Presbyterian Church and the liberal Westminster Presbyterian Church; Christ Episcopal Church; Trinity Lutheran Church; Buncombe Street United Methodist Church; and several others, including the local Conservative and Reform Jewish congregations (Richardson-Moore 2003c).

Although many Methodists had signed Wynn's ecumenical petition, the Greenville District of the United Methodist Church (UMC) went even further. As the only major Protestant body with substantial white and African-American membership, the UMC was in a strategic position. Thomas Bowman of St. Mark's noted that "we are an inclusive church, and we feel that Dr. King has set an example of being someone who's inclusive of the rights of all—not just blacks but of the rights of all." After the District's sixty-nine clergy voted unanimously for the holiday, Superintendent Gareth Scott explained that "we see it more as a day of remembering—of remembering what we were and how someone led us through that—not only him but many, many people, to become a more inclusive people, God's family" (Barnett 2003b).

Although some mainline clergy were clearly out in front, others were sympathetic, but chose to remain silent or work very quietly indeed. This tendency also characterized the county's dominant Southern Baptist churches. Of course, some of the most conservative Baptist clergy did not think well of King or the civil rights movement, but they refrained from any public statements to that effect. More often, representative Baptist pastors supported the holiday "personally," but avoided participating in the clergy mobilization. One minister of a mill village church favored the holiday, but had done nothing to advance the cause, either as a citizen or as a religious leader. "One must pick his battles," he told us, and "these were not battles that I am willing to fight." As an individual he could do little; if he attended Council meetings, no one would notice him if Jesse Jackson were also there. And no one followed the lead of his small, now struggling Baptist church: "they look to First Baptist to set the example." If parishioners asked, though, he would tell them that he favored the holiday. Still other pastors echoed the minister at a burgeoning rural Baptist church, who noted that the "holiday is a very divisive issue" and his people had "so many different beliefs." In any case, he refused to "use his sermons for any purpose other than expressing the word of God." Thus, whether out of a lack of political efficacy, concern for congregational harmony, or theological rejection of this-worldly politicking, most white Southern Baptist clergy remained aloof.

Similar factors inhibited other religious leaders. Like many growing communities, Greenville has several large, nondenominational megachurches, which are among the most racially integrated in the area. Their pastors often expressed "liberal" personal opinions about the King holiday, but for the same reasons as the Baptists, avoided visible activity. Catholic churches were also largely unmobilized. Although the Bishop of Charleston (who leads the diocese that covers the entire state of South Carolina) wrote County Council endorsing the holiday, this action went unnoticed in the media—and among Catholics. The priest of a predominantly African-American parish did try to muster Catholic support, but enjoyed only modest success. As he told us,

> I notified all Catholic Churches in the upstate. . . . One or two of the churches put something in their bulletins. I circulated petitions to all of the churches. Only one produced signatures. It was a

> very large church, and it only produced 75 signatures. This is just not a popular issue. With the exception of St. Anthony's the Catholic Church is a white church, and they just don't see it. They didn't even see it when it became an economic issue. Michelin and BMW said that they give their employees the day off, its part of their holiday package. And $150,000 is a very small amount to Greenville County. Yet, even when the council kept on coming up with lame excuses, people still did not see. This is racism.

Even this priest at St. Anthony's worried that the issue drew energy away from one they felt was far more important—abortion—and refused to circulate the petition among his own substantial Vietnamese flock. Islamic leaders gave an indirect endorsement through the Greenville Faith Communities United, but either saw no real stake in the holiday or feared becoming embroiled in any controversy so soon after September 11, 2001.

Meanwhile, what was happening within the fundamentalist community? Bob Jones University's (BJU) forces could be especially critical. Not only was the university directly "represented" on County Council by Bob Taylor, a BJU administrator (as well as by BJU alumnus Scott Case), its numerous graduates and staff were also prominent in the local GOP. Certainly no Council Republican could ignore their concerns. If these religious conservatives actually organized against the holiday, adoption would be much less likely.

Anyone familiar with BJU's long history of racial exclusion might anticipate automatic opposition, but this was not a foregone conclusion. In recent years President Bob Jones III had moderated the University's image, even ending the prohibition of interracial dating that had cost BJU its tax exemption in the early 1980s and more recently had been a hot issue in the 2000 Bush-McCain presidential primary battle. Support for the holiday might well serve this image-polishing purpose, but whether Jones could deliver was another matter. Although pundits often portray the university as a monolithic force, taking direction from the top, this response was seldom the case. For example, the "BJU crowd" frequently split among candidates in GOP primaries, often ignoring Jones's own favorite. Thus, it was unclear whether Jones would oppose or support the holiday—or whether his view would have much impact in either instance.

Initially, the holiday seemed a step too far, if not for Jones, then for university alumni and supporters. In an impromptu statement after a BJU assembly, Jones refused to endorse a holiday that violated his own Christian ideals: King was "grotesquely immoral, a communist sympathizer, and did not live by true Christian doctrine." Jones added that there were "other men of greater moral character who deserved a holiday." Although he did not "go public" at this point, his sentiments were accurately perceived by the BJU network. The major public spokesman for this view was the Reverend Stan Craig, pastor of the independent Choice Hills Baptist Church and leader of Citizens for Traditional Values, a group comprised mostly of fundamentalist clergy from the BJU network. Craig had long encouraged his people to participate in county politics and had no reservations expressing his views, calling King a communist sympathizer, and organizing a counter-petition to the one that Wynn circulated.

As religious leaders maneuvered, the business elite slowly awakened. As studies of civil rights controversies have often shown (Crain 1969), business involvement is often one critical ingredient in successful resolutions. In Greenville itself, peaceful school integration in 1970 had resulted from just such involvement, but in 2003 the Greenville business community was hardly unchallenged politically. By the early 1990s, a solid Council majority had emerged from rural and working-class resentment against the "tax and spend" development strategies of big business leaders (Ehrenhalt 1991). These forces had repeatedly defeated referenda authorizing tax increases and bond issues to build an arena, finance the public schools, and fund other civic projects. Although the business elite drew strength from the growing native and "immigrant" upper-middle class that had transformed the city of Greenville, this development had not yet altered the balance of power in the county.

Nevertheless, by late February 2003, business leaders began to weigh in. Bob Hughes, a developer and commercial builder, warned that the issue "is no longer about Martin Luther King. It is a symbol that the era of segregation is over, a symbol of the coming together of the races." Hughes's view was echoed by businesswoman Minor Mickel Shaw, heir to one of Greenville's most respected fortunes: "Martin Luther King was also about bringing people together; he was about peaceful reconciliation." Both Hughes and Shaw worried that Greenville would look backward to outsiders, with disastrous economic consequences. As Hughes put it, "everybody knows the Martin Luther King holiday is inevitable. These companies and business leaders outside the community don't understand why County

Council won't go ahead and pass it. It doesn't look like smart government." Tommy Wyche, founder of a prestigious Greenville law firm, complained that the county's failure "to recognize the significance of the civil rights movement gives it another black eye. This is taking a stand contrary to the rest of the world." Hayne Hipp, CEO of the media conglomerate Liberty Corporation, said, "every economic development prospect looking at Greenville . . . is talking about the Martin Luther King controversy." To add an intellectual element, President David Shi of Furman University used his weekly *Greenville News* column to endorse the holiday, returning to Greenville's school desegregation in 1970, which had been accomplished with what *The New York Times* called "grace and style." Shi lamented that both grace and style had disappeared in the current dispute. The *News* itself, a conservative newspaper, now vigorously challenged Case's cost estimates, noting that the Council spent far more on extraneous purposes such as travel and professional memberships. Hughes, Shaw, Wyche, Hipp, Shi and the *News* all placed their hopes in the citizens' committee that would seen be appointed (Young 2003).

By late February, then, all eyes were turned toward that committee. Republican Shelby and Democrat Norris had negotiated on the membership, with some input by BJU's Taylor. The outcome was either a masterpiece of anticipated coalition-building or a hopeless pastiche of irreconcilable antagonists. County Clerk of Court Paul Wickensimer, a widely respected former Councilor (who had once voted against a holiday) and BJU alumnus, chaired this panel. He was joined by Stephen Brown, a Southern Baptist conservative and past chair of the county GOP; Lisa Van Riper, a college instructor and veteran Republican pro-life activist; Chandra Dillard, a City Council Democrat and ardent holiday proponent; the Reverend Hall Hollifield, pastor of the Second Baptist Church of Greer; Rev. Ennis Fant, a pastor, past NAACP chair, and former Council member; Rev. Luonne Rouse, African-American pastor of a white Methodist congregation; Charles Harris, Michelin official and County Human Relations committeeman; and former Atlanta Braves pitcher José Álvarez. The committee's ethnic makeup was four whites, four blacks, and one Hispanic (Alongi 2003b).

Reactions to the announcement of the study committee varied. The NAACP's Paul Guy dismissed it as "irrelevant" and a "slap in the face," announcing that if the Council did not act by March 18, 2003, holiday proponents would begin an economic boycott of the County.

"If they want to sit there and take an economic hit, then we'll cripple the county. We'll cripple the tax base. That's my goal and objective. We'll bring in more national figures. We'll bring in an army." Presaging disagreement among black leaders, however, one of Guy's NAACP predecessors, Fant—himself a study committee member—said that he was "encouraged by the process . . . encouraged by the people on the panel . . . I think the community will be pleased by the end of the day." For the time being, at least, mainline church and civic leaders were optimistic and saw the panel as a vehicle for resolving the issue—if it acted quickly. Although Wickensimer hoped to produce a report before May, it would certainly miss the NAACP deadline. As Fant argued, a "winning" outcome could not be produced overnight.

The Conflict Is Joined

The appointment of the study committee certainly did not defuse the issue. Indeed, the most heated moment in this saga came as the Council held its regular biweekly meeting on March 3, 2003, which was attended by hundreds on both sides. This time the singing, preaching, and protests of the black churches were countered by a small group of people who waved Confederate flags and criticized Jackson, King, and holiday supporters. They represented the League of the South, secessionists seeking to revitalize "Old South" principles, including "true Christian tenets." Some League members were already inside, speaking about the religious basis of their opposition to anyone who would listen, calling Jackson and the NAACP terrorists and referring to King himself as a Communist and an adulterer. Once the Council meeting began, both sides waited expectantly as routine business was dispatched. Then the floor was opened for thirty minutes of public comment.

Almost instantly, bedlam ensued. There had been two signup sheets, one for those addressing routine Council business and one for the holiday issue. Some King proponents had signed the wrong form and Chair Henderson sent them—including Jackson—to the back of the King line, refusing to let them speak during the time allotted to those addressing routine business. (The *Greenville News* stoked the controversy by erroneously quoting Henderson as saying that "if people were not smart enough to sign the right list, they could wait." In fact, her exact words were "I feel like if someone can't read the list and figure out which list they're supposed to sign on, that they ought to go to the back of the line.")

When Butch Taylor of the Greenville County Taxpayers Association, a Council meeting "regular" and holiday opponent, began to speak, Jackson's entourage approached the podium, standing in line behind the other speakers. Taylor made a few racially charged comments, telling black listeners that "I did not sell your ancestors into slavery.... Your own ancestors sold your ancestors into slavery," citing a *National Geographic* article for proof. A shouting match ensued among some clergy in attendance. Revs. J. M. Fleming and Caesar Richburg berated Taylor, but Rev. Craig vigorously defended him. Once tempers had cooled a bit, Henderson asked Jesse Jackson to be seated until his turn came to speak. Still incensed at being relegated to the back, Jackson refused. Henderson repeated her request, and when Jackson remained adamant, she adjourned the meeting. This produced an uproar, as Jackson and Richburg led supporters in twenty minutes of "We Shall Overcome." Although most Councilors then went home, Democrats Flint, Norris, and Gibson stayed as Richburg told the crowd, "if we have to go to jail, we'll go to jail tonight." Jackson calmed the crowd and preached for a half hour on economic justice, racial profiling, school issues, and prison labor, as well as the holiday. Convinced that the Council had plotted to silence him, he warned, "We will speak when they allow us to speak. If not, we'll just speak anyhow. We will speak, and we will be heard" (Zacher and Barnett 2003c).

The next day, Flint and Norris held a press conference at County Square to muster support for the holiday. Rev. Craig interrupted them, complaining that the abrupt adjournment the night before had trampled on his civil rights, just before his turn to speak. Craig brandished his own petition signed by 133 fundamentalist clergy, a bit of theatre that produced a confrontation with Flint, who recalled his student days at the University of Alabama when George Wallace blocked the entrance of the first black student. After explaining that memory, Flint told them why "I support the Martin Luther King holiday. I don't think there's any doubt that Martin Luther King was successful in leading us to integration with a minimum amount of violence." The NAACP's Guy also felt that his side had been shut out, saying, "We have left our doors open to talk with the County Council, but I really do believe that on this issue there's not much room for negotiation." Craig obviously saw it differently: "I don't believe this issue is about Martin Luther King Jr. so much. I believe it's an issue of people forcing our committee and our community to do something without us having a voice in it." As this public confrontation illustrates, there seemed to be no common ground. Indeed, when a local mediation firm offered its services, both sides pointedly ignored it (Barnett 2003d).

The March 4 meeting disaster and aftermath led some antagonists to reconsider their stances. Henderson sought some middle ground in the March 11 issue of the *Greenville News:*

> As chairman, I am committed to working with the Democrats and Republicans of the council as well as all residents as we work out policies democratically. I am also committed to not allowing a vocal handful of partisans on either side to disrupt our progress toward a solution. . . . Arbitrary deadlines and public pressure are not helpful. They push the community further apart and reopen old divisions. The exchanges of words and sound bites also have not helped. I, as well, could have spoken with more care. For that, I apologize. . . . My hope and prayer is that we will come together as we have in the past to resolve this issue for a better Greenville.

Henderson was not the only one searching for negotiating space. Guy's predecessor as NAACP head, Horace Nash, complained that Guy had violated policy by not getting national office approval for the boycott: "We need to be careful with what we say now that emotions are so high and give the committee the chance to mediate this thing and try to come up with a solution." Guy retorted, "There is no threat. My position has always been to attempt to work together. It's the county council who is out of step. The NAACP is not out of step." And, in a thrust at the old-line black leadership, he added, "Now, if the old order in the black community cannot step to this new leadership, that's their problem, you see. We're moving forward."

Many black pastors echoed Nash's viewpoint and encouraged protestors to tone it down and give the study committee time. The Baptist Ministers Fellowship, instrumental in raising the holiday issue in the first place, now threw support behind the committee. "We see no need for any additional deadlines or public demonstrations between now and then," said its president, James Adams. "We are all bigger and better than violence and must provide an atmosphere whereby healing can begin" (Barnett 2003c). This stance was praised by Henderson, Study Committee Chairman Wickensimer, and by a *Greenville News* editorial saying that the "black Baptist ministers showed courage by urging an end to King day protests and allowing the committee to do its work."

The Baptist Ministers Fellowship did not specifically name Jackson or the NAACP, but they clearly wanted a moratorium on boycotts and marches. Guy, however, insisted that the protests would go on: "We commend the Baptist ministry association for their awareness of the situation and we support them in their endeavors. And we hope they will continue to support us in our endeavors." Jackson also rejected their call: "Those who don't want to protest have the right not to. Those who do, have the right to do so" (Alongi 2003a). As it turned out, the NAACP's March 18 march was postponed until April 26 because of the onset of war in Iraq. Guy announced that the protest would become a celebration if a holiday passed by that date. As if recognizing a public desire for greater civility, the Council's second March meeting was quite orderly, as law officers enforced strict rules on decorum. Paul Guy praised the rules, saying they produced "a nice, orderly process." Even Jackson said some kind things about the Study Committee, speculating that it would allow the anti-holiday protests to die down and opponents to "save face" (Zacher 2003c).

As Greenville debated the holiday and waited for the Committee report, the Council found itself isolated, even in the Upstate (Washington 2003). Two adjacent counties, Laurens and Pickens—neither a hotbed of civil rights activity—both created a paid holiday for employees, virtually without dissent, as did the small cities of Clinton, Mauldin, and Simpsonville (the latter two in Greenville County). Holiday proponents expected, perhaps understandably, that these actions would add to the momentum in Greenville, especially with some new political help. Although Republican Governor Mark Sanford declined to take sides, saying the issue was purely local, some noted Republicans, such as S.C. House Speaker David Wilkins, U.S. Representative Jim DeMint, and U.S. Senator Lindsay Graham were quietly passing the word that Greenville County should put the issue to rest (Hoover 2003).

The Citizens' Study Committee Reports

On March 26, the study committee reported. Despite its internal diversity, the committee demonstrated a rare degree of harmony. By all accounts, the heavily religious makeup of the panel had been an asset, as members began sessions with prayers for unity and divine guidance (Barnett 2003a). The prayers were answered. As one conservative Southern Baptist member, Rev. Hall Hollifield, put it, "If the people outside would take the attitude of these people here, I believe we can do something." The committee had been constrained less by its diverse membership than by its instructions. As a result, it came back with two options. The first would create a new fixed, paid holiday on the third Monday in January, calling it "Martin Luther King Jr. Holiday," effective in January 2004. This option represented a nod to holiday proponents, but ran up against the Council majority's preferences. The second option would convert an existing paid holiday (one of the days after Christmas, Thanksgiving, or Good Friday) to a "MLK Civil Rights Day," to be decided by county employees via secret ballot. As an additional gesture of good will, the Council would pass a resolution honoring several local civil rights leaders, all of them deceased (Bonnette 2003d).

Although most Committee members refrained from announcing their own preferences, some spoke up. Pro-life activist Lisa Van Riper advocated the first option, appealing to her usual Republican friends and allies on the Council in a March 28 *Greenville News* opted:

> Does recognition of the struggle and achievement have to take the form of a paid holiday? That was the course chosen and settled by our federal government, our state government and nearly all our county governments. To reinvent the standard of celebration at this point only invites questions about motives.

Former NAACP head Fant ironically told us that he saw the second option as more politically viable: "The key to No. 2 was basically everybody dumped all of their concerns in a pot—including the concerns of the council members. And that is the absolute best we could come up with trying to address every single concern that people had."

The initial public response was diverse, ranging all the way from support and gratitude to frustration. The Baptist Ministers Fellowship welcomed the proposals: "It is apparent that great collaboration went into the debate and that a fair and reasonable conclusion was reached. It is our hope that this process will serve as a model for handling highly contentious issues in the future." The BMF preferred option one, but thought that the second was "a fair compromise that addresses the concerns of all on both sides." The NAACP's Guy was less positive: "It sounds like they were trying to cook a soup. I don't know what kind of soup it was, but they put everything in it." He supported only the first option and was backed in this by some African-American pastors such as J. M. Flemming and Donald R. Smith (Zacher 2003a). The Greenville Taxpayers' Association was not satisfied, either: if the Council adopted either plan they would launch a petition drive for a public referendum. If successful, this would delay resolution until November 2004. Butch Taylor reiterated that "We do not want a Dr. Martin Luther King Jr. holiday in Greenville County—period. In my opinion he is not a person of honor, therefore we should not honor him with a holiday. Everybody in Greenville County has a right to vote on this. If you don't think people are upset, put a petition out there and see how upset people are."

Despite the diversity of the reaction, many community leaders saw the second option as the way out of the dilemma, and the Study Committee, representing activists from right to left, as showing the way. Council Chair Henderson immediately endorsed the report:

> I support the second recommendation as a fair and reasonable compromise. I believe it deserves the support of County Council. It does not add the cost of a new holiday. It would convert an existing county holiday into an MLK Civil Rights Day. It would not take away county employees' floating holiday. . . . Our community cannot afford continued division over a Martin Luther King Jr. holiday. We cannot afford to prolong the debate any longer. . . . The committee did its job well. Now I look for the County Council to act on the recommendations promptly, so that we as a community can continue to chart Greenville's future together.

Within days, the Council alignments had been clarified. Democrats Judy Gilstrap, Flint, Norris, and Lottie all preferred option one, but would clearly accept the compromise. On the other hand, four Republicans from mostly rural or working-class white districts—Joe Dill, Selby, Case, and Eric Beddingfield—opposed both options, although Beddingfield said that he "was still praying and deliberating." Republicans Dozier Brooks, Mark Kingsbury, and Taylor claimed to be uncommitted, with Taylor observing, "We have a lot of work to do." Taylor's professed openness hinted that the BJU forces might accept option two, following the lead of alumnus Wickensimer, who had shepherded the committee report. Nothing, as yet, was heard from Dr. Bob Jones III.

The business community quickly coalesced around the committee report. Three dozen business and civic leaders held a news conference urging the Council to adopt the holiday. As the *Greenville News* put it, "the group was a Who's Who of Greenville business, with diverse faces that bridged racial and political lines." Republicans such as Mayor Knox White and former (and future) U.S. Representative Bob Inglis held down the conservative end, while advertising executive Joe Erwin, soon to become state chair of the Democratic Party, anchored the left. Accounting executive George Short spoke for all: "if Greenville is going to build knowledge-based industries and jobs, we need to attract the best and brightest from around the world. And they need to know that they are welcome" (Zacher 2003b).

The Decision Is Made

Despite all the public pressure, the Council ignored both Committee options. Instead, it adopted a new scheme by Mark Kingsbury that gave employees five fixed holidays a year—and then allowed them to vote on five others. Kingsbury claimed his compromise responded to a petition by county employees opposed to shifting an existing holiday to a MLK Civil Rights Day. Drafted without input from either Council staff or Chair Henderson and the four Democrats, the proposal was rammed through by a 7–5 vote, virtually without discussion. Since most County employees were white, this plan would inevitably thwart any holiday. Study Committee members watched the proceedings in utter disbelief; indeed, Wickensimer's stunned visage summarized their reaction for television viewers (Zacher and Barnett 2003a).

The holiday proponents' responses varied. Jackson's forces left chambers for a rally at a nearby church, calling for an immediate economic boycott. They were joined by many in the Baptist Ministers Fellowship, who felt their conciliatory gestures had been mocked by the Council. The *Greenville News* blasted the Council in terms seldom employed in polite southern publications, and all the pro-holiday forces united in demanding that the Council reverse the decision at its next meeting. Two important new forces soon joined them: the Greenville Chamber of Commerce and Dr. Bob Jones III.

The Chamber of Commerce had remained quiet until the April 1 vote. The group represented a wide range of businesses, from large industrial enterprises to smaller entrepreneurial firms, making it difficult to achieve consensus. The Chamber also had testy relations with Council Republicans, who had recently terminated economic development contracts with the Chamber. Chamber leaders therefore avoided the early lobbying, but after the Kingsbury coup had decided to go public. Concerned that several corporations planning to relocate in Greenville were now having second thoughts, the Chamber sponsored a mass meeting of business, religious, and political leaders. Over three hundred appeared, representing major firms, including the international giants Michelin and BMW; mainline Protestant clergy, led once again by Wynn; Republican and Democratic political figures; and a host of black clergy and civil rights leaders. Close observers of Greenville politics could not recall a more impressive political coalition.

Most surprising of all, perhaps, was the simultaneous (but separate) endorsement of the Study Committee's second option by Dr. Bob Jones III in an April 11 *Greenville News* op-ed. Jones had not changed his mind about Martin Luther King Jr., with "his well-known and undisputed marital infidelities, his leftist political philosophies, his theological irregularities." If Jones had been on County Council, he "could have voted for the compromise resolution, because it took the focus away from Martin Luther King exclusively and placed it also on the civil rights movement." He said, "With a glad heart I could vote for a holiday that celebrates that." (Another reason for favoring the compromise was that Jackson did not like it!) The BJU president asked the Council to reconsider option two.

Despite the unprecedented mobilization of Greenville's religious, economic, and political elite, the Council refused to budge, refusing reconsideration by a party line vote, 8 to 4, with Henderson joining her GOP colleagues when it was clear the motion was lost. Indeed, Henderson was in an uncomfortable position. Although her willingness to compromise was in line with much of the GOP's elected leadership, it was unpopular among many grassroots activists. Although she joined pro-holiday members who tried later to revive the issue, Council rules prohibited reconsideration under normal parliamentary procedure for a full year (Zacher and Barnett 2003b).

Aftermath: Electoral Mobilization and Success

Activists adopted several tactics after the failure of the Study Committee compromise. Some continued to attend Council meetings and used the public forum to keep the issue alive. Others picketed Case's home, protesting the movement's *bête noir* (Buchanan 2003b). Civil rights leaders in the state legislature unsuccessfully introduced a bill requiring counties to observe all state holidays. Most visible, however, was a massive protest march on May 17, 2003, in downtown Greenville. Led by Jackson and national NAACP president Kweisi Mfume, the rally drew over ten thousand demonstrators to County Square, kicking off an economic boycott. The marchers included not only most of the African-American groups who had worked in uneasy alliance, but also many white supporters, including some who had marched with King himself in the heyday of the civil rights movement. But the largest demonstration in Greenville history left the Council unmoved and failed to influence county employees. On July 15, 2003, they voted to keep their traditional paid holidays, with the MLK Day option receiving only 271 votes, almost exactly the number of black employees. As a result, Greenville was left as the only Palmetto State county without an official holiday (Buchanan 2003a).

At this point, proponents turned to electoral politics, announcing an unprecedented venture to defeat the Council "antis" in the spring 2004 GOP primaries (tantamount to election for most County offices). At first blush, this campaign seemed quixotic: Republican members seemed quite in tune with their electoral base on this issue, as well as on other moral questions. The majority, however, had also antagonized important Republican constituencies beside the substantial GOP contingent supporting the holiday. The protracted warfare over economic development with the Chamber of Commerce had irked business leaders. The Council's fiscal austerity, the hallmark of the Republican majority, had left other residents dissatisfied with highway construction, street maintenance, and emergency medical services, especially in the burgeoning suburban areas. Many citizens had tired of the rancor and secrecy that often characterized Council operations.

As a result, primary challenges to some GOP members gained more impetus than the civil rights leaders—all of them Democrats—could ever have expected. Initially the most promising assault was mounted by business mogul Hayne Hipp against Case, whose fiscal tightfistedness and strict moral traditionalism critics saw as high barriers to more modern approaches to community issues. Hipp's concerns went far beyond the holiday issue to include a whole range of Council actions that threatened economic growth and civil comity. His wealth and business connections made him a formidable foe although he had only recently deserted his old Democratic affiliation for the GOP. As it turned out, the contest pitted Hipp's expensive media efforts against Case's grassroots mobilization.

Other Republicans faced opponents motivated by different concerns. In what proved to be a crucial contest, newcomer Tony Trout challenged Selby after the latter ignored a request to pave neighborhood streets, a failure Trout claimed was emblematic of Selby's poor constituency service. Similar complaints prompted challenges to Council chair Henderson by Jim Burns and to Dozier Brooks by Butch Kirven, a retired general in the National Guard. Even Taylor, representing the safely conservative "Bob Jones" precincts, attracted a primary opponent. Although the Republican challengers varied in age, length of residence in the area, and religious affiliation (all were active church people), they shared one stance: they wanted to see a King holiday. This issue was never the stated centerpiece of their primary campaigns, but inevitably the press drew the contrast.

In the end, the GOP primaries represented a victory for the pro-holiday forces. Case easily survived Hipp's well-financed and heavily publicized challenge, largely by mobilizing his own conservative religious base. Taylor handily defeated a token opponent, but Henderson and Brooks lost renomination bids to holiday supporters Burns and Kirven. Since Henderson had supported a holiday, the results shifted only one vote, leaving resolution to the outcome of a runoff between incumbent Selby and Trout. The first runoff went in Trout's favor by eighteen votes, but was overturned on Selby's appeal to the County GOP executive committee, ultimately confirmed by the state Republican Party and state Supreme Court. In the second runoff, however, Trout won decisively, giving holiday advocates at least a 7–5 Council margin, as all the (token) Democratic nominees in the general election supported the holiday (Szobody 2004).

Although many factors contributed to the final primary results, the King controversy clearly played a role. Many Democrats and independents voted in the GOP primaries, especially in the final Selby-Trout contest, where the number of African Americans voting far exceeded previous levels. (Indeed, Selby's successful appeal to the GOP authorities after the first runoff was based on Democrats who had clearly voted illegally, participating first in the Democratic primary and then in the GOP runoff.) The role of the religious community on both sides was much more muted, however, with little visible activity. Although some fundamentalist pastors endorsed Selby and a few black pastors encouraged parishioners to vote for Trout, most white clergy maintained their traditional aversion to overt electioneering.

The end, as they often say, was anticlimactic. After a modest civil rights march in downtown Greenville, a spate of interracial worship services, and a few pronouncements from afar by Jackson, the new Council quickly ended the controversy almost exactly two years after it had arisen. Following an invocation by Case, Trout's Public Services Committee voted 3–2 to adopt a new employee handbook including the King holiday, with the new GOP chair joining the two African-American councilors in favor. The next evening, on February 1, 2005, the entire Council adopted the handbook by a 7–5 vote, without discussion, and with the three new Republicans and the four holdover Democrats in favor (Szobody 2005; Szobody and Brutzman 2005).

Analysis and Conclusions

What can this unusual case tell us about the role of religious actors in community politics? To begin with, the episode is a useful reminder about the intersection of "policy types," because the King holiday issue does not fall neatly into the categories that often used social scientists to explain community decision-making. For many citizens on both sides, the controversy displayed large elements of morality or culture war politics, heavily influenced by religion (cf. Meier 1994; Sharp 1999). Many citizens viewed the decision to honor or not honor Dr. King as highly symbolic of community values. But such decisions also inevitably impinged on other community interests, such as economic development, as the antagonists debated the effects of any decision on the area's ability to attract new businesses and skilled workers. Although one can separate the *dramatis personae* into religious, business, or civic leaders, many actors fit in two or more categories and are closely linked by kinship, religious, or business ties to those in the others. As morality and economic politics are often linked, so too are religious and economic leaders.

With this caveat in mind, what can we say about the involvement of religious interests here? Clearly their most important role was agenda setting, putting the issue at the forefront of public and Council attention. Although black leaders had tried for years to raise the issue, not until the black clergy—including several civil rights leaders—made it a central focus did the holiday receive sustained community attention. Even that campaign might have miscarried, except for the substantial backing of the mainline white churches provided a critical link to the business leaders who were eventually activated. Granted, the business community had its own bones to pick with the County, but those concerns certainly did not instigate action on the holiday issue—quite to the contrary, they probably delayed involvement.

Religious leaders also played a vital role in the initial public mobilization. Although the black clergy produced more protesters at Council meetings, mainline pastors generated equally important publicity and directed the attention of many community leaders, often their own congregants, to the significance of the issue. For many whites, the mainline clergy legitimized the issue and made it an important priority. Some fundamentalist clergy sought to play a comparable role on the other side, but often found a less responsive public.

Despite the important agenda-setting and mobilization efforts by religious leaders, religious involvement was hardly universal. In fact, the case also illustrates factors that often inhibit clerical mobilization (Crawford and Olson 2001a; Djupe and Gilbert 2003; Guth, Green, Smidt, Kellstedt, and Poloma 1997). First, many clergy remained entirely uninvolved, whether out of theological strictures against political involvement, fears of conflict with (or within) one's congregation, or a sense of personal political inefficacy. This passivity was especially common among theological conservatives, who were often torn by this issue, but was shared by many others. Second, even among active clergy perspective diverged greatly, sometimes even within religious communities. For example, we find competing interests among African-American pastors, as some "traditional" clergy favored a more conciliatory strategy than that followed by Jackson and more aggressive ministers. Even the fundamentalist leaders were divided. Some, like Craig, fought vigorously against the holiday and sought to persuade his colleagues and congregation to do the same. Others, like Jones, struggled to reconcile personal moral sentiments with broader institutional and community interests. For most religious leaders, then, the issue raised important questions of personal theological perspective, organizational constraints, and political judgments.

At first glance the evolution of the issue resembles the classic civil rights struggles of the 1960s. The holiday movement was originated by black clergy and sustained primarily by African-American church members, with secular civil rights groups (often led by clergy) seeking leadership roles not always warranted by their actual membership. Once again, as in the 1960s, mainline churches joined the cause (Findlay 1993), albeit with one critical difference—this time the churches involved were from the affected community itself, not from other parts of the country. In the end, moreover, even some fundamentalists, including Jones, had sought a compromise. Thus, the ultimate religious coalition was much broader—and included more influential members of the racial majority—than was true four decades earlier.

The religious forces themselves could not control the outcome, however. Instead, they found it necessary to expand the scope of the conflict by bringing in influential outside parties (Schattschneider 1942; cf. Lipsky 1968). Although Jackson was a special case, given his personal ties to Greenville, the involvement by the national NAACP, some attention from the national media (especially in the form of a Public Broadcasting System filming crew), and the activity of state and national officials from both the Democratic and Republican parties certainly enlarged the circle of participants.

As in earlier civil rights controversies, the most crucial expansion brought in the local business community, especially when the economic implications of the Council's decision became apparent. Classic studies of civil rights conflicts often argued that successful resolution was most likely when business elites committed themselves to finding solutions (Crain 1969), a conclusion meshing with that scholarly generation's emphasis on the dominance of economic elites in local politics (Hunter 1953). By mid-2003 the local business community had decided that the Council had to adopt the holiday if Greenville were to continue to attract the high-tech and international corporations that had been so instrumental in its economic growth.

All of these analytic perspectives help us understand the debate over the King holiday. The moral character and the civil rights aspects of the issue mobilized large sections of the Greenville religious community behind the holiday proposal, the proponents successfully activated a broader coalition of religious groups, and the economic implications did the same for "secular" business leaders, many of them also active in mainline churches. Of course, this mobilization did not produce immediate victory. Despite the impressive range of the holiday movement, in some respects the mobilization was both incomplete and poorly timed. First, it did not include all the important actors in local politics, either religious or secular. The religious mobilization failed to activate most of the dominant Southern Baptist churches and clergy whose passivity was shared by leaders of several other groups. The intervention of some religious figures came too late: the initial outcome *might* have changed if Jones had announced support for the Study Committee's option two *before* it was voted down. Although some prominent business and professional people tried to garner support early on, most of the business community did not act until *after* the Council vote, apparently assuming that the Council could not ignore the swelling support for the holiday. Action by state GOP leaders to eliminate this embarrassing issue was also "too little," but was above all "too late."

The strategy of expanding the conflict also had negative effects. Although Jackson, the NAACP, and the national media brought greater outside attention to Greenville's deliberations, they probably delayed the final resolution. Indeed, a constant theme recurred in our interviews of leaders on all sides: the critical event that created the initial stalemate occurred quite early, namely, when Jackson first came to town to speak about the holiday. Jackson's refusal (and that of the NAACP) to endorse the Study Committee's work split the African-American community and hardened the resistance of the Council majority. In Jackson's absence, most participants privately agreed, the local actors might have resolved the issue much more quickly.

All this speculation assumes that the existing Council majority was reachable. But the holiday initially failed because of the makeup of the Council majority and the nature of their constituencies. Although the anticity attitude of most 1980s Councilors noted by Ehrenhalt (1991) was still present, a more important political transition had taken place. In 2003, the opponents of the holiday were mostly young, ideologically driven conservatives who represented well the anti-government sentiments of their rural, blue-collar and lower-middle class constituents. They effectively used those anti-tax, anti-spending sentiments to explain their opposition to the holiday, and although they did not resort to overt racial appeals, they utilized all the well-worn covert techniques of racial politics to build support.

Thus, the only hope for the holiday movement was to replace these Council members with others. Taking advantage of the full range of popular discontents, holiday proponents succeeded in swinging two crucial votes from the "no" to the "yes" column, reminding us again that elections are a powerful determinant of policy outcomes, whether those favored by religious interests, business elites, or other organizations. Although religious mobilization was least apparent in that arena, it had already played a critical role in the earlier stages of the policy process.

Chapter 8

Salt Lake City's Main Street Plaza Controversy

J. Quin Monson & Kara L. Norman

During the past several years, an enormous conflict erupted not only in Salt Lake City but also across the entire state of Utah over the sale of a block of Main Street in Salt Lake City to the Church of Jesus Christ of Latter-day Saints (Mormons).[1] The conflict began after a block of Main Street located between the two city blocks owned by the LDS Church was closed and transformed into a pedestrian plaza. The newly owned LDS Plaza sat between two blocks of particular importance to the LDS Church. One block houses the Salt Lake Temple and Tabernacle and the other contains the LDS Church Administration Building.

Because Utah's population is approximately two-thirds Mormon, the LDS Church and its members are significant players in Utah politics. The controversy and conflict over the sale of Main Street to the LDS Church may accurately be characterized as one of the most divisive and rancorous disputes to occur along religious lines in Utah over the last several decades. The disagreements effectively split the city and state along its religious and cultural divisions. Although the sale of the plaza was controversial, the controversy flared on October 9, 2002, when the 10th Circuit Court of Appeals in Denver voided some of the restrictions that the LDS Church had placed on behavior on the recently opened plaza. Immediately after the court's decision, protestors began to appear on the plaza, and the LDS Church called on the city to relinquish the public easement[2] on the property so that the church could resume the enforcement of behavioral restrictions and stop the protesting. The controversy escalated in December 2002 when Mayor Rocky Anderson announced that a compromise agreement had been negotiated that would result in the easement being sold to the LDS Church. The protestors stepped up their tactics, and word of the protesting, City Council deliberations, and other related activities dominated local news and opinion pages for several weeks. During the December 17, 2002, public hearings regarding Mayor Anderson's announcement that the easement would be sold to the church, protestors maintained their position and vowed to continue protesting on the plaza regardless of the consequences. Salt Lake citizens also expressed their disappointment in Mayor Anderson; many people openly denounced the mayor and said they would not support him in future elections (Salt Lake City Council Public Hearings 2002). Even the best attempts to settle the controversy surrounding Main Street could not eliminate all of the hard feelings and completely heal the community division.

This chapter presents an in-depth case study of the Main Street Plaza conflict resolution process that investigates the roles played by the various religious and secular interests involved in the controversy and how they interacted to produce a solution. First, we provide a brief overview of the religious and cultural divisions that exist in Utah and Salt Lake City using exit poll data from the 2003 Salt Lake City mayoral election. Second, we demonstrate that while Salt Lake City and the state of Utah share some characteristics, important differences also make the dynamics of religion and politics in Salt Lake City differ greatly from those we would observe statewide. Specifically, Mormons comprise a large majority of the state's population but actually make up a smaller proportion of Salt Lake City's population.[3] Third, we provide a detailed explanation of the events surrounding the Main Street Plaza controversy and the reasons behind its resolution. We find that because the heart of the controversy involved religious groups, nonreligious actors including Salt Lake City Mayor Anderson and the Alliance for Unity, a civic organization established (prior to the controversy) to bridge the religious and cultural divide that exits in Salt Lake City and Utah between Mormons and non-Mormons, played a critical role in bringing about a compromise solution. Finally, we link the Main Street Plaza case to existing theories on religion and community conflict resolution and elaborate on what our case can add to these theories.

Data and Methods

We utilize a variety of quantitative and qualitative data sources. These include a comprehensive analysis of journalists' accounts of the controversy in Salt Lake City's two major daily newspapers, the *Salt Lake Tribune* and the *Deseret Morning News.* Both papers have accessible and comprehensive electronic archives.[4]

Public opinion data for this paper come primarily from the 2003 Utah Colleges Exit Poll, conducted by faculty and students during the Salt Lake City mayoral election in November 2003 (Utah Colleges Exit Poll 2003). The 2003 mayoral election exit poll builds on a long-standing tradition of statewide exit polling in Utah, coordinated by Brigham Young University since 1982. The exit poll uses a stratified multi-stage, random sampling technique to select a representative cross section of voters leaving the polls on Election Day. Voters respond to a variety of questions related to their vote choice and public policy issues, as well as a full slate of demographic measures. Because of the controversy surrounding Main Street Plaza in 2002 and its possible implications for the 2003 mayoral election, the exit poll questionnaire contained several questions related to this matter, including questions about what kinds of activities should be allowed on the plaza, opinion about the settlement of the controversy, and voter approval of Mayor Anderson's handling of the issue.[5]

The research also includes eight in-depth interviews with people knowledgeable about or central to the controversy and its eventual resolution. These interviews allow for a deeper understanding of the divisiveness of the conflict itself. The interviews, furthermore, illustrate the diverging range of interests and opinions regarding the Main Street conflict that continue to exist in Salt Lake nearly six years after the initial sale.

The Context: The Religious Divide in Utah and Salt Lake City

Estimates of Utah's population put the proportion of Mormons in the state at about 62 percent (Canham 2004). Mormon Utahns are more politically active than their non-Mormon counterparts, so the proportion of Mormons to non-Mormons is slightly higher when just voters are considered. According to statewide exit poll data collected for Utah in 2002, Mormons comprise 71 percent of voters (Utah Colleges Exit Poll 2002). Consequently, "active" (practicing) Mormons hold nearly all of the major statewide offices and dominate the congressional delegation. Surveys of the state legislature routinely show that about eight of ten legislators are active Mormons (Bernick 2005). Whether in the state legislature or among the general public, the Mormon position generally prevails when the state of Utah encounters an issue where opinion is split sharply along Mormon and non-Mormon lines. This has been the case in recent years with alcohol control policy and a proposal to legalize some forms of gambling, for example (Campbell and Monson 2003).

The dynamics of Salt Lake City, however, are much different. Mormons comprise a minority of both the population of Salt Lake City and its electorate. According to the exit poll data, in the 2003 Salt Lake City mayoral election Mormons constituted 44 percent of voters (Utah Colleges Exit Poll 2003). Although a majority of the current City Council members are Mormon, neither current Mayor Rocky Anderson nor the two previous mayors are members of the LDS Church. In fact, Salt Lake City has not had a Mormon mayor since Ted Wilson in the 1980s.

Salt Lake City's religious demographics mean that if public opinion in the city is polarized along religious lines, the position or candidate that the majority of Mormons favor will more likely lose at the polls. This kind of religious polarization is precisely what prevailed in Salt Lake City's 2003 mayoral election. Table 8.1 presents the 2003 Salt Lake City mayoral vote by religion and "religious activity."[6] For ease of presentation, the religious preference categories have been divided into LDS and non-LDS and combined with level of religious activity.

Officially, Salt Lake City has nonpartisan elections, but both candidates in 2003 were Democrats. Although they held very similar positions on most of the issues, challenger Frank Pignanelli was clearly perceived as more friendly to the interests of Mormon voters, who overwhelmingly identify as Republicans (Pignanelli 2005). Regardless, incumbent Anderson received a majority of support from every group of non-LDS voters as well as from "not active" and "not very active" LDS voters. The reason the final vote was actually fairly close is that the largest group, "very active" LDS voters (34 percent of the overall electorate), voted overwhelming (88 percent) for Pignanelli. Of the much smaller group of self-identified, "somewhat active" Mormons, 61 percent voted for Pignanelli. Of the non-LDS groups, the two largest were the "not active" non-LDS and those who expressed no religious preference or chose not to answer. Of

Table 8.1
Religious Affiliation and Activity by the 2003 Salt Lake City Mayoral Vote (percents)

	Percent of all voters	Rocky Anderson	Frank Pignanelli
Very Active LDS	33.7	11.9	88.1
Somewhat Active LDS	5.5	39.2	60.8
Not Very Active LDS	2.9	56.2	43.8
Not Active LDS	1.7	64.6	35.4
Very Active non-LDS	10.4	68.2	31.8
Somewhat Active non-LDS	9.7	73.8	26.2
Not Very Active non-LDS	6.4	78.8	21.2
Not Active non-LDS	13.7	81.4	18.6
No religion/Prefer not to say	16.0	88.3	11.7
Total	100	53.7	46.3

Source: Utah Colleges Exit Poll [data]. 2003. Center for the Study of Elections and Democracy, Brigham Young University, Provo, Utah [producer and distributor]. N=3851

these voters, 81 and 88 percent voted for Anderson respectively. The 2003 mayoral election, therefore, is a good example of the strong possibility that Mormons will lose on their preferred political position when public opinion becomes highly polarized along Mormon and non-Mormon lines in Salt Lake City.

A key ingredient to the religious-based conflict in Salt Lake City is the perception that the LDS Church has a powerful influence over city politics and policy. The 2003 exit poll of Salt Lake City voters contained a question asking them to rate a list of groups on a five-point scale regarding their influence over public policy.[7] The perception that the LDS Church dominates the state politically is especially prevalent among non-Mormon Utahns (Sells 2005). Thus we expect respondents to rate the LDS Church highest in perceived power and also expect to find a difference in the perceptions of LDS Church power between LDS and non-LDS respondents. Table 8.2 presents the mean ratings of several groups thought to be powerful in Utah politics. As expected, the LDS Church is rated the highest at 4.35 (where

Table 8.2
Perceived Influence of Groups by Religious Affiliation
(mean scores)

Group	All	LDS	Non-LDS
American Civil Liberties Union (ACLU)	3.32	3.45	3.23
Utah Education Association (UEA)	3.22	3.3	3.16
Utah Association of Realtors (UAR)	2.86	2.72	2.97
LDS (Mormon) Church	4.35	4.12	4.53
Unitarian Church	2.17	2.43	1.99
Catholic Church	2.52	2.77	2.34

Source: Utah Colleges Exit Poll [data]. 2003. Center for the Study of Elections and Democracy, Brigham Young University, Provo, Utah [producer and distributor]. N ranges from 1216 to 1267 for all respondents, 705 to 728 for Non-LDS; 510 to 542 for LDS.

Note: An ANOVA test revealed that the difference in means between religious groups was statistically significant: F=10.402, p<0.001.

5 is "very powerful") and is the only entity with a rating above 4. It is worth noting that the other party to the legal dispute over Main Street Plaza was rated the lowest on the list at 2.17. This rate too is unsurprising. The First Unitarian Church in Salt Lake City has only one congregation with a small membership compared to other religious groups. The rating of 2.17 actually may be somewhat inflated by the visibility that the Unitarian Church achieved from their participation in the Main Street Plaza litigation.

Table 8.2 also presents the means for each group by LDS and non-LDS religious affiliation. While LDS respondents' average perception of LDS Church power was 4.12, non-Mormons' average perception of LDS Church power was 4.53. Furthermore, non-Mormons perceived the LDS Church as more powerful than any other group listed. Again, it is the only group rated above 4 on the scale, and 1.3 points separate the LDS Church from the next highest mean of 3.23 (for the ACLU). Conversely, Mormon voters perceived LDS Church power at an average of 4.12, only 0.66 points higher than the mean perception of power that Mormons gave the ACLU. An analysis of variance test reveals that the difference in means between perceptions of LDS power by Salt Lake's religious groups is statistically significant.[8]

Religious divisions affect political behavior and perceptions of power in Salt Lake City. With the religious demographics and political context of Salt Lake City in better focus, we can now turn to a description of what happened to ignite such a serious controversy regarding the Main Street Plaza. Understanding the dynamics of Salt Lake City in contrast to the rest of Utah shows why the LDS Church would need to participate so vigorously and actively to communicate its position on the controversy and work to persuade not only Mormons, but also at least some non-Mormons, that their position was tenable. It also helps bring into focus the reaction that many non-LDS residents have to the involvement of the LDS Church in public affairs.

The Main Street Plaza Story

Main Street Plaza is a block of land in downtown Salt Lake City that was sold to the LDS Church in April 1999. Immediately controversy surrounded the sale of the block, as citizens on each side of the issue divided themselves according to their opinion on the legality of the sale. The division occurred along primarily Mormon and non-Mormon lines and is considered one of the most divisive issues in the history of Salt Lake City. After nearly six years of legal battles among the LDS Church, the City of Salt Lake, and the ACLU, the controversy seems to have ended on October 3, 2005, when a three-judge panel rejected the ACLU's final lawsuit. In addition to the narrative here, we have included a brief timeline as an appendix to aid in keeping track of the sequence of events.[9]

The Players

Rocky Anderson was elected mayor of Salt Lake City in 1999 after the previous mayor, Deedee Corradini, and LDS Church President Gordon B. Hinckley had announced the proposed sale of Main Street to the LDS Church. A former attorney for the ACLU, Anderson spoke out against the Main Street Plaza sale after his election to office. Although he eventually brokered a compromise deal, Anderson was a critic of the sale and refused to vacate the city's easement to the plaza during the months immediately before the compromise. Even six years later, Mayor Anderson maintains that neither the City Council nor the LDS Church honestly dealt with the community when the sale was originally completed and before he became mayor (Anderson 2005).[10]

The Salt Lake City Council generally supported the position of the LDS Church during the controversy, with the votes on the Council usually breaking along religious lines: the five LDS Councilmembers sided with the church, while the two non-LDS Councilmembers typically sided against it. The City Council's actions remain a point of controversy. The Councilmembers almost always split along religious lines as they voted on various aspects of the controversy. Not surprisingly, they also split along religious lines in their assessment of their ability to separate their own religious beliefs from their views on Main Street Plaza. Councilmember Nancy Saxton, who is not Mormon, expressed her disappointment that the Council was unable to treat the LDS Church as they would any other entity in Salt Lake City (Saxton 2005). LDS Councilmember Carlton Christensen said that he tried to maintain his neutrality as much as possible (Christensen 2005). LDS Councilmember David Buhler simply answered "no" when asked whether his religion influenced his views (Buhler 2005).

H. David Burton, the Presiding Bishop of the LDS Church, served as the official church representative during the entire Main Street Plaza controversy. Bishop Burton asked the city to give up the easement, stating repeatedly that the church would not be satisfied without it (Snyder 2002b). The LDS Church maintains that their concerns regarding inappropriate behavior on the plaza were made clear from the time of the initial proposal in 1998 (Bills 2002; Church of Jesus Christ of Latter-day Saints 2002).

The central broker in attempting to resolve the conflict, the Alliance for Unity, was formed in September 2001 to promote a more accepting and unified community across religious, ethnic, and other boundaries throughout the state of Utah. The Alliance includes a diverse group of influential religious and secular leaders. When the Main Street Plaza controversy reached its apex, it facilitated discussion between the LDS Church, Salt Lake City, and other religious groups. The organization was founded by Mayor Anderson and Jon Huntsman, a wealthy and influential businessman in Salt Lake. Other prominent members include Elder Russell M. Ballard of the LDS Church, Baptist Rev. France Davis, Episcopal Bishop Carolyn Tanner Irish, Catholic Bishop George Niederaurer, businessman Spencer Eccles, and former judge Raymond Uno. The Alliance became vocal regarding the Main Street Plaza Controversy in December 2002, calling for a return to civility and eventually brokering and endorsing a proposed compromise that was later adopted.

The ACLU was one of the most ardent opponents of the terms of the sale of Main Street as well as the eventual compromise. The ACLU adamantly opposed the idea that the LDS Church could control the easement primarily on free speech grounds. Immediately following the sale of Main Street, the Utah ACLU started receiving calls from concerned citizens who questioned the legality of the city's sale. Initially, the ACLU responded that nothing was inherently wrong with a city selling a piece of land to a private organization (Clark 2005). Upon further study, however, the ACLU found reason to become involved in the controversy. Perhaps the ACLU involved itself most significantly through litigation surrounding the Main Street Plaza matter. The ACLU filed its first lawsuit in 1999, challenging the constitutionality of the sale on free speech grounds, and its second lawsuit in April 2000, challenging the sale of the easement on free speech grounds and alleging an unconstitutional entanglement of church and state.

The Sale of Main Street

The idea to build the plaza in downtown Salt Lake City originated as part of the 1962 Second Century Plan to revitalize the downtown area. The idea resurfaced in 1998 when a city official approached Bishop Burton about the possibility of selling the block of Main Street to the LDS Church. In late 1998 Hinckley and Mayor Deedee Corradini publicly announced a proposal for the city to sell a block of Main Street in Salt Lake City to the church. The proposal included a plan by the church to close the street and build a pedestrian plaza, complete with a reflecting pool and gardens that would connect two city blocks already owned by the church. One of the city blocks, known as Temple Square, is a place of great religious and historical significance to Mormons and contains the Salt Lake Temple and Tabernacle. It is also the largest tourist attraction in Utah. The other block houses the LDS Church Administration Building and the recently renovated Joseph Smith Building. The church was already in negotiations to purchase the subterranean rights below Main Street in order to build the underground parking garage included in the original Second Century Plan. Because construction of the parking garage would mean a long street closure due to construction, at some point negotiations with the city turned to the idea of closing the street permanently and building the pedestrian plaza.

In the spring of 1999, after debate over the sale, the City Council voted 5–2 along religious lines to approve the deal, and construction began. During the initial discussion before the planning commission and then before the City Council, the behavioral restrictions that the church had planned for the plaza once it opened to the public received some mention. Just how much of this discussion took place during the public forums and as part of the public record became a point of much contention later on. The City Council approved the sale in April 1999, with a set of easement restrictions they chose not to include in the deed.

In hindsight, the intentions of the LDS Church to restrict behavior to match its own standards and teachings are reflected in the record, but the City Council changed the terms of the sale recommended by the planning commission at the last minute to allow the church to restrict behavior that it found objectionable. This hasty change sparked the initial conflict. In particular, the LDS Church wanted to prohibit activities on the plaza that might normally occur in a city park or other public places around the city, such as sunbathing, smoking, and especially anti-Mormon protesting and distribution of anti-Mormon literature. Opponents of the sale later decried this last-minute change by the City Council and used it in federal court to attack the legality of the ordinance approving the sale.

The First Lawsuit

Immediately after the sale of Main Street to the LDS Church on November 16, 1999, the ACLU filed a lawsuit in federal court suing Salt Lake City regarding the constitutionality of the sale, specifically the behavioral restrictions that would limit free speech and expression. The conflict over the sale dealt with the confusion over whether or not Main Street was a public or private park. If the plaza were a traditional public park, the behavioral restrictions would be unconstitutional, but if the LDS Church owned the plaza, the behavioral restrictions would be legal. At issue were the terms of the easement maintained on the property by the city that allowed 24-hour access but also allowed the LDS Church to enforce its behavioral restrictions. The ACLU maintained that because the city kept an easement, the behavioral restrictions were unconstitutional. The city and the LDS Church maintained that the easement did not preclude the behavioral restrictions, pointing to other cities, such as Denver, where pedestrian walkways with free speech restrictions already existed (Fee 2002).[11]

Protest and Controversy

In the midst of the controversy, Rocky Anderson succeeded Deedee Corradini as mayor of Salt Lake City. Mayor Anderson was raised in an LDS family but no longer affiliates with the church. His initial statements about the plaza put him clearly in the camp favoring public access. On December 23, 2002, Mayor Anderson stated, "I don't think there's any question the city could insist upon retaining the easement" (May 2002a). His statements at the time indicate that he was straddling the fence between seeing the terms of the sale as outlined by the previous mayor through, while at the same time showing sympathy to the First Amendment and public access arguments of the ACLU. Initially he was unwilling to give up the city's easement to the plaza, stating repeatedly that "there is no way in my administration that the city will abandon any claim to public access" (Walsh 1999).

Despite the controversy over the terms of the sale, Main Street Plaza finally opened to the public in October of 2000. While a few limited confrontations occurred between protestors (testing the behavioral restrictions) and LDS Church security officials (enforcing them), the protests ended because the restrictions were legal at the time. Meanwhile, the pending federal court case moved forward, and in May 2001, U.S. District Court Judge Ted Stewart upheld the constitutionality of the church's behavioral restrictions, essentially by concluding that Main Street was not a public forum. The ACLU appealed the case to the 10th U.S. Circuit Court of Appeals in Denver.

Then, after nearly a year of relative silence, the conflict and controversy over Main Street Plaza began to heat up significantly. In October 2002 a three-judge panel of the 10th Circuit Court reversed Judge Stewart's decision and ruled that the plaza was a public forum. The LDS Church's behavioral restrictions, therefore, were unconstitutional. The judges recognized the difficulty of the situation they were creating for the parties involved. As Mayor Anderson put it, "The parties agreed to one term that was crucial to the church (which paid $8.2 million for the land) and another term that was crucial to the City—yet they could not both constitutionally be given effect. Either the restrictions or the easement had to go" (Anderson 2002:

86). The 10th Circuit also recognized the same possibilities, suggesting that the city could extinguish their easement on the plaza so that it would no longer be considered a public forum and the church's behavioral restrictions could be re-imposed. Alternatively, the court suggested that the city could create reasonable "time, place, and manner" restrictions that maintained First Amendment rights but also gave some protection to the church in recognition of the religious and spiritual significance of the plaza and its surroundings.

In response to the 10th Circuit Court's decision, Mayor Anderson again indicated that he would not support giving up the easement, stating that doing so would be a "betrayal" (May 2002b). Anderson indicated his support of "time, place, and manner" restrictions to regulate protest activity and began to formulate a set of restrictions that might be acceptable to all parties. The LDS Church's response to the 10th Circuit decision was also swift and clear—the church wanted the mayor and the City Council to follow the court's suggestion to give up the easement. To support their claims and generate support, the LDS Church then launched a major public relations campaign in mid-November. The church's public relations effort included releasing a packet of materials designed to tell their side of the story surrounding the creation of the plaza, and to press their case for turning over the easement as a viable solution (Church of Jesus Christ of Latter-day Saints 2002). In response to the church's public relations effort, the City Council offices were overloaded with phone calls—18,957 between November 20 and December 17, 2002 (Salt Lake City Council Public Hearings 2002). For a few days, the volume of calls was so high that some city employees were unable to make outgoing phone calls and resorted to using their cell phones to do their jobs (Ewing 2005).

It was then revealed in the press that prominent Utah businessman Jon Huntsman, an active and very wealthy Mormon who had a good relationship with both Mayor Anderson and LDS Church leaders, had been working behind the scenes to broker a compromise (Snyder 2002a). Even Huntsman struggled to bring the two sides to an agreement; his initial attempts failed to produce a compromise (Snyder 2002a). With no deal in sight, the controversy reached its climax in December 2002. In early December, Mayor Anderson presented a formal proposal for "time, place, and manner" restrictions, remaining unwilling to give up the city's easement. Mayor Anderson's proposal included limiting the public easement available for protestors on the plaza to the sidewalk on the eastern side of the plaza furthest away from the Salt Lake Temple. In addition, it included two smaller protest areas at the north and south ends of the plaza. The ACLU reluctantly approved the mayor's proposal but the LDS Church swiftly rejected it as soon as the details were made public.

The controversy grew more heated with every passing day. In early December 2002, the City Council was discussing whether the mayor's approval was necessary to decide whether the city could relinquish the Main Street easement to the church. Mayor Anderson threatened legal action if the Council attempted to do so. The ACLU promised a lawsuit if the city sold the easement, and the church was insisting that the city do just that. The City Council responded by voting to vacate the easement; Mayor Anderson released a "time, place, and manner" proposal three days later. Once again, compromise did not appear to be in the works. Following the opposing decisions from both the City Council and the mayor, the Alliance for Unity began its involvement in the affair by calling for a return to civility.

The Compromise

Mayor Anderson finally concluded that the LDS Church would never agree to "his time, place, and manner" restrictions proposal (Anderson 2002, 2005). At this point the controversy was taking a heavy toll on the mayor both personally and in terms of his standing in public opinion polls (Fantin 2002). His public statements up until that point indicated virtually no movement in his position that the city would not give up the easement. He began to feel pressure from many sides, including enormous pressure from the church. Then, on Friday, December 13, 2002, Mayor Anderson first conceived of a compromise proposal in which the city would give up the easement in exchange for two and a half acres of land the church held adjacent to a west side Salt Lake City community center.

The sequence of events that followed on the weekend of December 14–15 is not clearly known. The public record is incomplete; our eight interviewees offered different accounts; and some parties to the compromise declined to be interviewed. What is known is that the mayor met with Jon Huntsman to discuss his proposal. Some months earlier, Anderson and Huntsman were the cochairs of the Alliance for Unity, the group created independently of the plaza controversy to improve community relations in Utah and foster understanding and better relationships between diverse groups. One of the main reasons for the formation of the Alliance for Unity was to bridge a growing gap between Mormons and non-Mormons in Salt Lake City. Many prominent Mormons were members of the Alliance, including Huntsman, Elder Ballard (a member of the church's elite Quorum of the Twelve Apostles), and Bishop Burton—the church leader charged with overseeing LDS financial and business asset, and the church official most visibly involved in projects involving downtown Salt Lake City. In addition to Anderson, the non-Mormon membership of the Alliance also included the leadership of the Catholic Diocese of Salt Lake City and the largest Episcopal congregation in town. The presence of prominent Mormons together with other major religious leaders gave the Alliance instant credibility.

Although the Alliance for Unity became involved in the battle late in the game, its impact was felt immediately. Mayor Anderson's compromise was aided by the Alliance's ability to negotiate something for the city in return for relinquishing the easement. Over that weekend in December, members of the Alliance met with both Mayor Anderson and LDS Church leaders in December to hammer out the details of the compromise. In the end, the city would trade the easement for two and a half acres in west Salt Lake and five million dollars to be used for building a community center. On Sunday, December 15, 2002, the Alliance met and voted to support the proposal. Mayor Anderson made a formal announcement regarding the compromise the next day with both Bishop Burton and Huntsman at his side. Clearly, the Alliance facilitated the compromise. That same day, the *Salt Lake Tribune* published the results of a poll conducted on December 9–12 that indicated a sharp decline in Anderson's approval as well as declining support for his reelection, particularly among Mormon respondents (Fantin 2002).

With a new compromise reached between the city and the LDS Church, the plaza issue heated up again and produced what was perhaps the most tumultuous day of protesting during the entire controversy. On December 17, 2002, the day after the compromise announcement, a small group of protestors and street preachers gathered on the plaza and chose a location for their protest directly in front of the Salt Lake Temple. Their position obscured a popular location for wedding parties to have their pictures taken with the temple in the background. With local television news cameras rolling, the protestors refused to move to accommodate wedding party photos and then shouted obscenities and offensive comments through bullhorns. These protests were given lengthy and prominent coverage on the local evening newscasts, overshadowing the public hearings taking place in the City Council chamber the same evening to discuss the compromise proposal. The visual imagery was powerful—a young bride on her wedding day was reduced to tears by the protestors, and her mother went on camera to plead with the protestors to be reasonable, asking, "Is this what you would want for your daughter's wedding day?"

While there are no opinion surveys to gauge the immediate effect of this series of events, the combined effect of the endorsement of Mayor Anderson's "land for peace" proposal by the Alliance for Unity, combined with the ugliness of the subsequent protesting, seemed to work in tandem to coalesce public opinion in favor of resolving the compromise. For LDS Church leaders and prominent Mormon members of the Alliance for Unity, the prospect of years of ongoing ugly protest at the heart of the church's most sacred space, the Salt Lake Temple, likely prompted their desire to offer whatever was necessary to dissolve the easement and end the protesting. Even the *Salt Lake Tribune*, whose independence from the LDS Church is widely accepted,[12] condemned the ugliness of the protesting, calling it "offensive" and saying, "Handing out religious leaflets is one thing. Shouting insults at young brides on what should be the most perfect day of their lives is another. Picketing against church policy on, say, academic freedom is one thing. Loudly implying that another person's deeply held beliefs are a ticket to hell is another" ("With Friends Like These" 2002).

The endorsement of the proposal by the LDS leadership, combined with the spectacle of the protests, likely prompted the Mormon rank and file to support the compromise. Conversely, for all but the most ardent opponents of the LDS Church, and even some who placed a very high value on First Amendment freedom of speech rights, the personalization and ugliness of the protesting may have resulted in a reconsideration of opposition. No one stepped forward to defend the most egregious actions of the protestors. Many initial opponents of the mayor's compromise proposal may have realized that if the easement were to remain, the effect on long-term relations between Mormons and non-Mormons in Salt Lake City could suffer each time such protests took place.

Public opinion polling about the compromise eventually turned in favor of the mayor's decision to relinquish the easement. The proportion favoring the settlement, while not overwhelming, was clearly a majority.[13] A year later, the 2003 Utah Colleges Exit Poll revealed that 61 percent of voters "agreed" or "strongly agreed" with the eventual plaza settlement.[14] Just like the mayoral vote, opinion on the settlement divides along religious lines. Table 8.3 presents a crosstabulation of the settlement question by religious affiliation and activity.

Opinion is clearly split along religious lines, with an overwhelming majority of "very active" Mormons agreeing with the settlement and a majority of non-Mormons disagreeing with it. A substantial minority of non-Mormons, however, favored the compromise, including 43 percent of "very active" non-Mormons, which reveals

Table 8.3

Religious Affiliation and Activity by Agreement with Main Street Plaza Settlement (percents)

	Strongly Agree	Agree	Strongly Disagree	Disagree	Don't know/ "prefer not to say"
in LDS					
Very Active	69.4	25.2	1.7	1.5	2.2
Somewhat Active	52.5	35.0	2.5	6.3	3.8
Not Very Active	39.0	31.7	9.8	7.3	12.2
Not Active	37.9	34.5	20.7	6.9	0
in non-LDS					
Very Active	17.3	25.9	25.9	27.2	3.7
Somewhat Active	10.3	28.3	24.8	30.3	6.2
Not Very Active	12.1	29.7	25.3	28.6	4.4
Not Active	5.0	27.4	31.3	31.8	4.5
Prefer not to say	9.7	27.7	25.1	29.7	7.7
Total	33.6	27.5	16.6	18.0	4.3

Source: Utah Colleges Exit Poll [data]. 2003. Center for the Study of Elections and Democracy, Brigham Young University, Provo, Utah [producer and distributor], N=1405.

that many people of faith outside the Mormon tradition approved of the eventual resolution of the controversy.

One consequence of the Main Street Plaza controversy, however, is the significant deterioration of the relationship between Mormons and non-Mormons in Salt Lake City. The consensus view of those we interviewed was that interreligious relations had broken down, suggesting that the controversy clearly affected those most closely involved in it (Anderson 2005; Buhler 2005; Christensen 2005; Goldsmith 2005; Pignanelli 2005; Saxton 2005). This sense also carried over to the public. A year after the compromise was announced, when asked if relations between Mormons and non-Mormons were made better or worse by the controversy, 51 percent of Salt Lake City voters believed that the controversy had worsened relations, while only 9 percent believed relations were better, and 30 percent thought there had been no change.[15]

Understanding Community Conflict through the Lens of the Main Street Plaza Debate

The Main Street Plaza controversy presents a case where the Alliance for Unity, a nonreligious and nongovernmental group that included representatives from all the major religious groups in Salt Lake City, combined with shifting public opinion to enable a compromise between a reluctant mayor and a dominant religious presence. Ultimately the mayor blinked when public opinion turned against him and his role in the controversy. The compromise solution, brokered by Huntsman and the Alliance for Unity, was a way to end a divisive dispute while all of the major parties walked away with something. The ugly protests on the plaza also helped to convince some reluctant groups in the public to support the mayor's proposal and ultimately resulted in a reframing of the controversy.

The role that the Alliance for Unity played in resolving the conflict makes this case so unique. Religious leaders typically play central roles in compromise and conflict resolution. In the Salt Lake City case, the dominant (but minority) religion was a party to the conflict and held a position with little room for movement. This case shows us that a civic-oriented group can play a major role in aiding communication and compromise between two seemingly intractable positions. Huntsman and Mayor Anderson formed the Alliance for Unity before the plaza controversy boiled over into a major battle, but the organization took a major role in a time of crisis and served to bridge a communication gap. The emergence of the Alliance-endorsed compromise provided a major step toward the eventual resolution of the controversy.

While the Alliance for Unity played an important role in the resolution of the conflict, many factors contributed to its divisiveness and longevity. As E. E. Schattschneider (1960) has explained, the scope, level of visibility, intensity, and direction of the conflict shapes the dynamics of any conflict. The Main Street Plaza controversy exemplified these criteria. The scope was large, with various religious organizations, the city government, and the ACLU together representing a large percentage of the community. The reluctance of the major parties to compromise, the rancorous public hearings, and the heated rhetoric best evidenced the intensity of the conflict. The longstanding religious divisions in Salt Lake City provided a strong foundation for division around the Main Street issue and "put a strain on relations such that they may never fully be able to recover" (Christensen 2005). These divisions also enhanced the visibility of the issue, generating significant press and publicity.

Another interesting lesson from the Main Street Plaza controversy is that while the scope and direction of the conflict are important factors, framing the conflict also matters greatly to the outcome. In this case, the major frames included the LDS Church's claim to property rights versus the claim by the mayor, the ACLU, evangelical street preachers, First Unitarian Church, and others to free speech and freedom of expression. While the LDS Church lost the initial legal battle when the 10th Circuit Court upheld the existence of First Amendment rights on the easement, it won the ensuing public relations battle through a combination of the church's own efforts to mobilize public opinion—and especially after a small subset of zealous protestors overstepped the bounds of acceptable social behavior in the eyes of the community. Our public opinion data show that while a significant minority of Salt Lake residents opposed the settlement, a majority favored it. The results in Table 8.3 indicate that a large majority of LDS residents supported the settlement, as did a significant minority of non-LDS residents, especially the most religiously committed. The pivotal non-LDS supporters who produced a majority in support of the settlement likely surfaced in the wake of the ugly protesting in December 2002.

The long-standing divisive religious context in Salt Lake City, which is so profoundly shaped by the presence of a single dominant, powerful religion, may have produced a situation initially in which many religiously committed non-Mormons were inclined to side with the ACLU in protecting freedom of expression and free speech because they identified themselves as a religious minority. When free expression crossed the line of socially acceptable behavior, however, the countervailing frame presented by the LDS Church of preserving the plaza as a place of quiet reflection took precedence. Within a few months of the compromise, a group of evangelical Protestant ministers in Salt Lake City gathered near LDS Church headquarters to express their disapproval of the most egregious behavior of a small number of protestors. It was no longer a question of absolute freedom of expression, but rather how opinions are expressed. One minister stated, "They say they're Christian evangelists sharing the good news of Jesus Christ, but are doing it in a way that is so hurtful and harmful we just can't sit by and be silent" (Mikita 2003).

The unique factors present in the Main Street Plaza controversy lead us in new directions regarding our understanding of the behavior of religious actors in politics. Prior work on clergy activism focuses primarily on characteristics intrinsic to individual participants (such as theological orientation or ideology) to explain the behavior of individual actors (Guth, Green, Smidt, Kellstedt, and Poloma 1997). This emphasis is likely, at least in part, because of a focus on national issues potentially involving clergy from many denominations. In the Main Street Plaza case, the behavior of the various actors likely had much less to do with individual-level characteristics. Instead, the local context better explains it, as Paul Djupe and Christopher Gilbert (2003) would argue. The longstanding history of divisive relations between Mormons and their neighbors in Salt Lake City and the framing of the conflict can do much to explain the behavior of the actors involved.

Appendix

A Timeline of Major Events in the Main Street Plaza Controversy

Date	*Event*
Dec. 1998	Public announcement of a proposal to sell Main Street block to LDS Church.
April 12, 1999	The City Council votes 5–2 to approve the closure and sale of the block of Main Street to the LDS Church for $8.1 million.
May 4, 1999	The local ACLU chapter threatens litigation.
May 9, 1999	The LDS Church begins construction of the plaza.
Nov. 16, 1999	The ACLU sues Salt Lake City in federal court, challenging the constitutionality of the terms of the sale. At issue are the terms of the easement maintained on the property by the city that allows 24-hour access but also allows the LDS Church to enforce behavioral restrictions.
Jan. 2000	Mayor Rocky Anderson takes office.
April 13, 2000	The ACLU sues Salt Lake City in state court, challenging the legality of the city ordinance approving the sale of Main Street because of changes in the behavioral restrictions allowed on the plaza by the City Council, but not allowed by the city planning commission.
Oct. 7, 2000	The Main Street Plaza opens with behavioral restrictions in place.
May 4, 2001	U.S. District Court Judge Ted Stewart upholds the constitutionality of the church's behavioral restrictions by essentially stating that Main Street is not a public forum. The case is appealed to the 10th Circuit.
Oct. 9, 2002	A three-judge panel of the 10th U.S. Circuit Court of Appeals reverses Judge Stewart's decision and rules that the plaza is a public forum and the behavioral restrictions are unconstitutional. The panel suggests two legal solutions. The city could extinguish their easement on the property so that it is no longer a public forum, or the city could create reasonable "time, place, and manner" restrictions. Mayor Anderson says he will not give up the easement but would support the creation of "time, place, and manner" restrictions to regulate protest activity.
Oct. 13, 2002	Mayor Anderson says that he would consider conveying the easement to the LDS Church if 24-hour public access is guaranteed.

Oct. 18, 2002	The ACLU urges the adoption of "time, place, and manner" restrictions.
Oct. 22, 2002	Mayor Anderson concludes there is no way to give up easement legally and again suggests the consideration of time, place, and manner restrictions.
Nov. 14, 2002	The full 10th Circuit refuses to rehear the plaza case.
Nov. 16, 2002	The LDS Church launches Public Relations campaign in Salt Lake City.
Dec. 6, 2002	After prominent Utah businessman Jon Huntsman fails to broker a compromise between the city and the LDS Church, Mayor Anderson formally proposes a set of time, place, and manner restrictions.
Fri., Dec. 13, 2002	Mayor Anderson first conceives a proposal to give up the city's plaza easement in exchange for two acres of LDS Church property on Salt Lake City's west side for the construction of a community center.
Sat. & Sun. Dec. 14–15, 2002	Mayor Anderson meets over the weekend with fellow cochair Jon Huntsman of the Alliance for Unity, a group of prominent community civic, business, and religious leaders. The Alliance meets on Sunday to vote its approval of the compromise.
Mon., Dec. 16, 2002	The *Salt Lake Tribune* publishes a poll conducted December 9–12 that shows a steep decline in approval for Mayor Anderson. After first appearing in newspapers over the weekend, Mayor Anderson formally announces the compromise proposal with Alliance for Unity cochair Huntsman and LDS Church Presiding Bishop Burton at his side to simultaneously endorse it.
Dec. 17, 2002	A tumultuous day of activity on the plaza occurs as a small group of protestors shout obscenities at a wedding party outside of the Salt Lake Temple adjacent to the plaza. The protestors also refuse to move their protest to accommodate wedding pictures. A tearful bride and her mother are featured prominently on evening newscasts and newspaper coverage.
April 9, 2003	The Salt Lake City Planning Commission votes to recommend against giving up the easement on the plaza.
June 11, 2003	After a set of public hearings, some of which are televised live, the Salt Lake City Council endorses the compromise proposal and votes to give up the city's easement on the plaza.

July 28, 2003	After the details of the compromise are finalized, the LDS Church regains control over the plaza when the easement is officially extinguished.
Aug. 7, 2003	The ACLU again sues Salt Lake City over the process followed in eliminating the city's easement on the plaza.
May 3, 2004	U.S. District Judge Dale Kimball upholds the land-for-easement swap between the city and the LDS Church.
May 22, 2004	ACLU files notice of appeal to the 10th Circuit.
October 3, 2005	10th Circuit Court upholds the district court decision. Shortly after the parties involved decide not to appeal, the dispute is officially over.

Part IV

RACE RELATIONS

Chapter 9

From Riots to Reconciliation

The Religious Interests Involved in Healing Cincinnati after Racial Unrest

Anand Edward Sokhey

The city of Cincinnati is no stranger to the spotlight, having been on the front lines of national debates involving morality and family values for decades. Battles over the distribution of Larry Flynt's *Hustler* magazine, the display of Robert Mapplethorpe's photography, the establishment of parental advisory labels on music albums, and the passage of gay rights legislation have shaped the contemporary political culture of the city. Nestled along the Ohio River at the confluence of the states of Ohio, Indiana, and Kentucky, the greater Cincinnati area has come to be regarded as conservative and traditional in its general outlook, a sentiment famously characterized by Mark Twain: "When the end of the world comes, I want to be in Cincinnati because it's always twenty years behind the times" (Lazare 2001).[1]

In 2001 Cincinnati again received national and international media attention. This time, however, the extra press did not come as a result of the city's proactive efforts on moral issues (Button, Rienzo, and Wald 1997; Sharp 1999). Instead, the world watched as Cincinnati played host to racial unrest. On April 7, 2001, the fatal shooting of a young, unarmed African-American man, Timothy Thomas, by white police officer Steven Roach sparked intense protesting and sporadic violence. Thomas was the fifteenth black man killed by the Cincinnati police since 1995 (Horn 2001c). His death came just weeks after the American Civil Liberties Union (ACLU) and a local organization, the Cincinnati Black United Front (CBUF), filed a racial profiling suit in federal court against the Cincinnati Police Department (Adams

2001). The events bore at least a superficial resemblance to those that had occurred approximately ten years earlier in Los Angeles: an encounter between white police officers and a black man brought widespread racial tensions to the surface.

Research Methods: The 2002–2003 Cincinnati Clergy Study

I rely heavily on print accounts of the violence in Cincinnati and its aftermath, since most of the engagement of religious interests with racial reconciliation following the riots was hidden from the view of the general public. I also use a mail survey of clergy in Cincinnati-area churches, temples, and mosques conducted in the fall and winter of 2002–2003[2] to document how Cincinnati religious leaders contributed to the resolution of the city's racial problems in the first two years following the riots. Surveys were sent out to 539 houses of worship randomly selected from the list provided in the Cincinnati Bell Yellow Pages (this sample represents just under half of the listings). Three waves were mailed in order to obtain a sample large enough from which to draw substantive conclusions. In the end, 109 clergy returned surveys, resulting in a response rate of approximately 20 percent.[3]

Several of the returned surveys from the first two waves arrived with comments mentioning the location of the respondent clergy's parish, and the extent to which its members were directly affected (or unaffected) by the rioting. These sentiments prompted a more thorough investigation of the impact of proximity: Did being removed from the action allow clergy to be removed from these issues? After the data set was complete, I measured the distance of each responding clergyperson's house of worship from a set address in the Over-the-Rhine neighborhood, which was the epicenter of the violence (see appendix for variable coding).

Finally, I also conducted extensive phone interviews with religious leaders from several Cincinnati-area churches under the condition of anonymity. The clergy I chose to interview were selected to achieve variance both in terms of proximity to the riots and denomination. Therefore, the interviews covered a broad geographic and theological range. These interviews provided valuable insights into clerical activity and the efficacy of the organizations active in the city concerning racial reconciliation after the riots.

In this chapter, I inquire about the nature and patterns of involvement among community leaders, addressing three familiar questions: (1) What was the level of local political engagement among Cincinnati's religious leaders, and in what activities did they participate? (2) What are the resources available from church, denominational, and community sources that these religious leaders have at their disposal? Are these resources under or outside the clergy's control? Finally, (3) how are these religious leaders mobilized to participate in local political issues, and how do they in turn mobilize support among their followers? I close the chapter with a discussion of the empirical findings, grounding the action (and inaction) of Cincinnati-area clergy and organizations in broader theoretical frameworks.

Racial Unrest in Over-the-Rhine

Immediately following the shooting of Timothy Thomas in April 2001, rioting broke out in the downtown neighborhood of Over-the-Rhine (Hampel, Hollinshed, and O'Neill 2001; Milicia 2001; Winternitz 2001). Once home to a variety of ethnic immigrant groups including Germans, Irish, and Italians, today Over-the-Rhine is largely African-American and stocked with vacant buildings and low-income housing (Adams 2001). By 2001 the neighborhood had become known as a hotbed of illegal drug activity, hosting a population of only 7,600 residents (a sharp decline from years past), but averaging about 2,300 drug arrests a year since 1995. This image was reinforced by the neighborhood's portrayal in the award-winning 2000 film *Traffic* (Lazare 2001). For three days, violence and protests filled the streets of the poverty-stricken Over-the-Rhine area; acts of vandalism and looting soon spread to at least half a dozen other city neighborhoods, while police in riot gear patrolled the streets. The mayor of Cincinnati, Charlie Luken, imposed an 8:00 p.m. to 6:00 a.m. curfew on April 12, which finally helped to restore order and bring some semblance of calm to the city (Garretson 2001).

As the violence subsided, the Queen City catalyzed a nationwide conversation about police conduct and race relations. Local and national religious leaders, including Revs. Al Sharpton and Jesse Jackson, arrived to offer their services in efforts toward reconciliation, as well as confrontation. Later, former President Bill Clinton offered his services to the city (Goudreau and Bonfield 2002). Other organizations, including the CBUF and the local chapter of the NAACP, emerged united and determined to keep the nation's eyes on

Cincinnati while pushing for local social and political change (MacDonald 2001).

As high-profile figures descended on the city, a flurry of activity began. Community leaders and organizations (some led or comprised local religious leaders), city-appointed committees, and local media outlets started the work of promoting understanding, change, and reconciliation. In May 2001, Mayor Luken, a white Democrat, formed a commission, Cincinnati Community Action Now (CCAN), to examine race relations in the city, as well as the concomitant issues of housing and neighborhood development (Cincinnati Community Action Now 2002). Like many northern cities, the urban core of Cincinnati is heavily Democratic; it is only the surrounding suburbs that give Cincinnati its Republican reputation. Meanwhile, the Cincinnati Human Relations Commission conducted a series of public meetings that brought together groups of people to talk about race relations in the city. The ARIA Group, a conflict resolution firm that was called in to mediate the racial profiling lawsuit among the ACLU, the CBUF, and the city of Cincinnati (and that has also worked in the Middle East), gathered opinions on police-community relations from over 3,500 area citizens (Goetz 2001).

In the months immediately following the riots, the situation in some parts of the city continued to worsen. As a general mistrust lingered between the African-American community and the Cincinnati Police Department, the police responded to the increased public scrutiny by decreasing patrols in certain urban neighborhoods (Horn 2001a). This police work slowdown resulted in a spike in criminal activity, with homicides jumping from forty in 2000 to sixty-one in 2001; twenty-three alone occurred in the summer after the riots (Horn 2001a; Prendergast 2002). Tensions only mounted in the coming months, as officer Stephen Roach was found not guilty of negligent homicide in the death of Timothy Thomas. This verdict was followed by the acquittal of two white Cincinnati police officers who were involved in the November 2000 death of another black man, Roger Owensby Jr., who asphyxiated while being held in police custody (Horn 2001b).

In late 2001, frustrated with what they perceived to be the city's inadequate and slow response to the riots, and spurred on by the outcomes of the criminal trials of police officers, the CBUF launched an economic boycott against the city with the support of Stonewall Cincinnati (a gay rights organization), Coalition for a Just Cincinnati, and the Coalition of Concerned Citizens for Justice (Aldridge 2002). Over the course of the first six months, it was estimated that the boycott cost the city nearly eleven million dollars (Aldridge and Anglen 2002), especially as several high-profile entertainers, including Bill Cosby, Wynton Marsalis, and the Temptations canceled scheduled performances in Cincinnati. The boycott effectively kept Cincinnati's racial troubles on the national pages long after the rioting had ended ("Arts Association" 2003).

A Tale of Two Cincinnatis

The riots left Cincinnati with a rather unflattering national reputation. It was no longer seen as just a conservative conurbation resistant to change, but also as an area behind the times in dealing with issues of race and ethnicity. One United Church of Christ minister surveyed for this study remarked: "The lid has finally come off what is and has been the issue in Cincinnati for generations. Race relations will always be an issue in this particular area, more so than in other cities." Another respondent described the problems in the city as "complex and with deeply rooted traditionalism holding both the African-American community and the white community in a Gordian knot."

To an extent these impressions of the city seem incongruent with certain aspects of its past. In some ways Cincinnati has played an important historical role in advancing race relations. Its Lane Theological Seminary was the site of eighteen days of debates in 1834 that helped to initiate, shape, and propel national dialogue over slavery (Findsen 1999; Gilder Lehrman Center 2003). The city was also a major stop on the Underground Railroad, a fact that Harriet Beecher Stowe observed while living there in the 1830s and that influenced her classic work *Uncle Tom's Cabin* ("Aboard the Underground Railroad" 2006). Some have argued that it is false to claim that Cincinnati's race problems are uniquely serious, since deeply rooted racial problems continue to plague many major cities as well. As Richard Newman, a research officer at the W. E. B. Du Bois Institute at Harvard University noted, "Cincinnati is not alone. . . . It's only emblematic of what the situation is in every American city" (Goetz 2001). Perhaps a dichotomous characterization of the city is appropriate, given that Cincinnati has truly been a place where North meets South.

Reconciliation Five Years Out

Nearly five years later, Cincinnati is on the mend, yet still marked by divisions and intransigence. The suit brought by the ACLU and the CBUF in 2001 prompted a yearlong investigation by the Department of Justice. In April 2002, the Cincinnati Police Department signed an agreement with the United States Department of Justice specifying new regulations for the use of force as well as the appointment of an independent monitor to oversee internal policy changes ("Cincinnati Signs Pact" 2002). While changes have been made, they have not been without controversy. For instance, the city's police department failed several times to meet Justice Department guidelines when submitting revised use of force policies for review (Flannery 2003).

Although homicide rates are still higher than in years past, overall crime is currently down in Cincinnati (Cook 2006); and today the city has its first African-American mayor, Mark Mallory. As efforts at change were made and time passed, the boycott essentially dissolved and convention and other business rebounded. Even the organizers of the boycott, including the leadership of the CBUF, have acknowledged this fact (Alltucker and Aldridge 2004).

In 2004, the National Underground Railroad Freedom Center opened on Cincinnati's riverfront, commemorating the African-American struggle for freedom and equality and serving as an important symbol of understanding and healing. A 2005 survey of Cincinnati residents commissioned by the Center, in conjunction with the National Council for Community and Justice and Cincinnati's Xavier University, found that although the city's racial divisions remain significant, "younger residents, whether black or white, are increasingly willing to bridge that divide through ongoing dialogue and aggressive denunciation of overt discriminatory behaviors" (National Underground Railroad Freedom Center 2005).

The Role of Religious Leaders in the Cincinnati Community Conflict

The race riots left Cincinnati divided and in need of healing, but they also opened a window of opportunity for leadership. Some local religious leaders eagerly answered this call for guidance. They played (and continue to play) an integral and public part in this most recent episode of the Cincinnati story, whether talking about issues from the pulpit, contacting local officials or media outlets, serving on local clergy councils, or hosting discussion groups on race relations. It would be foolish, however, to think that all clergy were involved in such activities at the same rates. Some, of course, evaded the issue entirely. In particular, preliminary investigations indicated that clergy and congregations in the suburbs felt less personally affected by the riots. Just as there was tremendous variance in terms of attention and engagement, there has also been much disagreement as to the appropriate course(s) of action in the wake of the unrest. For example, some religious leaders lent their support to groups, most notably the CBUF, that (among other things) pushed for the economic boycott of downtown Cincinnati. However, the actions of the CBUF in particular (and other groups allied with it) were the source of much controversy within both the city's African-American community and greater Cincinnati. The picture of religious involvement in racial reconciliation is one of a spectrum of activity, differentiated in public expression by frequency and approach.

The Engagement, Opinions, and Actions of Cincinnati Clergy

How much attention did Cincinnati's religious leaders pay to issues of race, reconciliation, and misconduct? How did contacts from groups such as the CBUF and CCAN affect their engagement?

Overall, nearly 70 percent of area clergy reported having paid "a great deal" or "quite a bit" of attention to racial reconciliation issues and events since the April 2001 riots, whereas just under half believed that their congregation had paid the same amount of attention. Table 9.1 presents clergy engagement and their perceptions of the congregation's engagement with reconciliation categorized by both the denomination and the predominant race/ethnicity of the respondent's church. As we might expect, the numbers break down differently by religious tradition and race, with reports from clergy in predominantly black churches being somewhat distinctive from other clergy on most questions.[4] The ministers of African-American Protestant churches reported the highest level of engagement with racial reconciliation events and issues since April 2001 (nearly 80 percent), followed by Cincinnati's Catholic, evangelical, and mainline Protestant clergy.

Clergy of African-American Protestant churches also reported in the highest percentage (70 percent) that their members paid a lot of attention to race-related issues, which is far more than the next highest group, Catholic clergy. On the other hand, along with

Table 9.1
Clergy Engagement and Clergy Perceptions of Engagement by Denomination and Predominant Race/Ethnicity of Church
(percent reporting "a great deal" or "quite a bit" of attention paid)

Variables	Mainline	Catholic	Jewish	Evangelical	White	Black
Personal	62.7	75.0	100.0	64.3	66.3	77.8
Congregational	37.2	56.3	33.3	44.4	42.4	70.6
Denominational	61.9	75.0	33.3	30.0	55.1	50.0
Local elected officials	51.3	81.3	100.0	60.9	60.8	53.3
TV media	78.6	87.5	100.0	84.0	81.9	60.0
Newspapers	76.7	87.5	100.0	80.0	79.8	62.5
Number of cases	44	16	3	28	86	18

Source: The 2002–2003 Cincinnati Clergy Study, Total N=109

mainline Protestant clergy, clergy in black Protestant congregations reported at a lower level that local elected officials had paid either "a great deal" or "quite a bit" of attention to racial reconciliation issues and events. It is worth noting that racial distinctions also extended into perceptions of the Cincinnati media. Although clergy across denominations reported that local media paid "much" attention to reconciliation issues after the April 2001 riots, a sizably lower percentage of clergy in black churches thought the same thing.

The fact that the confluence of religion and politics is often especially pronounced in the African-American communities has been well documented (Harris 1999; Kohut, Green, Keeter, and Toth 2000; Lincoln and Mamiya 1990; Morris 1984). We would expect, therefore, that a violent conflict between blacks and whites, especially one adversely affecting black neighborhoods, would grab the attention of clergy in African-American churches, and it does. These findings (reported in Table 9.1) display a marked difference in reported clergy engagement by race, with some additional structuring of attention according to religious tradition. Clergy in black churches reported that they, as well as their congregation, had been highly engaged at higher rates than did clergy in non-black churches. They also reported at lower rates that local elected officials, the media, and their denominations had been engaged.

Outside black churches, the results thus far lead us to infer that a fair amount of attention was given to issues of race and reconciliation across the broader religious spectrum. Differences between levels of clergy and congregational engagement were greater in non-black churches, hinting at potential barriers to activism for these clergy.

Opinions

It appears that many Cincinnati-area clergy were paying attention to reconciliatory issues and events in the first two years after the riots. What, however, did these leaders think about these matters? Overall, nearly 70 percent of Cincinnati clergy questioned *did not* think that the rioting of April 2001 was justified. Likewise, 60 percent disagreed with the statement that "the police are largely to blame for the riots," and approximately the same percentage reported that the economic boycott of Cincinnati had done more harm than good. However, close to 60 percent of all clergy reported that the Cincinnati city government had not dealt adequately with the city's racial unrest. And, while a few clergy thought race relations had improved since the riots, Cincinnati-area religious leaders overwhelmingly adopted a prophetic stance of holding the community to account, with close to 90 percent agreeing that "churches should be more involved in racial reconciliation."

We might expect that clergy in white churches would see the events of April 2001 (and concomitant social justice issues) differently than would clergy in black churches. This hunch is supported by results in Table 9.2, which again breaks down clergy responses by both race and religious tradition.

A cursory inspection of the last two columns of this table reveals widespread differences in opinion between the clergy in black and white churches on a variety of race-related issues. While the solidarity displayed among religious leaders in black churches is indicative of the nature of this conflict, it can also be seen as the logical and expected response of clergy who sometimes see themselves as defenders of a distinct community. Although only 10 percent of clergy in white churches reported that the rioting was justified, close to 45 percent of clergy in black churches agreed that violent protest was warranted. Half the clergy in black churches blamed the police for the

Table 9.2
Clergy Opinions on Statements Concerning Race Relations by Movement and Predominant Race/Ethnicity of Church of Clergy (percent reporting agreement)

Variable	Mainline	Catholic	Jewish	Evangelical	White	Black
More resources should be devoted to the black community	64.2	50.0	100.0	23.1	50.6	94.4
The rioting was justified	14.3	31.3	0.0	3.7	10.7	43.8
Race relations have improved since the riots	16.3	25.0	0.0	19.2	18.8	5.9
The police are largely to blame for the riots	19.0	6.3	33.3	0.0	11.9	50.0
Black clergy exploited the riots for personal gain	30.2	37.5	0.0	51.9	34.1	5.6
Churches should be more involved in racial reconciliation	93.0	75.0	100.0	77.7	86.0	93.8
The economic boycott of Cincinnati did more harm than good	62.3	68.9	33.3	74.1	67.1	29.4
Cincinnati city council has dealt with the crisis adequately	9.3	37.5	0.0	18.5	15.3	5.6

Source: The 2002–2003 Cincinnati Clergy Study, Total N=109

Note: Each question is coded on a five-point Likert scale: 1=strongly agree, 2=agree, 3=not sure/neutral, 4=disagree, 5=strongly disagree. 'Agree' is categories one and two collapsed. Table 1 reports the number of observations by denomination and race; the number of observations used to create these percentages may vary slightly, as not all respondents answered every item.

problems in the city, while only about 12 percent of clergy in white churches agreed. Also, while close to 70 percent of clergy in white churches viewed the economic boycott of the city as having done more harm than good, a much smaller percentage (approximately 30 percent) of clergy in black churches expressed the same sentiment.

Virtually all clergy agreed that race relations within the city had not improved since the riots—and that the city government had not played an effective role in solving the problem. Among religious traditions, Catholics emerged as the most optimistic on both of these fronts, with a fourth reporting that race relations had improved and nearly 40 percent thinking that the city council had adequately addressed the racial unrest. Interestingly, about one-third of clergy in white churches thought that black clergy had exploited the city's racial situation for personal gain. Half of clergy in white churches supported allocating more resources to the African-American community, though this number was low compared to the 95 percent of clergy in black churches who answered in the affirmative on this item.

Since organized interests played an obvious and important role in the story of the Cincinnati riots, clergy were also asked to provide opinions on the effectiveness of various groups involved in resolving (or as some clergy indicated, intensifying) the racial crisis. Questions were included on prominent organizations including the CBUF (the most controversial organization), the local and national NAACP, several religious organizations, and both black and white Cincinnati-area churches in general. Again, there was great variation in opinion, and striking differences between the clergy of white and black churches.

Close to 70 percent of all religious leaders described the CBUF as having been *ineffective* in promoting racial reconciliation within Cincinnati (results not shown). Somewhat surprisingly, clergy in black and white churches nearly agreed on this point, with well over 60 percent of each expressing the opinion that the CBUF had not been productive in achieving reconciliation (see Table 9.3). A sizable percentage of clergy in both black and white churches also indicated that the NAACP (both local and national) had been ineffective in solving the city's problems; a larger percentage of clergy in predominantly black churches labeled this organization as ineffective.

Regarding how churches handled the reconciliatory process, approximately 40 percent of all clergy surveyed reported that

Table 9.3
The Opinions of Clergy in Predominantly White and Black Churches on Groups Promoting Racial Reconciliation (percent calling them effective/ineffective)

	African American			*White*		
	Eff.	Don't Know	Ineff.	Eff.	Don't Know	Ineff.
Group of Concerned Clergy	23.5	23.5	53.0	39.8	34.9	25.3
National NAACP	23.5	11.8	64.7	23.8	32.5	43.8
Cincinnati NAACP	29.4	11.8	58.8	27.2	30.9	41.9
Cincinnati Black United Front	29.4	5.9	64.7	12.3	19.8	67.9
ACLU	11.8	23.5	64.7	10.0	36.3	53.8
Cincinnati Community Action Now	41.1	23.5	35.3	29.1	35.4	35.4
Metropolitan Area Religious Coalition	17.6	29.5	52.9	41.5	30.5	28.0
Citizen's Police Review Panel	17.6	23.5	58.8	26.8	32.9	40.2
Black Churches in Cincinnati	23.5	23.5	53.0	44.4	23.5	32.1
White Churches in Cincinnati	11.8	17.6	70.6	17.3	25.9	56.8

Source: The 2002–2003 Cincinnati Clergy Study, Total N=109

Note: Each question is coded on a five-point Likert scale: 1=very effective, 2=effective, 3=ineffective, 4=very ineffective, 5=don't know. 'Effective' is categories 1 and 2 collapsed; 'Ineffective' is categories 3 and 4 collapsed.

Cincinnati's black churches had been *effective* in promoting racial reconciliation; only 15 percent of all clergy reported the same sentiment about white churches (results not shown). Looking at responses to these items by race (see Table 9.3), 70 percent of clergy in black churches reported that white Cincinnati-area churches had been ineffective in mitigating racial tensions. Interestingly, clergy in white churches largely agreed: well over half reported that white churches had not been effective in promoting racial reconciliation. At the same time, nearly half of the clergy in white churches reported that black Cincinnati-area churches had been effective in promoting racial reconciliation, a higher percentage than the meager self-assessment by clergy in black churches.

One pattern that clearly emerges in Table 9.3 is that many clergy were highly critical of the response to the riots, holding the community to high standards. Clergy in African-American churches were quite critical of the churches and organizations that shared the race of their congregation. They were more critical of the NAACP than clergy in white churches and almost equally as critical of the CBUF as were the clergy of white churches. Also, as another measure of engagement, clergy in black churches appeared more opinionated and certain about their judgments of groups than were clergy of white churches; they marked "don't know" at considerably lower rates (see Table 9.3).

Activities

Clergy are informed, critical observers of their communities, but they only matter to politics to the extent they make their views known. Therefore, I now examine the activities in which these clergy participated. How did the city's clergy contribute to the resolution of the racial crisis?

To gauge the impact of the riots on the activities of Cincinnati clergy, I asked respondents to indicate whether they had performed a number of different activities both before and after the events of April 2001. As Table 9.4 indicates, the percentage of clergy reporting activity increased for *all* types of activity after the riots, from hosting discussion groups to encouraging political activity among members of their congregation. What is most intriguing is the rather small increase across the board. Indeed, at first glance it seems that congregations were either engaged with these issues or they were not, and the riots did not drastically change their levels of interest. This points to the importance of geography in defining organizational priorities, as will become clear.

Overall, Cincinnati's religious leaders engaged in quite a bit of cue-giving activity after the riots, speaking out about race-related issues both publicly and from the pulpit with regularity. Outside public speech, however, clergy were not as involved in other types of activity with quite the same frequency: three-fifths of all clergy reported "rarely" or "never" contacting a local official, and close to 85 percent reported "rarely" or "never" writing to a newspaper editor.

Table 9.4
Clergy Race-Related Activities before and after April 2001 Riots (percent reporting activity)

Variables	Before April 2001	After April 2001	Percentage Point Increase
Encouraged church member participation in community action	52.1	64.6	12.5
Held discussion groups in church on race relations	37.2	53.5	16.3
Hosted a worship service dedicated to race relations	35.1	43.4	8.3
Hosted a community leader to discuss race-related issues	26.1	33.0	6.9
Encouraged church members to contact local government officials	25.3	40.4	15.1
Hosted a community leader of a race other than that predominant in your church	23.4	25.3	1.9

Source: The 2002–2003 Cincinnati Clergy Study, Total N=109

Note: For each activity, clergy were asked to report "yes" or "no" to whether they had performed the activity both before the April, 2001 riots, and after the riots.

Local organizational activity was a bit more common, with sizable percentages of clergy reporting serving on clergy councils or boards and participating in discussion groups. Not surprisingly, clergy reported engaging in unconventional activities at lower rates, though the one-third of clergy who reported "often" or "sometimes" participating in rallies, demonstrations, or marches is astounding when compared to other clergy samples (Djupe and Gilbert 2003; Guth, Green, Smidt, Kellstedt, and Poloma 1997). Many Cincinnati-area clergy attempted to force public recognition of their concerns in ways that typically are deemed unconventional.

Table 9.5 presents selected clergy actions by religious tradition and race. The table indicates that cue-giving activities were frequent across racial categories and denominations; a higher percentage of clergy spoke out about race-related issues more often in church than in public. While a sizable portion of Cincinnati clergy reported serving on a local board or council, the percentages were not appreciably different between clergy in black and white churches. Across denominations, the highest percentage of reported involvement in this type of activity came from mainline Protestant religious leaders (after the unanimous participation of the small sample of three rabbis).

The greatest disjuncture in reported activity between clergy of black and white churches came in unconventional activities. While only 5 percent of the religious leaders in predominantly white churches reported participating in the economic boycott of Cincinnati, over half of the respondent clergy from black churches reported

Table 9.5

Clergy Frequency of Activity in Selected Reconciliation Issues Since April 2001 by Denomination and Predominant Race/Ethnicity (percent reporting activity)

Variables	Mainline	Catholic	Jewish	Evangelical	White	Black
Publicly take a stand on race relations	76.7	75.0	100.0	63.0	73.0	76.5
In a sermon, take a stand on race relations	74.4	86.7	100.0	70.4	76.1	88.9
Participate in the economic boycott of Cincinnati	9.3	—	—	—	4.5	53.0
Serve on a local board or council	46.3	25.0	100.0	18.2	34.9	35.3
Contact a local government official	27.9	56.3	100.0	37.0	38.2	41.2

Source: The 2002–2003 Cincinnati Clergy Study, Total N=109

Note: Each is coded 1=often, 2=sometimes, 3=rarely, 4=never. “Activity” is the collapse of categories 1 and 2.

participating. The dramatic differences in rates of participation in this controversial action highlight the fact that a confluence of racial, congregational, and community factors shaped concerns and action among Cincinnati-area clergy in the wake of the April 2001 unrest.

Explanations: Resources, Motivation, Recruitment, and Distance

Understanding how Cincinnati clergy varied in their levels of social and political activism necessitates knowing and considering the resources, material and otherwise, that they had at their disposal; their motives for action; their channels of recruitment into public life; and other practical factors, such as their church's experience with the conflict (proximity to the violence). Having described what Cincinnati-area leaders seem to have thought, done, and paid attention to in the wake of the riots, I now take a step back to examine these possible explanations individually before testing them simultaneously.

Resources

In the broadest sense, resources refer to both the material and the intangible. Support from the congregation, denomination, and community are important determinants of clergy action, sometimes provided in the form of genuine encouragement and receptiveness to clergy action and sometimes in passive resistance—or even open antagonism (Crawford, Olson, and Deckman 2001; Olson, Crawford, and Deckman 2005). Of course, support may also come in the form of money, materials, and assistance; that is, the congregation and community may offer their time and abilities to religious leaders by volunteering to help organize and participate in activities.

To get an idea of the resources that clergy had at their disposal, respondents were asked to compare their congregations to others in the community on several points, including income and social status. Over 60 percent of all Cincinnati clergy surveyed indicated that their congregation was nearly equal in income and social status to the other congregations within the community; nearly 30 percent reported that their congregation members had higher incomes and greater social status than those in other congregations. There are some differences by race: roughly 5 percent of clergy in predominantly white churches reported that their congregation was lower in income and social status than surrounding churches, while over three times that amount (about 19 percent) of clergy in black churches reported that their congregation was poorer than the surrounding community.

Other resources that clergy frequently draw upon to help accomplish their theological, social, and political goals are the abilities and energies of their congregations. Over half of all Cincinnati clergy reported that the members of their congregation were involved in the church and community at the same level as the members of other surrounding congregations. A slightly higher percentage of clergy in white churches rated their members as more active in church and the community than the members of surrounding churches, while a slightly higher percentage of clergy in black churches rated their members as more involved in political activity than the surrounding community.

Motivation for Involvement

Although congregational resources play a part in determining clerical activism, other factors also shaped involvement. Motivation for clergy activism surely comes from personal political and theological beliefs, but also from the demands (and possible sanctions) of the denominational hierarchy, the congregation, the community, and other organizations. For example, one survey respondent described experiencing backlash after speaking about the racial unrest in Cincinnati: "Some families left the church after I spoke about race relations in a sermon, but I am still planning sermons this year to cover several topics: homosexuality, race relations, and environmental threats." Clergy sometimes must tread lightly as they move between their personal priorities and ministering to the congregation, though for some a prophetic role is worth pursuing even in the face of resistance (Olson, Crawford, and Deckman 2005), as this respondent's comments indicate.

Cincinnati-area clergy were asked to indicate the degree to which certain factors encouraged or discouraged their involvement in racial reconciliation efforts after April 2001. Above all else, nearly 85 percent of all clergy stated that their own theological beliefs encouraged them to work on reconciliation in the city. This factor was followed by political beliefs (at about 70 percent), then the demands of the congregation, the demands of leaders within the denomination, and the attitudes of other clergy (each at around 50 percent). With the exception of job demands, few clergy reported that any factors discouraged their involvement in racial reconciliation activities.

Table 9.6 presents clergy reports of motivating factors by race and denomination, and across all items, the percentage of clergy indicating encouragement across different sources in black and white churches was more or less comparable. An important exception comes with regard to the congregation, community organizations, and the attitudes of other clergy, where a sizably higher percentage of clergy in black churches reported that these factors encouraged them to participate in reconciliatory efforts. This finding suggests that clergy in black Cincinnati churches had social networks that were more supportive of action than did clergy in white churches.

Table 9.6

Clergy Reported Motivation for Involvement in Reconciliation Efforts by Denomination and Predominant Race/Ethnicity of Church (percent reporting factor encouraged)

Motivating Factors[a]	Mainline	Catholic	Jewish	Evangelical	White	Black
The attitudes of my congregation	37.2	68.8	66.6	37.0	43.8	70.6
Community organizations	48.8	53.3	100.0	28.0	45.2	62.5
The attitudes of other clergy	54.8	50.0	100.0	38.5	50.6	62.5
Leaders of my denomination	58.1	75.0	—	31.6	55.0	33.3
My own political beliefs	79.1	81.3	100.0	42.3	69.0	70.6
My own theological beliefs	90.5	68.8	100.0	69.2	85.1	81.2
Demands of my job	31.0	37.5	33.3	3.8	24.1	26.7
Neighborhood residents	26.8	25.0	—	11.5	21.0	43.8

Source: The 2002–2003 Cincinnati Clergy Study, Total N=109

[a] Each is coded on a five-point scale: 1=strongly encourage, 2=encourage, 3=neutral, 4=discourage, 5=strongly discourage. 'Encourage' is categories 1 and 2 collapsed.

Recruitment to Action

In addition to a complex constellation of forces motivating the work for racial reconciliation, direct recruitment into political activity may also explain levels of activism among clergy. Table 9.7 reports the results from a series of questions asking Cincinnati religious leaders if they were contacted about reconciliation issues from a number of different sources.

A little less than one-third of all clergy reported that the local media contacted them, and this number was similar for clergy of both black and white churches. Higher percentages of clergy from predominantly black churches said that local ministerial organizations, community organizations, and members of their congregation contacted them. Matched with the results reported in Table 9.7, we begin to get a strong sense that clergy in black churches were receiving cues from more sources than clergy in predominantly white churches. We might expect this finding in light of the historically significant political role of the black church and the fact that the African-American community was (and is) the primary stakeholder in this conflict.

Distance from the Conflict

One additional factor that may help to explain Cincinnati clergy's social and political activism was their church's actual experience with the conflict, which I operationalize by looking at its physical distance from the riots. Table 9.8 presents correlations between the measured distance from clergy's churches to the epicenter of the

Table 9.7
Clergy Contacts about Racial Reconciliation Issues
(percent reporting being contacted by each entity)

Variables	Overall	White	Black
Your denominational hierarchy	52.7	52.9	50.0
A local clergy council	57.1	55.2	66.7
A community organization	59.4	55.7	77.8
A group of church members	30.8	29.5	37.5
Local media	28.0	28.1	27.8

Source: The 2002–2003 Cincinnati Clergy Study.

Table 9.8
Correlations between Church Distance from the Riots and Engagement /Selected Activities (Pearson Correlations)

Engagement	Distance From the Riots
Attention given by self	0.280**
Attention given by your congregation	0.349**
Reconciliation Activities	
Publicly take a stand on race relations	0.203*
In a sermon, take a stand on race relations	0.249**
Serve on a local board or council	0.234**
Contact a local government official	0.311**

Source: The 2002–2003 Cincinnati Clergy Study. Total N=109. ** $p<0.01$, * $p<0.05$

Notes: Engagement questions asked, "How much attention has been paid to reconciliation issues by the following?" These variables are coded: 1=a great deal of attention, 2=quite a bit, 3=some, 4=very little, 5=none. Activity variables asked clergy "how often they participated in the following." These are coded: 1=Often, 2=Sometimes, 3=Rarely, 4=Never. Distance was measured from an address in Over-the-Rhine (1243 Elm St., Cincinnati, Oh 45202—the neighborhood where the rioting was centered) to churches using Yahoo Yellow pages.

rioting (the downtown neighborhood of Over-the-Rhine) and several measures of clergy engagement and activity.

The strong and statistically significant relationships suggest that physical distance was connected both to psychological distance and involvement (see appendix for coding). Cincinnati clergy whose churches were located further away from the violence paid less attention. Likewise, clergy closer to the riots reported higher rates of participation in local councils, higher rates of contacting government officials, and speaking out more frequently on race relations (both in public and from the pulpit).

The findings make intuitive sense, for we would expect higher levels of engagement and activity among clergy whose congregations and communities were closer to the conflict or may have experienced portions of it firsthand. In a sense, these results indicate that distance encapsulates many of the other findings discussed above. Religious leaders near the violence were in social locations that dictated certain roles—clergy as community leaders and as representatives

(Olson 2000)—that provided the web of congregational and organizational resources that both encouraged (or more likely, demanded) and sustained clergy interest and activity in reconciliation-related tasks. That being said, it is important to keep in mind that this relationship was probably a bit different for clergy in black churches, where regardless of proximity there was likely a perception that Cincinnati's African-American community itself was at issue in the conflict, and not simply the Over-the-Rhine neighborhood.

Testing Explanations of Clergy Activism

Having described the distributions of opinion, engagement, and resources among Cincinnati-area clergy, I now examine how these and other factors structured the reconciliatory activities of these religious leaders. Table 9.9 presents multivariate regression estimates for a clergy activity index composed of twelve activities (see the appendix for full question wording and coding). These activities cover a wide range, including direct and indirect (such as writing a letter to a newspaper and contacting government officials, respectively), cue giving (such as taking a stand on race relations), local/group (such as serving on a clergy council), and the unconventional (such as protesting). I also estimate two components of the index: one predicting community-oriented activities and the other predicting individualistic activity (the separate indices were formed based on the results of a factor analysis: data not reported).

Expectations: A Summary

The three models are set up to examine whether the influences on clergy action are different for overall activity, community-oriented activity, and more individualistic reconciliatory actions. In line with the sections above, I expect clergy's levels of engagement with the conflict to emerge as a significant predictor for all types of activity, along with their opinions on the role of religion in resolving the conflict, and not surprisingly, the dominant race of their church. For the community index in particular, I expect external factors to matter in the structuring of activity, including the social location in which clergy find themselves (as measured by the proximity of the church to the riots) and recruitment attempts in the form of contacts from local media and the denomination. Individual activity, on the other hand, should be more sensitive to church-specific factors,

Table 9.9

Estimated Reconciliatory Activity of Cincinnati Clergy on an Activity Index and Selected Components of the Index (OLS Regression Estimates)

	Activity Index		Community Activity		Individual Activity	
Variables	Coeff.	(S.E.)	Coeff.	(S.E.)	Coeff.	(S.E.)
Personal Attributes						
Age	0.047	(0.025)*	0.108	(0.086)	0.152	(0.062)**
Sex	0.014	(0.060)	-0.002	(0.205)	0.005	(0.146)
Congregation						
Similar race/ethnicity	-0.032	(0.023)	-0.080	(0.077)	-0.096	(0.055)*
Worship attendance	0.000	(0.000)	0.000	(0.000)*	0.000	(0.000)
Years with church	-0.005	(0.003)[0.121]	-0.023	(0.012)**	-0.006	(0.008)
White	-0.119	(0.059)**	-0.064	(0.201)	-0.217	(0.143)
Miles from riots	0.008	(0.004)**	0.026	(0.013)**	0.011	(0.009)
Engagement						
Personal interest	0.046	(0.023)**	0.205	(0.077)***	0.058	(0.055)
Recruitment						
Attitudes of congregation	0.032	(0.030)	0.024	(0.102)	0.129	(0.073)*
Demands of job	0.054	(0.024)**	0.121	(0.082)	0.145	(0.058)**
Contacted by denomination	0.054	(0.045)	0.317	(0.154)**	0.134	(0.109)
Contacted by local media	0.118	(0.046)***	0.337	(0.157)**	0.191	(0.111)*
Opinions						
Churches should be involved	0.116	(0.033)***	0.209	(0.113)*	0.339	(0.081)***
Constant	0.483	(0.171)	0.250	(0.584)	0.313	(0.415)
Number of cases	90		90		90	
Adjusted R^2	0.595		0.476		0.553	
Standard error of the estimate	0.181		0.618		0.440	

Source: The 2002–2003 Cincinnati Clergy Study. See Appendix for variable coding.
*** p<0.01, ** p<0.05, * p<0.10.

with clergy adjusting their actions on race in response to the attitudes and racial/ethnic composition of their congregation.

Full Model

The first model predicts the overall reconciliatory activity of Cincinnati clergy (see Table 9.9, first column). It is worth noting that the model performs reasonably well, explaining about 60 percent of the variance in the clergy activity index. The results underscore the importance of personal orientations, as clergy who were more interested in reconciliatory issues and who thought religion should be involved in Cincinnati's racial reconciliation efforts are predicted to display higher levels of activity. Although denominational factors do not achieve statistical significance, the demands of the clergy's job do: clergy reporting that their jobs encouraged political involvement are predicted to be more active. Clergy in black churches are also predicted to have taken part in higher levels of activity, along with those contacted by the local media. Finally, the distance from a church to the riots emerges as a significant predictor, functioning as a summary measure that incorporates many of these explanations: greater distance predicts less activity.

Community Action Model

The second model (see Table 9.9, second column) examines the community-oriented reconciliatory actions of Cincinnati clergy. The dependent variable is a component of the index used in the previous model wherein the activities being predicted involve organizing and public participation (such as joining a demonstration and attending a community meeting).

As in the model for overall activity, the community model performs fairly well, explaining just under half of the variance in the community activity index. Personal orientations are again statistically significant covariates, with personal interest and the feeling that religion should be involved in reconciliation efforts both predicting higher levels of activity. Although it did not achieve statistical significance in the overall activity model, being contacted by the denomination helps to structure the community activities of clergy, as does a religious leader's length of tenure in his or her congregation (such clergy are often more invested in the community and have more avenues to express their views: Olson 2000). Notably, a church's distance from the riots again emerges as a significant predictor of clerical action, depressing action.

Individual Activity Model

The final model (see Table 9.9, right column) predicts the individualistic reconciliatory activities of Cincinnati clergy. As with the community activity model, the dependent variable is again a component of the overall activity index, though the focus here is on more personal- and in-church-oriented activities (such as taking a stand on race relations in a sermon or contacting a local government official).

All in all, the model performs well, explaining about 55 percent of the variance in the individual activity index. As in both the overall and community activity models, clergy's personal opinions about the role of religion in solving racial problems proves to be a significant predictor (though personal interest, surprisingly, is not significant). Interestingly, distance is also not a factor in the model, but age is, with older religious leaders predicted to participate in more activities.

Clergy who reported that their job discourages political involvement are predicted to engage in fewer individual activities. As expected (Olson, Crawford, and Deckman 2005), discouragement from the congregation also appears to dampen individual activity, as do certain characteristics of the congregation, namely if the congregation is racially/ethnically heterogeneous.

Discussion

The literature in religion and politics has noted the tendency of religious officials to involve themselves in what Charles Euchner (1996) calls "extraordinary politics," by which he means conflicts involving race or moral issues that demand the attention of local governments and that often draw forth "non-conventional" protest activities from groups. The situation in Cincinnati certainly matched this description. One local pastor commented specifically on the mix of organizations and individuals working in the city after the riots: "Some groups used the crisis to promote agendas, but there is a groundswell of smaller groups and individuals who work tirelessly to promote healing and better relations." As a site of past battles in an ongoing culture war (Hunter 1991), Cincinnati provided, and continues to provide, fertile ground for religious interests to work for social and political change.

Toward A Theory of Clergy Political Behavior

Although Cincinnati provides us with a unique opportunity to document a religious response, studies have noted the frequent involvement of religious leaders in resolving community crises (Sharp 1986, 1999; Steggart 1975). The actions of Cincinnati clergy, therefore, are not unique; indeed, they fall in line with an extensive history of religious involvement in local, state, and national politics (Fowler, Hertzke, Olson, and den Dulk 2004; Noll 1990).

The case of Cincinnati reminds us that clergy interface with social and political issues in a variety of ways, performing a multitude of actions from preaching to protest as they act in various roles (Crawford and Olson 2001a). Religious leaders have the opportunity to exert influence by acting as opinion leaders within their congregations (Beatty and Walter 1989; Morris 1984). Even when working outside of their congregations or denominations, clergy have the ability to recruit and mobilize individuals to support their causes (Crawford, Olson, and Deckman 2001; Olson, Crawford, and Deckman 2005). For some religious leaders, especially those in the churches of marginalized groups, this influence may be driven by the self-assigned or congregationally imposed role of community representative (Djupe and Gilbert 2002a, 2003; Jelen 2001; Morris 1984; Olson 2000).

What motivated Cincinnati clergy's reconciliatory actions in the wake of the April 2001 unrest? Broadly speaking, attempts to explain the political participation of clergy have focused on whether motivation for action comes from within the individual, from the cultural and organizational milieu, or from a combination of both. The former is a more psychological approach that "focuses on ideas, values, beliefs, norms, and ideologies, and the impact of these internal phenomena on social action" (Sharp 1999: 8; Guth et al. 1997). The latter stresses the impact that social interaction, cultural influences, and organizational mobilization have in generating action (Crawford and Olson 2001a, 2001b; Djupe and Gilbert 2002a, 2003; Sharp 1999; Olson 2000; Olson, Crawford, and Deckman 2005).

At the mass level, it is widely accepted that a combination of resorces, engagement, and recruitment motivates participation (Verba, Schlozman and Brady 1995). A person needs to be self-motivated and self-aware in order to respond to recruitment attempts and participate in political activities (see also Crawford, Olson, and Deckman 2001; Djupe and Grant 2001; Rosenstone and Hansen 1993; Sharp 1999). Although the same general forces act on clergy to produce action, the structure of influences—and their particular meanings—is quite different in the case of religious elites, as the Cincinnati findings indicate. James Guth and colleagues (1997) suggest that mainly internal, psychological influences drive clergy to participate in political activity. Ernest Campbell and Thomas Pettigrew (1959) proposed that three areas affect clerical participation: personal beliefs, the congregation, and the denomination. Paul Djupe and Christopher Gilbert (2003) add a fourth explanatory factor: secular, community influences.

Explaining the Empirics

Given the literature on the political behavior of religious elites, we would expect that the reconciliatory activities of Cincinnati clergy result from personal interests and theological orientations, conditioned and supplemented by the needs and influences of the congregation, the denomination, and the community. By virtue of their positions, these religious officials mediate the relationships between the city, the congregation, and their church (Blizzard 1956). Thus, it only makes sense that their involvement in response to a community crisis would be influenced both by personal orientations and a mix of external influences and factors, including available resources and recruitment into action (or discouragement), especially from congregational and community sources (Crawford, Olson, and Deckman 2001; Olson, Crawford, and Deckman 2005). Both the descriptive tables and multivariate analyses of Cincinnati-area clergy strongly support this manifold theoretical explanation of clerical political activism, especially the community factor.

Across the three activity models, clergy's personal views concerning the role of the religion in promoting racial reconciliation were a consistent and significant predictor of all types of reconciliatory activity (as expected). Beyond clergy's views of religion and their personal engagement with the racial situation, recruitment also proved to be important as clergy responded to media contacts, their denominations, and their congregations. Modeling different types of reconciliatory activities separately produced somewhat different findings, indicating that for these clergy the nature of the reconciliatory activity structured the influences (see Table 9.9). For example, when it came to involvement in community-oriented activities, including participating in local meetings, or perhaps attending demonstrations, being contacted by the denomination is indeed what mattered, as did the clergyperson's length of tenure within the church and the distance of the church from the riots. On the other hand, for individualistic activities, the attitudes and composition of the congregation stood out as significant influences (although the congregation's distance from the violence did not). Clearly, some of the city's clergy continued to navigate troubled waters when mixing religion and politics after April 2001 (as they surely did before the racial crisis as well), feeling freer to speak out if the congregation was ethnically homogeneous and when the laity openly supported their political activism (see Table 9.9).

In the case of community reconciliatory activity, my findings illustrate that clergy are pulled simultaneously by multiple forces: their personal desires for action and the pressures of the church denominational hierarchy, as well as the demands and constraints of the congregation (this dynamic is consistent with the findings of Olson, Crawford, and Deckman 2005). The finding regarding distance from the riots speaks to levels of engagement and recruitment, but also gives us insight into the fourth important factor mentioned above: community pressures. As Laura Olson (2000) has also observed, the location of the church dictates not only its clergy's concerns, but also the agenda of its congregation and the network of organizational affiliations that will instigate and maintain the organization's involvement in social and political issues. Thus, the fact that clergy who serve churches situated in close proximity to the riots were involved in community reconciliatory activities at higher rates is no surprise, for many of these religious leaders likely already viewed themselves as community representatives since they had been working in a context rich with social needs, calls for action, and opportunities for involvement.

Of course, the racial makeup of various congregations in the city also served to highlight the impact of community pressures, albeit in a different way. Given that the Cincinnati community conflict formed around issues of race and racism (Michaud 2001; Bowers 2002), black Cincinnatians had more at stake in the outcome regardless of whether or not they lived near the rioting. The results of this study indicate that the racial unrest in Cincinnati awakened the community factor that is deeply embedded in African-American churches (Assensoh and Alex-Assensoh 2001; Harris 1999; Lincoln and Mamiya 1990; Morris 1984). Clergy in black Cincinnati churches emerged as defenders of a distinct African-American community and exhibited high levels of racial reconciliatory involvement, matched with distinctive opinion patterns.

Conclusion

In the portion of the survey that welcomed additional comments, one respondent remarked: "Riot? Rebellion? Civil protest? All of the above? The events of April 2001 are too narrowly categorized by the term riot." While this study has not aimed to debate the meaning of the terms "racial reconciliation" or "riot," this clergyperson's comment has relevance in another sense. Just as no single term adequately captured the situation in Cincinnati, no one factor adequately explains the political behavior of the city's clergy in the wake of the violence. This investigation has verified the linkages discussed in the literature on the political activity of religious leaders, while at the same time it has contributed to that literature by detailing the connections between organized interests, churches, clergy, and church context. Cincinnati clergy did not decide to become involved in reconciliatory activities in a vacuum; a variety of forces that differed by race, denomination, and physical proximity to the violence drove them.

There has been a longstanding debate about the "suburban captivity" of religious bodies (Winter 1966). Churches outside of major cities have been accused of ignoring the political needs of urban areas and shrugging off their shared responsibilities for societal issues. While this research has supported that notion to a certain extent (with clergy in churches further from the riots reporting less engagement with and activity on racial reconciliation), I do find that there was considerable activity throughout the Cincinnati religious community (as well as influences and forces maintaining the suburban/urban divide).

The role of religion in American society has been well established, if only to note its many forms. As Robert Wuthnow writes, "Religion interacts with political life in America in countless ways, from obvious institutional ties to practices that express religious sensibilities though far removed from conventional religious settings" (1988: ix).

While the activity of the Cincinnati religious community in resolving the city's racial crisis certainly cannot easily be categorized, it does nevertheless point to the positive and important role that religious interests play in driving and resolving community conflicts. In issues involving race, dominant religious interests largely overlap in their views and have legitimacy not found elsewhere (although perhaps not the same desired methods). Despite the high hurdles of resources and constraints of apathy and opposition, clergy across religious families have exercised their prophetic voice to help heal Cincinnati, and Cincinnati has begun to come around.

Appendix: Variable Coding

Note: Variables are listed in the order presented in Table 9.9.

Age: "What year were you born?" 1=1900–1939, 2=1940–1950, 3=1951–1960, 4=1961–1975.

Sex: 1=female, 2=male.

Similar race/ethnicity of church: "Do members of your church, on the whole, share a similar ethnic/racial background?" 1=almost all members do, 2=most, but not all, 3=less than a majority do, 4=no, it's mixed.

Worship attendance: "About how many people attend an average worship service?" (Number)

White: "What is the predominant ethnicity/race of your church?" 1=black, 0=white (excluding Hispanic and "other")

Miles from riots: Measured from 1243 Elm St. Cincinnati, OH 45202 (in Over-the-Rhine, downtown Cincinnati).

Personal engagement: "How much attention have you paid to racial reconciliation issues and events since the April 2001 riots in Cincinnati?" 1=a great deal, 2=quite a bit, 3=some, 4=very little, 5=none.

Attitudes of congregation: "Some clergy are more politically involved than others for a variety of reasons. How did the following factors generally encourage or discourage your involvement in racial reconciliation in Cincinnati after the riots? The attitudes of my congregation." 1=strongly encourage, 2=encourage, 3=neutral, 4=discourage, 5=strongly discourage.

Demands of job: "Some clergy are more politically involved than others for a variety of reasons. How did the following factors generally encourage or discourage your involvement in racial reconciliation in Cincinnati after the riots? Demands of my job." 1=strongly encourage, 2=encourage, 3=neutral, 4=discourage, 5=strongly discourage.

Contacted by denomination/local media: "Citizens are often contacted by groups providing them information designed to influence their activity or to solicit their opinions. Since the riots, were you contacted by any of the following groups concerning race relations?" 1=yes, 2=no.

Churches should be involved: "Please tell us whether you agree or disagree with the following statements about race relations: Churches should be more involved in racial reconciliation."

1=strongly agree, 2=agree, 3=not sure/neutral, 4=disagree, 5=strongly disagree

Activity index: An additive index, ranging from 12 to 48, including the following statements, each coded 1=often, 2=sometimes, 3=rarely, 4=never. "Since the race riots of April 2001, how often have you participated in any of the following activities dealing with racial reconciliation in Cincinnati? publicly (not in a sermon) take a stand on race relations, publicly (not in a sermon) support a city leader, in a sermon take a stand on race relations, deliver a sermon on a controversial social/political issue, participate in the economic boycott of Cincinnati businesses, participate in a local/community group, serve on a local board or council, serve on a local clergy council, participate in a rally, demonstration or march, contact a local government official, attend a community meeting, and write a letter to a newspaper editor or an op-ed piece."

Community activity index: An additive index, ranging from 5 to 20, including the following statements, each coded 1=often, 2=sometimes, 3=rarely, 4=never. "Since the race riots of April 2001, how often have you participated in any of the following activities dealing with racial reconciliation in Cincinnati? Participate in a local political/community group, serve on a local board or council, serve on a local clergy council, participate in a rally, demonstration, or march, attend a community meeting."

Individual activity index: An additive index, ranging from 6 to 24, including the following statements, each coded 1=often, 2=sometimes, 3=rarely, 4=never. Since the race riots of April 2001, how often have you participated in any of the following activities dealing with racial reconciliation in Cincinnati? Publicly (not in a sermon) take a stand on race relations, publicly (not in a sermon) support a city leader, in a sermon take a stand on race relations, deliver a sermon on another controversial social/political issue, contact a local government official, and write a letter to a newspaper or op-ed piece."

Chapter 10

Unity in the Face of the Faceless

Clergy Opposition to the Ku Klux Klan in Northwest Arkansas

Frankyn C. Niles

Every time we come to town, something good happens. Because we came, all the church groups got together.

—*Jeffrey Berry, National Imperial Wizard of the Church of the American Knights of the KKK*

Whenever the Ku Klux Klan comes to town, there is apt to be conflict, especially if the town they come to is Siloam Springs, Arkansas. Struggling to distance themselves from lingering southern stereotypes, residents of this small (population 11,000) yet growing community on the Arkansas-Oklahoma border remember August 5, 2000 as the day the Klan held a rally in front of City Hall. A local Klan member, believing the city was discriminating against him, invited Rev. Jeffrey Berry, the often-violent leader of the Indiana-based Church of the American Knights of the KKK, to stage a demonstration (Hayworth 2000). In the months prior to the rally, city leaders asked members of the Siloam Springs Ministerial Alliance (hereinafter referred to as the SSMA), an alliance of white, male, and primarily evangelical ministers, to mobilize their parishioners to pray for a peaceful rally and to avoid the event altogether (Clergy Interview #6, hereinafter CI6). SSMA members heard the plea and, with an unprecedented level of unity, mobilized their parishioners to participate in a series of visible, yet peaceful, protest activities against the Klan.

Clergy viewed their mobilization efforts as successful, especially when compared to previous efforts to organize other parish activities, such as the National Day of Prayer and a series of Walks for Jesus (CI5). While the precise number of those who participated in the religiously sponsored events preceding the Klan rally was not tallied, most of the ministers estimated that between 20 and 25 percent of their parishioners were actively involved in anti-Klan activities. Perhaps most notably, only about two hundred spectators turned out for the rally, most of whom were from other communities in Northwest Arkansas. As one pastor told me, "We prayed that Siloam Springs, for the most part, would ignore [the Klan]. From that aspect, it was very successful" (CI1).

That the clergy of the SSMA opposed the Klan is, perhaps, not surprising; local ministerial organizations (MOs)—formal or informal gatherings of clergy of one or more faiths in a community—have often spoken against racism and intolerance, making them important avenues for social and political reform (Morris 1984; Wood 2002). For instance, in 1957 in Little Rock, Arkansas, MOs were instrumental in organizing resistance against anti-integrationists (Campbell and Pettigrew 1959), while in other locales they spoke out against lynching (Miller 1957). More recently, clergy associations have been credited with helping end desegregation policies in hotels and restaurants in St. Louis (Djupe and Gilbert 2003), and in Boston, a black MO has created ad hoc committees for endorsing African-American candidates (Jennings 2005).

What is puzzling about the Siloam Springs case is that the SSMA historically had not promoted social activism. Moreover, in the years leading up to the Klan demonstration, the SSMA had been largely inactive, with activities limited to monthly meetings and raising support for a local benevolence fund through offerings at a yearly community worship service. In fact, because of a lack of leadership and clear vision, most ministers considered attendance at SSMA meetings to be a waste of time. One SSMA member explained: "We wanted to lead the community, but we weren't doing it" (CI1). So, other than convening poorly attended and poorly considered monthly meetings, and occasionally promoting public religious dialogue, the SSMA had never engaged in social protest.

This chapter aims (1) to understand how and why SSMA clergy chose to address the Klan rally and (2) to identify the strategies they used to mobilize their parishioners. I also explore how the threat posed by the Klan shaped the response of the SSMA to the rally, as well as the efficacy of that response. I rely on data from seven interviews with SSMA clergy, two interviews with local officials, and local media coverage of the Klan rally. Beyond these immediate aims, this case study offers an opportunity to explore how community conflict structures the creation of political agendas in religious organizations, which speaks more generally to the question of how social context shapes the expression of collective religious interest.[1] The analysis is guided by various tributaries of social movement theory, each of which has been used previously to understand religious organizations (Lienesch 1982; Moen 1994; Niles 2003; Wald, Silverman, and Fridy 2005; Williams 2000; Wolcott 1982). Applied to the SSMA, this theoretical perspective suggests that collective action occurs at the intersection of organizational resources and member motivations (Morris and Mueller 1992). Organizational influence is in large part shaped by how well leaders anticipate and respond to community opportunities and their ability to marshal support for their agenda (Eisinger 1973).

Siloam Springs: Idyllic Yet Isolated

The city of Siloam Springs is located in Northwest Arkansas, one of the fastest growing and economically vibrant areas of the state.[2] The region is home to numerous corporate giants, such as Wal-Mart, Tyson Foods, and J. B. Hunt, as well as the flagship campus of the University of Arkansas. Owing to the economic stimulation provided by these employers, a substantial amount of economic and community development has occurred over the past decade, especially along the "I-540 corridor," an area extending from Bentonville in the north to Fayetteville in the south along the I-540 freeway. Unquestionably, this swath of property is the hub of economic, if not cultural, activity in Western Arkansas, boasting a relatively high standard of living. According to United States Census data,[3] when compared to other regions in Arkansas, communities in the Northwest are consistently ranked among the highest in terms of median family income, percentage with a college degree, and employee wages. Moreover, because of plentiful production and service jobs, unemployment is very low in the region.

Siloam Springs is the fourth largest city in Northwest Arkansas, located twenty-five miles east of the I-540 corridor. In many ways, the city mirrors the rest of Northwest Arkansas, providing a relatively high standard of living: consistently it ranks above the state average in terms of median family income, is home to international industries such as La-Z-Boy and Allen Canning, a regionally recognized liberal arts college (John Brown University), and low unemployment. Additionally, like other communities in Northwest Arkansas, Siloam Springs is racially homogeneous: 85 percent of the population are white, 10 percent Hispanic, and 0.5 percent (53 individuals) African-American. Politically, residents are overwhelmingly Republican and ideologically conservative.

Siloam Springs is also a deeply religious community. Upon entering the city, one is greeted by a sign that reads, "Welcome to Siloam Springs: Where Jesus Christ is Lord." There are nearly sixty churches in the city (most are evangelical Protestant congregations), and on any given Sunday morning or Wednesday evening, church parking lots are filled with cars of the committed.

Despite being located in one of the fastest growing and economically vibrant regions in the state, if not the country, the city is geographically and socially isolated from the bustling I-540 corridor. As a result, Siloam Springs remains remarkably rural, lacking many of the economic, social, and cultural accoutrements associated with urban development. For example, the city lacks a movie theater, a bakery, and fine dining restaurants; only recently has it had a gourmet coffee shop open. As one journalist recently noted, "Driving . . . towards Siloam Springs, things aren't much different than they were 20 years ago" (Roebuck 2003). At the same time, because of a low crime rate, its proximity to the Ozark Mountains, and its "friendly atmosphere" many consider Siloam Springs idyllic and an ideal place to live.[4]

Much to the chagrin of civic leaders, the geographical isolation of Siloam Springs has led most cultural and political elites, including major media outlets located in the region, to forget the city. Illustrating this concern, a city council member remarked,

> We are still not garnering the attention and respect that a growing community like Siloam Springs deserves. With many large industries like Allen Canning, Simmons Foods, . . . we should be seeing more of the media attention from Northwest Arkansas. Northwest Arkansas is more than Fayetteville, Rogers, Springdale, and Bentonville (Roebuck 2003).

Because of this lack of visibility, business leaders in Siloam Springs have been unable to attract larger businesses and white-collar workers, resulting in slower economic growth than what other cities in

Northwest Arkansas have experienced (COI2). Equally important, and foremost in the minds of civic leaders when they first learned that the Klan was planning to hold a rally in the city, social isolation further entrenches in visitors' minds the notion that Siloam Springs is an underdeveloped, racially bigoted town where, as one pastor remarked, "everybody walks barefoot and marries their cousin" (CI1).

In all, despite cherishing their small-town way of life, residents of Siloam Springs are acutely aware of the stigma associated with living in what is largely a rural southern town. But while many in Siloam Springs see underdevelopment as something to be celebrated, one senses anxiety, especially among younger and more educated residents, when comparisons are made between the city and more prosperous and developed communities in the region.

In light of these anxieties and the desire on the part of many residents to combat lingering racist stereotypes, it is not at all surprising that when the media descended on Siloam Springs to report on the Klan rally (all major networks came), religious leaders, as well as most other residents in the community, were deeply concerned. One pastor told me, "This is the first time the media has come to town. . . . We didn't want to be nationally identified as [being] the place that had the Klan rally" (CI2). Another clergy member quipped, "For those of us who consider Northwest Arkansas a separate state from the rest of Arkansas . . . it was horrible" (CI6). This same pastor also expressed worry that the Klan rally was "going to tie the [city] to 'Alabamans' and 'Mississippians' . . . and further entrench in people's minds [the idea] that [Siloam Springs] is a little backwater, southern town" (CI6). To be sure, many clergy in the SSMA expressed opposition to the Klan because they believed that their silence would harm both the community and their status as religious leaders.

Data and Research Design

The primary data source for this study consists of face-to-face interviews with seven members (current and former) of the SSMA and two city officials. Pertinent information from newspaper articles and SSMA documents supplement these data. Interviews were conducted during June and July 2003, either in the respondent's office or at John Brown University. All respondents were guaranteed anonymity. Each interview lasted between one and two hours and proceeded using a series of open-ended questions.

Respondents for the study were identified using a combination of newspaper reports and clergy queries. All clergy interviewed were white males with an average age in the mid-forties. Tenure of the clergy in their congregations ranged from five to over twenty-five years, with an average tenure of ten years. Most of the clergy were also highly educated: two had earned doctorates and five possessed master's degrees. Five of the ministers represented conservative, evangelical denominations, while two of the clergy presided over mainline Protestant churches. Except for the two ministers from the mainline Protestant churches, each clergy member considered himself theologically conservative.

Because a man named Tom Yoakum—the individual who invited the Klan to Siloam Springs—continues to harass community residents, it is essential to maintain the anonymity of the respondents.[5] In fact, one minister refused to be interviewed because of concerns about retaliation. For this reason, any identifying denominational or professional labels are omitted in subsequent analysis. Within the text, clergy interviews are signified by the initials "CI" followed by a unique number assigned to each respondent (e.g., CI2). Similarly, interviews with city officials are identified by "COI" followed by a number (e.g., COI1). In an effort to minimize clutter in the presentation, only direct quotations from respondents or, in some instances, paraphrases are cited in the text.

While the identities of the key actors involved in organizing the anti-Klan protest are readily identifiable from news reports, I avoid the direct use of names except in a few instances. Furthermore, because Yoakum has a history of violence and harassment (he was tried sixteen times in 2002 and 2003 for a range of matters including threatening to kill a Wal-Mart manager: Mero 2001b), I judged it too hazardous to interview him personally.

A Drowning and a Dad: The Non-Racial Roots of the Klan Rally

On Sunday, May 21, 2000, the seventeen-year-old son of Tom Yoakum—a longtime resident of the Siloam Spring's community and a member of the Church of the American Knights of the Ku Klux Klan—drowned while swimming in a local creek. Despite repeated attempts by fire department paramedics to resuscitate the boy, he was pronounced dead at a local hospital. After his son's death, Yoakum accused the emergency crews who had responded to the accident of letting his son die—using bullhorns and fliers, as well as the local media (Bradford 2001). Despite the repeated attempts of city officials (including the mayor, city administrator, and fire chief) and clergy to assure Yoakum of the fidelity of the emergency crews, his harassment of community leaders increased throughout the summer of 2000.

Yoakum was especially antagonistic towards local police officials. Much of this animosity stemmed from an incident that occurred during the funeral for his son. According to police reports, a member of the "Mexican Mafia," a group of hooligans in Siloam Springs, arrived at the ceremony "toting baseball bats" and was generally disruptive (Branam 2000). Yoakum interpreted this display of aggression as "terrorist acts." The perpetrator was arrested and charged with felony aggravated assault, though the prosecutor subsequently reduced the charges. This reduction further fueled Yoakum's belief that city officials—in this case, the police and prosecutors were discriminating against him and his family.

To protest his mistreatment by the Siloam Springs community, Tom Yoakum invited Rev. Jeffrey Berry, the Indiana-based Klan leader, to hold a rally in Siloam Springs. Rev. Berry organized the rally with the impression he was coming to town because of problems with gangs and drugs, and believed that "the police don't want to get involved because they will be sued for discrimination" (Hayworth 2000). Despite the apparent misunderstanding between Yoakum and Rev. Berry, the latter secured the necessary permits from the City of Siloam Springs and scheduled a rally to be held in front of City Hall on August 5, 2000, publicizing the event in the media and in flyers.

City and Religious Leaders Respond

In response to the planned rally, local, state, and national law enforcement agencies, including the Federal Bureau of Investigation and the Bureau of Alcohol, Tobacco, and Firearms, were enlisted by the Siloam Springs Chief of Police to help draft a contingency plan in the event violence erupted, and also to provide their services during the rally itself. In the days before the event, city workers also canvassed area streets, alerting residents about the upcoming event. Because Jeffrey Berry had a history of inciting violence at rallies—rumors were circulating that young persons in the area were planning a series of drive-by shootings during the rally—city officials hoped planning beforehand would minimize the likelihood of escalation (CI6).

Civic leaders were also keenly aware that the arrival of the Klan would result in negative publicity for the city. One official was worried that the rally would harm the image of the city, leaving, in his words, a "black eye on the community"(CO1). In the local media alone, there were more than fifteen stories devoted to the rally and Tom Yoakum. To limit the negative impact the rally might have on Siloam Springs, city leaders devised a simple plan—they wanted area residents to avoid the event, remaining away from the downtown area during the hours of the demonstration. According to one city official, the reasoning behind this strategy was simple: if the "community stayed away from the rally . . . [there] would be little publicity or conflict surrounding it" (Flowers 2000c). More candidly, the mayor of Siloam Springs, M. L. "Moose" Van Poucke, commented, "What happens if the media shows up, and there is nobody there? You all around go 'OK' and leave" (Flowers 2000c). Ultimately, city officials wanted the demonstration to be a "non-event," limiting any collateral damage that might occur (CO1; CI3; CI6).

Political leaders communicated their agenda through local media outlets. At the same time, in an effort to gain access to religious adherents in Siloam Springs (a large percentage of the local population), they also contacted clergy in the SSMA. One pastor recalled that a local official asked him to encourage his parishioners to stay away from the rally (CI6), while another minister told me that the Siloam Springs Police Chief requested that he "pray for confusion on the part of the demonstrators so that violence would not occur" (CI4). In response to these requests, but also independent of them, SSMA clergy met to devise a protest strategy.[6] Recalling the planning period, one pastor commented, "we felt like it was important to have some sort of response . . . but we didn't want it to be a confrontational kind of response" (CI1). According to news reports, SSMA leaders wanted to send a message "of tolerance and peace [yet wanted to] . . . convince the Klan members they [were] not welcome in Siloam Springs" (Flowers 2000a). With these immediate objectives in mind, instead of organizing a counter-rally, which many feared would only foment tensions, the SSMA implemented a two-pronged protest strategy consisting of a series of peaceful demonstrations during the week prior to the rally and sponsoring prayer meetings in local churches during the event.

Clergy Motivations

What motivated clergy to oppose the Klan in the first place? While the SSMA clearly responded to the agenda conveyed by political elites, religious leaders also pursued their course of action with a set of organizational goals firmly in place. Reeling from years of inactivity, as we shall see, these goals provided guidance for SSMA clergy as they designed their response to the Klan and sustained the organization throughout this period of protest.

Building the SSMA and Seeking Spiritual Influence

First, clergy chose to address the Klan rally because they saw it as an opportunity to work together on a project of public interest, and in the process, to legitimize the organization and support the spiritual life of Siloam Springs. Since its 1965 founding, the SSMA largely had remained a marginalized member of the local religious community. Because of high clergy turnover, the organization failed to meet regularly and was unable to attract a committed cadre of members.[7]

Furthermore, because of a lack of leadership and a clearly articulated set of goals—according to the original constitution, the SSMA was formed to promote the diffuse goals of "Christian fellowship" and "moral improvement of the community" (Siloam Springs Area Ministerial Fellowship Constitution 1975)—the organization lacked a sustained and systematic agenda of social engagement. This lack of social engagement meant that many in the community viewed the SSMA as irrelevant. For example, when I asked one city official what he thought of the SSMA, he replied, "The ministerial alliance is really a joke . . . they don't do much of anything" (COI2). While less dismissive, members of the SSMA also described their own experience with the organization in less than glowing terms. Recalling the years before the rally, one minister mentioned, "To be honest, I've always considered the SSMA to be a waste of time. There was no purpose [and] no relationships [among pastors]" (CI1).

All of this changed, however, in 1999 when a new president was elected to lead the SSMA. Having been involved in a MO previously and being relatively new to the community, he, along with a core group of seven to ten religious leaders, set out to build the organization and to bring about spiritual renewal in the city. Evangelical in orientation (a reflection of the dominant theological culture in the community), according to members, the primary goals of the

SSMA during that time were to "break down walls between denominations" (CI2), "unify" the clergy and the community (CI1; CI5), and help "transform . . . Siloam Springs once again into a place of healing" (CI2).

To accomplish these goals, between 1999 and the summer of 2000, the SSMA began to meet regularly. At the same time, leaders convened a fall retreat for clergy, organized "pulpit swaps" between congregations, and sponsored well-attended community worship services. During this time, the SSMA also composed a new constitution, calling upon "leaders and congregations of the Church of Siloam Springs to . . . pray and work together for the Christ-centered transformation of individuals, couples, and families" (Siloam Springs Area Christian Ministerial Fellowship Constitution 2000).8 According to clergy, these goals resonated with members of the SSMA and, by the summer of 2000, relationships among members of the SSMA were starting to be established (CI2). At the same time, clergy developed a sense of "togetherness" (CI1), a conviction that they were collectively responsible for the spiritual life of Siloam Springs, and a desire to "have one voice on key issues that might come about" (CI5). During this time, the SSMA also gained a visible presence in the community, with one pastor recalling that before the rally, "parishioners were beginning to see the various congregations unified" (CI1).

Although Siloam Springs clergy wished to act with "unity" during the early months of 2000, according to one pastor, at that time it was still "just a concept" (CI1). When SSMA leaders heard about the impending Klan rally, they saw it as an important opportunity to engage the community in a way that would allow for the expression of their newfound commitments, providing a platform upon which coordinated social activism could occur. One minister told me he viewed the SSMA's involvement in anti-Klan protests as an opportunity to do "something visible . . . to demonstrate the unity of the Church of Siloam Springs" (CI4). Similarly, yet with more strategic nuance, another pastor remarked that organizing the anti-Klan events "gave us [SSMA] something to latch on to . . . something to focus on outside of church" (CI1), admitting later that without the rallying point of the demonstration, he was unsure what would have happened to the organization (CI1).

Clergy as Community Protectors

Second, as community leaders, clergy felt they had a responsibility to confront the threat posed by the Klan. To be sure, theological considerations motivated clergy. For example, one pastor mentioned that he believed that racism is inherently "sinful" (CI2), and thus, to stand by, as one pastor said, "as evangelical churches did during the 1960s . . . on the racial issue" (CI4) would be wrong.

At the same time, each minister I interviewed saw the rally as an attack on the city of Siloam Springs and their way of life. Clergy echoed many of the concerns voiced by political officials, worrying that the arrival of the Klan would result in a public relations disaster. With great indignation, one pastor defended the SSMA's course of action, saying, "we are gatekeepers of the city. . . . How dare these guys come in. . . . This [rally] was going to give us a black eye" (CI6). More directly, another minister said that the SSMA opposed the Klan because "we [could not] just sit idle when someone comes into our town where we are shepherds. . . . As citizens of this community, we didn't want people to think this is who we are" (CI2).

That clergy wished to play a protective role in their community is not surprising; clergy often engage politics to protect their parishes from threatening events (Djupe and Gilbert 2003; Smith and Harris 2005). What is especially interesting about the current case is the vigor with which clergy approached the protective task and the acute sense of anxiety that the rally appears to have engendered. Beyond the obvious worry associated with a Klan rally, much of the anxiety that clergy experienced was a function of residing in Siloam Springs, Arkansas, a southern city whose residents cherish their way of life yet wish to distance themselves from lingering regional stereotypes.

Jericho Revisited: SSMA Protests the Klan

Building upon these motivational substrates, SSMA clergy organized a series of community-wide protest events during the week before the rally. According to clergy, the activities were intended to send a visible yet peaceful message of opposition to the Klan and, according to one pastor, helped "buffer [and] diffuse anger" that was growing among many in the community in response to the rally (CI6).

First, on the Sunday before the demonstration, the SSMA hosted a "Concert of Prayer." Over four hundred people attended the event, including a speaker from the prominent evangelical men's organization Promise Keepers, with pastors from the community leading participants in prayer for the community and city leaders (CI1). During this time, congregants were also given the opportunity to pray together in small groups.

Second, on each evening during the week preceding the rally, the SSMA organized a series of "prayer walks" around the city administration building, the site of the planned rally. Pastors described the prayer walk route to parishioners through flyers and church bulletin inserts. Between fifty and one hundred protestors participated each night, praying about a variety of topics, including the need for peace and unity in the city and, in the words of one participant, for "Mr. Yoakum [to] come to Christ" (CI1). SSMA members believed that praying would protect city residents from violence and provide wisdom to city officials (CI1; CI6). One minister prayed that the demonstrators would be denied the necessary permits to hold the rally, believing that if he prayed earnestly enough, God would answer his request (CI1). Also seeking divine intervention, another city resident was reported as "praying for rain" on the day of the event (Branam 2000).

Beyond achieving the intended spiritual goals, clergy designed the prayer walks to forge a sense of solidarity among city residents and to portray a peaceful yet resolute image of the community to the Klan and to the media (CI1; CI2; CI6). One pastor commented that the prayer walks were intended to "show community unity and show that churches can work together" (Flowers 2000a). While the extent to which the prayer walks achieved these objectives is unclear, there is some evidence the strategy worked: religious protests were prominently featured in news stories about the rally. From the perspective of leaders in the SSMA, the prayer walks succeeded in achieving the goal of "breaking down barriers" between people of faith (CI1), believing those who participated in the walks developed a sense of "kinship" and camaraderie (CI1).

Finally, recall that in the weeks before the Klan rally, clergy appealed to their parishioners to stay away from it. While simply remaining at home during the rally would have sufficed, providing an alternative activity with some thematic continuity seemed a better option to the Siloam Springs clergy. Therefore they organized a series of prayer services to be held during the time of the rally. Hosted by prominent area churches, clergy reported that hundreds of religious adherents attended the services, praying for the police, the demonstrators, and the community (CI3).

The Klan Rally: A Non-Event

As it turned out, instead of rain (for which the hopeful town resident had prayed), the morning of August 5, 2000, broke clear and bright; by the beginning of the rally, the temperature was unusually hot, exceeding a hundred degrees by mid-afternoon. Approximately two hundred spectators, including a few dozen counter-demonstrators from other cities in Arkansas, and about forty Klan members, twelve of whom were brought to Siloam Springs by Indiana Klan leader Jeffrey Berry, endured the stifling heat. The major media outlets in the area also turned out to cover the event. The rally was scheduled from 1:00 p.m. to 3:00 p.m. But owing to the excessive heat, members of the Klan began leaving the demonstration area by 2:25 p.m., with many removing their hoods for fear of heat exhaustion (Flowers 2000b; COI1).

The police presence at the rally was exceedingly strong. Uniformed officers patrolled on foot and on motorcycles while sheriff K-9 units searched the demonstration area and a sheriff's helicopter flew overhead (Flowers 2000b). The Arkansas National Guard was also on hand in case a riot broke out. Other than a few spectators becoming outraged over some of the more inflammatory statements made by members of the Klan, no incidents of violence were reported during the rally and no arrests were made.

Unquestionably, the peacefulness of the Klan rally was a function of careful planning by the Siloam Springs Police Department. As Benton County Sheriff Andy Lee suggested, "Siloam Springs [Police Chief] Al Gregory did his homework and reached out and got the assistance he needed to make it clear to the Klan demonstrators that there would be no nonsense" (Bell and Jones 2000). At the same time, the likelihood of violence was minimized by the fact that so few spectators or counter-demonstrators attended the rally. Indeed, the number of those attending the rally fell far short of law enforcement officials' estimates, suggesting that city leaders achieved their goal of keeping most residents away from the rally.

The fact that few city residents attended the rally was a function of SSMA clergy's ability to convince their parishioners to avoid the rally by either staying home or attending church-sponsored events.

Communicating their strategy through the newly established religious networks (CI3), SSMA clergy were able to replicate their plan of peaceful protest in congregations throughout Siloam Springs, staying visible to city leaders and clergy alike. For example, a few weeks before the rally, the Mayor of Siloam Springs noted, "many churches . . . in the city have their own functions at the same time as the Klan rally . . . but they are away from the rally site" (Flowers 2000c). Illustrating the response of the clergy, one local Hispanic pastor who was not a member of the SSMA stated that he "wanted no part of the rally." Instead, he organized a prayer meeting on the day of the rally (Flowers 2000c).

Clergy mobilized parishioners to participate in their sponsored events by using a mixture of spiritual and cultural narratives. Exploiting the deep-seated social anxieties exposed by the Klan, clergy—both from their pulpits (although no pastor devoted an entire sermon to the topic) and in flyers distributed around town—conveyed the message that opposing the Klan was both a religious and a civic responsibility of parishioners. For example, pastors encouraged parishioners to become involved in the prayer walks and used a variety of religiously grounded arguments, including telling their flocks, "the KKK is not a Christian organization" (CI2); "the perpetrators need prayer" (CI3); prayer will help bring about "confusion" on the part of the Klan (CI1), and that praying "is a great way for all our churches to come together in unity" (CI).

Clergy employed protective themes, suggesting, as one minister did, that peacefully opposing the Klan is "something we can do positive for our community" (CI3). More directly, another pastor recalled telling his parishioners that the Klan rally was in reality "an attack on his home," suggesting that parishioners needed to oppose the threat actively (CI6). While the extent to which all clergy used these narratives when discussing the Klan from the pulpit is unknown, most SSMA clergy acknowledged that they urged their parishioners be involved in the anti-Klan events in order to benefit the community.

In the end, the Klan rally was largely the "non-event" political and religious leaders had envisioned. From the SSMA's perspective, rather than dividing the community, the rally actually unified the town (and especially its clergy) to an unprecedented extent. Assessing the effect of the rally, one city official commented that perhaps the rally had tarnished the image of the city, but had not "given it a black eye." Instead, the community had responded by demonstrating unity and tolerance (COI1).

After the Rally: The Decline of the SSMA

Despite its role in organizing protest against the Klan, by the winter of 2000, the SSMA once again entered a period of decline. Even though leaders in the organization desired to "maintain a sense of being together" (CI3), once the crisis was over, clergy involvement in the SSMA waned. Only recently, in large part because of the efforts of one prominent Siloam Springs minister, has the SSMA started to meet again regularly and discuss future goals. Nevertheless, in the months after the Klan rally, as one minister told me, "it came to a point where [the SSMA] came close to dying" (CI1). The moribund status of the SSMA largely resulted from internal conflicts concerning the future direction and goals of the SSMA, differences in theological commitments among members, and perhaps most importantly, a lack of clear purpose. Many of the ministers I interviewed claimed that they had exerted substantial amounts of energy leading up to the Klan rally; however, when a "new cause" did not materialize, and because leadership was lacking, clergy chose to withdraw from the SSMA and focus on more pressing issues in their own congregations.

A Theoretical Evaluation: Placing the SSMA in Context

When asked why they succeeded in mobilizing their parishioners to participate in the anti-Klan activities, many Siloam Springs pastors suggested it was because the Klan posed a tangible threat to the community. A closer reading of the data, however, suggests that this humble assessment only provides one part of the explanation. Indeed, the evidence, as well as a good bit of theory, suggests that the success of the SSMA was due in large part to the ability of pastors to mobilize their parishioners. Given the level of perceived threat that permeated the community, this mobilization is perhaps not surprising. Nevertheless, it was the clergy's own ability to create messages that resonated with those in the pews that made the social threat posed by the Klan operational.

Collective Framing: Creating Mobilizing Messages

According to collective framing theory, one tributary of social movement theory, opinion leaders mobilize support for an agenda by constructing and conveying a set of grievances that resonate with potential supporters (Snow and Benford 1992). To achieve this end, leaders of social movements employ frames, which according to Snow and Benford are "interpretive schemata that 'simplify the world' by selectively punctuating and encoding . . . situations, events and experiences . . . within one's present and past environment" (1992: 137). More than simple schema, however, frames define problems, diagnose causes, make moral judgments, and suggest remedies (Entman 1993: 52).

Because clergy are also community members, they can draw upon relevant cultural and religious resources that might include beliefs, ideologies, values, myths, and fears when creating their messages. They are also especially capable of identifying culpable agents and proposing actionable solutions (Snow 2004). By selecting narratives that resonate with people's experiences and require "religious intervention," clergy move the faithful to action. For example, in a study of clergy involvement in anti-drug programs, James Cavendish (2001) finds that clergy mobilized parishioners using a combination of political and religious themes. According to Cavendish, this suggests that "participation is increased when framing strategies try to incorporate themes that are salient among diverse audiences" (2001: 222).

It is useful to note that while the content of grievances is socially constructed, they may actually reflect longstanding concerns in the community. Illustrative of this view is the notion that a perceived external threat is the key to successful mobilization efforts (Mueller 1992). According to Taylor and Whittier (1992), conflict is a key variable that affects the mobilization success of social movement leaders. In communities where threat is high, movement leaders will be more successful at attributing blame, suggesting solutions, and ultimately motivating collective action. In this way, framing theory suggests that creating resonant messages depends upon both agency and social context: leaders and social context both matter.

Clergy in the SSMA succeeded in their mobilization efforts because they were able to identify and frame the conflict posed by the Klan rally in such a way that it resonated with parishioners. Recall that residents of Siloam Springs are highly religious and fiercely loyal to their community, but that they simultaneously wish to distance themselves from "small town Southern stereotypes" (CI1). As a result, many in the community believed the Klan posed a credible threat. As religious leaders and members of the community, clergy were able to successfully exploit these social anxieties while also appealing to a set of broadly held conservative religious beliefs, such as those related to unity, reconciliation, and the utility of using prayer to solve social problems (CI2; CI3). For example, a flyer announcing the downtown prayer walks encouraged parishioners to pray for "God's restraint upon those who would sow discord in our community" (Flowers 2000a). Consistent with collective framing theory, by emphasizing the community threat posed by the Klan and proposing solutions that would address the threat in a way that was religiously credible and socially desirable, clergy successfully mobilized a substantial percentage of their parishioners to protest peacefully against the Klan.

Social Networks: Internal Infrastructures and Social Protest

While framing was perhaps the proximate cause of the SSMA's successful mobilization, structural and ideational changes that occurred in the SSMA between 1999 and 2000 provided the resources necessary for social protest to occur. These changes facilitated the creation of collective action in the organization. According to resource mobilization theory, because social movement organizations (SMOs)—the visible component of the movement (McAdam, McCarthy, and Zald 1996)—are typically voluntaristic, lacking consistent access to human or material resources, one of the primary tasks that social movement leaders face is securing the necessary resources, such as money, expertise, or labor, that make collective action possible (Klandermans 2001). In this view, organizational success, which is typically defined in terms of a narrow set of purposive goals, is a function of "resource availability . . . preference structures, and entrepreneurial attempts to meet preference demands" (McCarthy and Zald 1977: 1236).[9]

One of the most important resources that a social movement can avail itself of is the social infrastructure provided by pre-existing networks among movement affiliates (McAdam, McCarthy, and Zald 1996; Snow, Zurcher, and Ekland-Olson 1980). Research on the civil rights movement (McAdam 1982; Morris 1984), the feminist movement (Freeman 1975), and neighborhood organizing (Boyte 1981) demonstrates that social organizing most likely occurs where there are pre-existing relationships among movement activists (McCarthy 1987). When connections exist among movement supporters, mobilization is less costly in terms of securing human and material resources, and communicating goals and strategies within the SMO is greatly facilitated.

Religious communities are especially likely to exhibit a dense web of internal networks (McCarthy 1987). Because "building community" is normative in many religious traditions, participants in faith communities will seek out connections with coreligionists. As a result, faith-based organizations, such as churches, can facilitate the organizational growth and social activism of MOs by providing congregational and denominational resources, with social networks being most efficacious concerning issues around which consensus is easily reached.

One of the most important findings of this chapter is that the networks that existed among members of the SSMA and between congregations and the organization facilitated the rapid mobilization of clergy and parishioners in opposition to the Klan. Recall that after the implementation of growth initiatives in 1999, such as weekly prayer meetings and the concomitant desire on the part of clergy to be unified, the internal infrastructure of the SSMA was enhanced significantly. When asked why organizing resistance to the Klan had proceeded so smoothly, one pastor suggested that it was because "there was an existing structure, weak as it was, that pulled together in a matter of weeks" (CI3). Indeed, after first hearing about the proposed Klan rally, a core group of ministers—the same ones who regularly prayed together—met to plan a course of action. Thereafter, they communicated the plan with others using an existing SSMA telephone list. With clergy networks firmly established, a timely and ongoing response was possible. According to one pastor, without the existence of such networks, communicating the group's protest strategy would have been nearly impossible (CI3).

Congregations were also integral components in the networks established among clergy between 1999 and 2000, providing important human and material resources to the SSMA and facilitating communication with parishioners. Indeed, clergy used their churches as the primary platform from which they launched their anti-Klan initiatives, communicating their protest plan to parishioners from their pulpits, using church facilities to produce flyers, soliciting congregants to help organize the prayer walks, and holding anti-Klan events at their churches, including the prayer services on the day of the rally.

Ultimately, of course, SSMA leaders could not sustain this level of organizational cohesion and social involvement. After the Klan rally, amid internal conflicts concerning the direction of the SSMA, clergy withdrew from the organization. This ebb and flow of activity is entirely predictable. Social movement theory predicts that once a crisis is resolved without being replaced by new, tangible goals, few opportunities exist for group cohesion and, as a result, disintegration of the organization is likely (Colquhoun and Martin 2001).

Opportunity Structures: Social Context and Agenda Setting

Finally, in addition the influence of organizational and individual factors, forces external to the organization shaped collective action in the SSMA. Indeed, one of the central features of the theory used in this chapter is that a SMO, and by extension, a MO, is an open system, influencing and being influenced by the surrounding environment (Balser 1997; McAdam, McCarthy, and Zald 1996).[10] The local socio-political environment might structure the organized expression of religious interests in two ways: by providing opportunities for political involvement and by shaping the strategies used by religious elites to mobilize support for protest activities.

According to Herbert Kitschelt, political opportunity structures are "specific configuration[s] of resources, institutional arrangements and historical precedents for social mobilization, which facilitate the development of protest movements in some instances and constrain[s] them in others" (1986: 58). In this view, opportunities (or barriers) exist in the immediate socio-political environment of a SMO that make political action more or less likely.

While a great deal of disagreement exists in the literature over how best to conceptualize the notion of "opportunity structures" (Meyer and Minkoff 2004), scholars generally agree that SMO leaders, either consciously or unconsciously, respond to structural changes in the opportunities available in a community, such as those arising from legislation or from demographic changes, or by opportunities created by political elites or political events (Tarrow 1996, 1998; see also Eisinger 1973). Regardless of the precise causal mechanism, according to Meyer and Minkoff, political opportunities are largely ephemeral (effectively) and exogenous to the SMO, suggesting that such organizations "are composed of . . . more or less rational, entrepreneurial, and perceptive organizers who are consequently more or less responsive to changes in political opportunity" (2004: 1464).

The findings of this chapter support the central tenets of political opportunity theory, suggesting an important method for understanding the behavior of other MOs. One of the consistent themes of this chapter is that the social threat posed by the Klan shaped the way in which the SSMA clergy addressed the rally. Believing the rally was an attack on their community and an affront to their religious values, SSMA clergy intentionally designed their response to the Klan to project an image of peace and unity. Prayer walks and community worship services were designed to evidence both. At the same time, ministers also saw the rally as an opportunity to engage in meaningful collective action while also enhancing the visibility of the SSMA.

Clergy in the SSMA also responded to an agenda promulgated by individuals outside the organization. Recall that the mayor and police officials, recognizing the important access religious leaders have to community residents in a town as devout as Siloam Springs, contacted SSMA leaders in hopes of forestalling a violent response to the Klan. The evidence presented in this chapter suggests that, at least initially, much of the SSMA's response to the rally reflected the political goals articulated by city officials. It is safe to conclude that the favorable response of the SSMA to this agenda setting occurred because ministers were convinced that their involvement in anti-Klan activities would genuinely benefit the community. Recall that before the rally was announced, SSMA clergy expressed a desire to preserve the community. At least at a conceptual level, there was symmetry between the goals articulated by city leaders in the weeks before the Klan rally and the long-term goals of the SSMA. This symmetry, in effect, primed religious leaders to be aware and receptive to cues provided by political elites (Zaller 1992).

Conclusion

In this chapter, I have endeavored to understand how and why SSMA clergy opposed the Ku Klux Klan rally held in Siloam Springs, Arkansas, in August 2000, achieving a measure of collective action and influence heretofore unseen. Results suggest that organizational resources (especially social networks), a cadre of members desiring to establish unity among clergy and provide for the spiritual wellbeing of the community, and agenda-setting by political elites helped shape the response of the SSMA to the rally. At the same time, the very nature of the threat posed by the Klan—a threat to public safety, public image, and the legitimacy of clergy as religious leaders—was a determining factor in the creation and implementation of the SSMA's protest strategy.

In a similar way, the local political and social environment provided the materials used by clergy to mobilize parishioners. Drawing upon a host of social anxieties imposed by the local social context and exposed by the arrival of the Klan, and using both secular and spiritual narratives as motivational themes, clergy were able to convey their messages in such a way that parishioners willingly engaged in protest.

In the end, by providing an organizational structure in which peaceful protest was possible, the SSMA succeeded in advancing its primary agenda of unifying the community and legitimizing themselves as religious leaders. Ultimately, the symbolic threat posed by the Klan provided much of the impetus behind the organizational efforts of the SSMA during the summer of 2000, structuring the strategies that religious leaders used to mobilize the faithful to protest the rally.

This study provides one example of how local political conflict shapes clergy political behavior. My findings suggest that it was the type of threat that the Klan posed that drove the response of the SSMA. In this way, this study adds to the existing literature that explores the social basis of clergy political involvement, yet does so with one important twist—it explores how social context shapes *collective* clergy behavior in MOs, one of the most common, yet understudied, ways in which religious professionals engage politics. Specifically, this research provides some preliminary insights into how local political conflict and the broader social context structure the identification and mobilization of political agendas within MOs, how collective action is achieved in these organizations, and how MO leaders frame their messages. This study also suggests that scholars should avoid divorcing the study of social engagement of MO clergy from the process of organizational development, as collective clergy interests are located at the intersection of these two imperatives.

If we take James Guth's recent observation seriously—that scholars have yet to "map the rest of the clergy's organizational world . . . [and that] the impact of local organizational affiliation is also largely unexplored" (2001: 39–40)—exploring causes and consequence of the MO political engagement will yield important substantive and theoretical dividends. Fruitful areas of inquiry might include (1) exploring the organizational characteristics that structure MO political engagement, paying particular attention to the impact that group diversity, size, and leadership structures have on internal agenda setting; (2) determining how MOs function in different social contexts, identifying the types of issues they address and why; (3) exploring in greater depth how face-to-face interactions in these groups are translated into collective action (see Walsh 2004); (4) analyzing more extensively the relationship between governmental agencies and MOs, with particular attention to understanding how agenda setting by political elites shapes the protest activities of MOs, as well as their involvement in the delivery of local social services (Cnaan 2002; Livezey 2000); and (5) exploring the different sorts of strategies MO leaders use to effect social change. Because civic leaders and parishioners alike increasingly call upon these religious organizations to provide a religious voice on pressing political and social issues, such an approach will yield important substantive and theoretical dividends, providing insights into how religious interests shape American society.

CONCLUSION

Chapter 11

A Meditation on and Meta-analysis of the Public Presence of Religious Interests

Paul A. Djupe & Laura R. Olson

In this volume, we set out to take stock of the public intersections of religion and politics in the United States, tell some engaging stories, and build evidence to assess the theoretical work that has been completed during the first generation of empirical religion and politics inquiry. In the same way in which each of the foregoing chapters is constructed, we saved a full discussion of the theoretical implications of this work for last. Instead of summarizing the preceding chapters, we now undertake a meta-analysis of the collected findings of the volume. Three guiding research questions unite the chapters. First, what motivates organized religious interests to confront public problems? Second, do religious interests cooperate with one another to confront public problems, and what barriers exist that might hinder them from doing so? Third, how effective are religious interests when they choose to confront public problems? Before attempting to specify the lessons of the case studies, we begin with an assessment of the literature. How well does the extant literature on religion and politics address these questions? What is the state of the religion and politics literature?

The Religion and Politics Literature

The religion and politics literature maintains at least an implicitly pluralist belief system (Truman 1951), although it has not used that language in a long time. Intramural differences in approach have aligned loyalties more reliably. And more than most political science subfields, the religion and politics subfield continues to address a plural set of research questions, all under one tent. In the absence of self-interested motives that might provide a reason for adopting an Olsonian framework (but see Djupe 2001; Djupe and Gilbert 2002b; Djupe, Olson, and Gilbert 2005), religion and politics scholars have approached the notion of "religious interests" in various ways, such as vast lobbying groups (or potential lobbies) and as a force that might convert political potential into action. Scholars also have explored the factors that affect the cohesion of religious groups, as well as the place of religiously based attitudes (still equated with "interests") in citizens' political calculi.

One motivation for this volume was the unit-of-analysis problem in religion and politics research. Until now, very little research has treated multiple levels of analysis simultaneously, and too little attention has been paid to the communities in which questions of representation are generated. We are therefore left with questions about the role of various intermediaries involved in mobilization—questions that concerned both David Truman (1951) and Mancur Olson (1965)—and the environmental forces that impinge on representation (Gray and Lowery 1996b).

Taking a look at the political function of religious interests in communities is akin to examining "systems," such as state interest group systems (Gray and Lowery 1996b). Systems respond to their own pressures but should also showcase the aggregate of micro-level processes, thus providing a test of the full range of theory (see Gray and Lowery 1993). But "many properties of interest-group systems . . . emerge only at the population-level. . . . Thus, population-level properties of interest-group systems are unlikely to be explained as mere aggregations of mobilization outcomes" (Lowery and Gray 1995: 2). At the very least, studies are underspecified if they do not include community (system)-level factors, even if they do not study communities per se as the unit of analysis.

Such questions about the system level of politics are of considerable normative importance and have occupied a distinguished group of scholars: James Madison, Alexis de Tocqueville, Arthur Bentley, and John Dewey. As David Lowery and Virginia Gray (1995) synthesize these questions, the primary concern should be with the *density* and *diversity* of representation (though Gray and Lowery are concerned with *organizational representation* solely). To what extent are interests organized, and how homogeneous is the resulting interest population?

Of course, the trick for students of systems is to operationalize a baseline of interests to assess the degree to which mobilization ("reproductive effort") and environmental constraints ("carrying capacity") influence organizational representation or other types ("survival"). The baseline measures are typically crude: population size, economic diversity, societal wealth (Hunter, Wilson, and Runk 1991; Gray and Lowery 1996a).

Operationalizing the baseline, however, is neither the only problem nor the most severe. Organizations registered with the state to lobby are hardly the only ones involved in public affairs, although they certainly comprise an important subset. For instance, Sidney Verba, Kay Lehman Schlozman, and Henry Brady (1995; see also Leighley 1996) revealed that nearly a majority of individuals who contact an elected representative are *not* motivated by group recruitment, for instance, but also that a healthy proportion of people writing letters to representatives undertake this action on the job, in churches, or in other organizations that are (almost always) not registered to lobby government. And, of course, representation flows through various channels besides direct communication: through intermediary elites (such as clergy), public opinion measures, mass media, and protest.

The problems are just as prevalent in religion and politics research, where the population of interests is difficult to identify (there is certainly no list of registrants). We focus almost exclusively on one type of actor at a time; we often sample actors across systems without gathering system-level variables; and we almost never gather information about other actors within relevant systems. One might be tempted to claim that religion and politics scholars work blindfolded, feeling the elephant in small portions and failing to identify the species or even the genus of the beast. Of course, this claim would be an unfair and inaccurate judgment since religion and politics scholarship is wide-ranging. Studies at one level often attempt to gain some measure of other relevant actors and forces; and many scholars have read widely and thought hard to assemble general theories of religion and politics.

In this volume, we specified a design to address many of these problems. We mandated an encompassing definition of religious interests and invited contributors to measure system-level (community-level) and group- and individual-level factors, as well as the interrelation between interests, within a system. Then, with multiple case studies presented in the volume, we have assembled a diverse sample of systems, although our sample is nonrandom and not without other challenges.[1] In any event, before attempting to synthesize the lessons of our study and adding to the cacophony of voices, we examine other theories advanced in the religion and politics literature according to the principles laid out in the discussion above.

Psychological Approaches

Psychological perspectives have been advanced primarily by John Green, Ted Jelen, and Clyde Wilcox (Green 1999; Green, Guth, and Wilcox 1998; Jelen 1993a; Wilcox 1989; Wilcox, Jelen, and Leege 1993), but also feature prominently in the study of religious influences on African Americans (Calhoun-Brown 1996; Harris 1999). Psychological perspectives view the key attachment point between religious faith and political commitments as the individual's identification with religious reference groups, which might be a denomination, a leader, or a movement. Within this framework, identities can build and sustain movements and facilitate the pursuit of agendas. As Green summarizes, "Collective identity is a cognitive encapsulation of group values, group attachments, and orientations toward group action. [It is] . . . relevant to the mobilization of resources for the movement activity" (1999: 154).

Research on identity relationships has been pursued primarily in the context of the Christian Right. Identity relationships promote voting for Christian Right candidates and lending support to the Christian Right movement and its leaders (Green 1999; Jelen 1993a). But how do such identity relationships perform when the links are neither obvious nor traditional? What are the mechanisms of influence? For instance, does identity promote support of the recent increase in environmental concern among evangelicals (Janofsky 2005)? Research on the politics of African-American churches suggests that the answer is no (see Harris 1999).

The dominant models of African-American church influence place religion first and psychological factors, especially group consciousness (Miller, Gurin, Gurin, and Malanchuk 1981), as both an outcome (Reese and Brown 1995) and an intermediary between organizational resources and political participation (Calhoun-

Brown 1996, 1998; Harris 1999). However, intriguing research has suggested that religiosity is largely endogenous to the church context, undermining the independent influence of religiosity on political behavior (Cavendish, Welch, and Leege 1998). Furthermore, decades of research have produced considerable disagreement (or at least inconsistency) about what aspects of African-American religion promote race consciousness. The older literature agrees, however, that there is a general relationship between religiosity and black consciousness. Even so, more recent research has found that group consciousness variables have no effect in explaining participation.[2] Nancy Burns and colleagues (2001: 302) offer an explanation: "Blacks who are race conscious are more likely to be active on behalf of issues involving either civil rights, in general, or Blacks, in particular." While race consciousness may affect the specific political aims of African Americans, it may be irrelevant in promoting other political activity once various elements of civic voluntarism are accounted for (Verba, Schlozman, and Brady 1995). Hence, a purely psychological approach is unlikely to catch the effects of religion when a candidate or issue does not prominently display an identity marker. To make this concrete, identity measures clearly promoted voting for Rev. Jesse Jackson, but not for John Kerry (nor Michael Dukakis, Al Gore, or even Bill Clinton).

Cultural Approaches

A more expansive treatment of psychological approaches is represented in *The Politics of Cultural Differences*, in which David Leege and colleagues (2002) assert a cultural theory of electoral politics. Leege and colleagues note that social choice models often skip preference formation, while most social psychological approaches do not allow for the short-term manipulation of symbols applicable to people with particular "demographic attributes" such as religion, gender, and class (2002: 252). The theory offered by Leege and colleagues is, in essence, that office seekers manipulate cultural symbols to segment the electorate, mobilizing some, demobilizing others, and reframing debates in favorable terms. Cultural arguments gain their impetus through societal disturbances, social change, and events, although an entrepreneur must recognize and invest in them. In this way, one might say that Leege and colleagues are to Truman (1951) what Robert Salisbury (1969) is to Olson (1965). This insertion of the importance of an entrepreneur provides additional clarity about the mechanisms driving changes in the use of cultural symbols, avoiding reliance on a *deus ex machina.*

The potency and plausibility of this cultural argument are difficult to deny. Because Leege and colleagues focused on electoral outcomes, theirs is a cultural theory of electoral politics not a general theory of religious influence. The mechanisms of religious influence are not clearly specified in their theory, and their findings would be difficult to apply to nonelectoral politics, perhaps because voting is such an individualistic act (Giles and Dantico 1982; but see Kenny 1992; Leighley 1990). Most of the work in the present volume, however, encompasses more (or at least a different part) of the political universe than elections alone.

Furthermore, religious communities are often mobilized to action even when the most politically salient symbols in a conflict are not rooted in religion. In order for Leege's theory to hold, those mobilizing symbols must be considered cultural, and we think it would be a stretch to call threats to the community cultural, for example. Moreover, we would argue that a cultural theory cannot account for why some religious groups are in the forefront, as opposed to in the backseat, on similar issues. Neither can a cultural theory account for the organizational impediments to action that religious actors so frequently encounter, nor for the important roles of the various intermediaries between symbol and action. A certain elegance surrounds the practiced delivery, clean lines, and studied moves of electoral campaigns, particularly presidential campaigns, whereas community conflict usually conveys the elegance of a rugby scrum. Perhaps we need a more brute theory to account for its movements.

Social Psychological Approaches

Theories of Christian Right mobilization that emphasize the fundamental differences in religiosity between various religious groups have long dominated the religion and politics subfield. This collection of theories, which may be termed social psychological, holds that individuals with higher levels of religious commitment, conservative (although the term "orthodox" is often used) theological views, and moral traditionalism are mobilized to fight against elements in American society that are less committed to religion or are outright secular. Those with more religious commitment affiliate with the Republican Party, while more secular persons cast their support to the Democratic Party, creating a cultural two-party cleavage fraught with both religious and political undertones (Green, Guth, Kellstedt, and Smidt 1996; Guth, Green, Smidt, Kellstedt, and Poloma 1997; Guth, Kellstedt, Smidt, and Green 1998; Hunter 1991; Jelen 1993a: 179; Kohut, Green, Keeter, and Toth 2000; Layman 2001; Wuthnow 1988).

It almost goes without saying that culture wars arguments do not perform particularly well in the mass public (DiMaggio, Evans, and Bryson 1996; Evans 2003; Fiorina 2005; Williams 1997). Many scholars of religion and politics argue that "values conflict does not necessarily make for 'culture wars'" (Fowler, Hertzke, Olson, and den Dulk 2004: 79), but the framework does work for at least a sizable minority of the population (Green et al. 1996 conclude as much). The religious commitment perspective goes beyond laying the foundation for culture wars, of course, by attempting to explain generally the role of religion in politics.

Paul Djupe and Christopher Gilbert (2004) took this perspective to task, undermining the model's articulation of religious communities and its empirical foundations. They argue that individuals identify with congregations rather than denominations, let alone broad religious traditions. Religious commitment perspectives assume a uniform message content within congregations grouped under a certain religious tradition, which hides often-significant divisions within religious traditions, not to mention denominations, and even churches. Certainly uniformity can be found across churches, especially when the wider society imposes it, such as among Jews and Muslims (though only after September 11, 2001: see Djupe and Green, 2007; Djupe, McDaniel, and Neiheisel, 2007). But uniformity should not be treated as an assumption.

Finally, empirical results regularly produce patterns that do not square with the assumptions of the model. Essentially, Djupe and Gilbert (2004) conclude that the political implications of religion are learned in one's congregation (see also Wald, Owen, and Hill 1988, 1990). Assessing commitment through a general set of religious beliefs will produce consistent results only when the congregations' own beliefs have not strayed too far from the momentum of traditional understandings of faith. In the end, religious commitment is more politically relevant in evangelical Protestant churches than in mainline Protestant churches, for instance, where lowered boundaries to the world have allowed a greater drift in theology and the relation of theology to the world's problems (see Olson, 2007). In addition, religious commitment leaves no room for representation of the community (see Crawford and Olson 2001b; Olson 2000). If it is added, no theoretical guidance exists for its operation.

Social Movement Approaches

Some scholars have argued that the political rise of Christian conservatives is rooted in various "status politics" theories (sometimes called "collective grievance" theories in social movement parlance). Such theories pose that the Christian Right emerged as a besieged subculture's response to perceived threats from secular society (Hertzke 1993; Oldfield 1996; Wald, Owen, and Hill 1989). When used to explain individual behavior, however, the "echoes of discontent" (Hertzke 1993) that are said to emanate from this traditionalist backlash against modernization have had little explanatory power. In their review of previous research, Wald, Owen, and Hill found that "measures of status discontent . . . performed quite badly" (1989: 3). Wald and colleagues find that status explanations hold their own after shifting a number of operational definitions and making the important link that personal status is tied to relevant social groups.

More recent tests of status politics theories, perhaps more appropriately operationalized at the system level, have found some support for the notion that religious activism occurs in areas where the religious group constitutes something of a minority. One such study found that resource and opportunity perspectives (also known as "political process": McAdam 1982) overlap considerably with "discontent" theories in explaining the emergence of Christian Right political candidates (Green, Guth, and Hill 1993).

In their attempt to provide a comprehensive theory of the presence of religion in public life, Kenneth Wald, Adam Silverman, and Kevin Fridy (2005) suggest that the engagement of religious groups in politics may best be understood by using elements of social movement theory, particularly by investigating religious groups' motives, means, and opportunities to participate (2005: 124). Motives, or grievances, flow from the clash of society and cultural identities, which establish groups and group norms (see also Wildavsky 1987). Means constitute the "organizational capacity" to bring grievances into the political sphere and are generally thought to include the intensity of grievances, leadership, money and material, networks, and physical meeting space (Wald, Silverman, and Fridy 2005: 131; Zald and McCarthy 1987). Groups operate within a political system that provides many points of access that either invite or discourage group claims at different times (Leege, Wald, Krueger, and Mueller 2002; McAdam 1982; Wald, Silverman, and Fridy 2005).

The theory that Wald and colleagues (2002) advance solves many of the problems that plague other theories discussed to this point. Their theory is flexible with regard to actors since social movements, such as "the Christian Right . . . [, consist] of leaders, organizations, activists, members, sympathizers, and distinct constituencies from which potential members are drawn" (Smidt and Penning 1997: 269). Wald and colleagues agree with Leege and colleagues about political motives and their wellspring in societal disturbances, but they are also rather flexible about what might qualify as a motive (which also is a weakness of the theory since it has a tendency toward tautology). They move beyond social psychological and psychological perspectives to incorporate organizational resources situated in a particular system, which, taken together, provide great analytic power.

We argue that Wald and colleagues do not go far enough in two areas. First, religious interests overlap and interrelate, which can compound or confound their political potency. Religious influence on salient actors is *contingent* upon the relationships they have with other actors.[3] These relationships can be vertical: A clergyperson almost always has the means, motives, and opportunities to participate but may often be constrained in action by their congregations, denominations, or communities (Crawford, Olson, and Deckman 2001; Djupe and Gilbert 2003; Olson, Crawford, and Deckman 2005). This array of constraints is not merely another way of labeling mobilization, nor does shoehorning it into motives prove analytically helpful.

Second, as Lowery and Gray (1995) argue (although at a different level of aggregation), there are also horizontal, constraining relationships: the public presence of an organization is driven by the interaction between environmental constraints and organizational properties. One implication is that this interdependence tends to drive groups to carve out unique, sustaining niches (Gray and Lowery 1996b) that may result in peculiar types of political participation or group structures. While this perspective demands that we pay attention to how the community defines opportunity, it also indicates that the environment affects means and motives and their translation into presence.

Contextual Approaches

One set of theories that attempts to resolve at least some of these problems is a branch of contextual analysis (see Huckfeldt and Sprague 1995) adapted to fit religious organizations (and perhaps all organizations). Interestingly, in this recent development, contextual analysis is only now beginning to study the effects of Truman's (1951) understanding of individuals as members of extended, overlapping groups. One incarnation of this theory attempts to understand how churches affect the politics of church members (Djupe and Gilbert 2005), employing a four-part theory in which the four parts are interrelated and function contingent on system-level factors. In essence, four generic aspects of the church environment (social networks, small groups, clergy, and the congregation as a whole) can provide information to members and hence wield political significance. The degree to which the church provides political information is contingent on their position in the community, with those feeling underrepresented in community affairs more likely to engage in providing this information. Moreover, a politicized church environment activates the potential influence of the other parts.

Further, the contextual approach incorporates the formation of motives and neatly ties it to means and mobilization. The specific contexts in which civic skills are developed (especially church small groups: Djupe and Gilbert 2006; Leege 1988; Wuthnow 1994) are also the critical milieu where influential political information can flow and shape opinions. The interests of a church also depend upon the community in this model, partly because the church is conceptualized as part of the community and as a communication network among community members rather than merely a symbolic representation of religious beliefs.

Although the predictions above were not developed to meet the demands of the organizational ecology literature, they dovetail nicely with the expectation that reproductive effort is density-dependent—mobilizational efforts depend on environmental constraints (Rosenstone and Hansen 1993). Although the contextual theory discussed above was developed to apply to churches, a very similar construction may be (and has been: Djupe and Gilbert 2003) applied to clergy. This breadth suggests that the contextual approach is applicable across actors, although the theory works best in face-to-face communities. And while Djupe and Gilbert's contextual theory was not formulated to explain system-level attributes, Gary and Lowery (1996a) note that population diversity in representation at the system level is the sum of density-dependent reproductive efforts for all the relevant organizational types (which would include churches). Thus, to understand the amount of political activity of religious interests, one needs to add up the results of the interaction between environmental constraints and each interest community.

While Gray and Lowery (1996b, among others, such as Truman 1951; Heinz, Laumann, Nelson, and Salisbury 1993; Schlozman and Tierney 1986; and Walker 1991) would claim that studying systems is the most fruitful approach, we will not advise jumping the individualist ship for the system-level vessel. Consequential dynamics in and between the myriad relevant religious groups remain unexplored; but religion and politics scholarship should take into account system-level attributes that affect group processes, as well as the levels and types of representation that result from them. Now we turn to the lessons of the case studies in order to provide some data to assess the validity of the above discussion.

The Foundations of This Study

Why did we choose to build this volume around community case studies? We were struck by the fact that religion and politics intersect at the local level at least as much as they do on the national stage and over similar issues. Until now, however, little scholarship has systematically addressed the role of religious actors in local-level political activism (but see Deckman 2004), especially beyond the electoral context, even though a local milieu allows researchers greater access and reliability in making causal claims. Individual studies of religious activism, moreover, overwhelmingly have focused on one type of religious actor at a time: the organizational hierarchy of a denomination or religious tradition; an interest group with religious ties; clergy and other religious leaders; or congregation members. While there are sensible reasons to limit the focus of a study exclusively to one type of actor, in practice different types of religious actors are often in contact with one another when they attempt to address public problems (Crawford, Olson, and Deckman 2001). That religious interests at any level often interact with non-religious interests (Crawford, Olson, and Deckman 2001), such as political parties, governments, businesses, and others is, moreover, a fact with which the literature needs to come to full grips. Case studies are valuable tools to address these concerns when they attempt to tell a comprehensive story about the functioning of religious interests in a local-level conflict.

To conduct this meta-analysis, we use the foregoing chapters as our data. Thinking at the outset about what making general claims about religious interests would require, we insisted on several uniform design components in all contributions to this volume:

- Each chapter is based on a tangible community issue so that all of the actors would have the same point of reference.
- Each contributor was to include the full range of actors involved with the issue in order to bridge the unit-of-analysis divide, primarily between individuals and groups.
- Because each chapter is supposed to tell a complete story, authors are not constrained by the need to generate their own theory and instead were free to allow their observations to speak to established theories.
- Each contribution includes a diverse range of religious interests, and the chapters are situated in a diverse range of communities.

We aimed to draw upon the high internal validity of case studies while building external validity by including a wide range of cases, selected on the basis of two criteria: issue content and community.

A depiction of some of the gross descriptors of the chapters, or "the data," is presented in Table 11.1. The issues cover a wide range of content, but also exposure. Issues steeped in morality politics (Meier 1994), such as gay marriage, are represented, but so too are social justice concerns such as homelessness and the establishment of a Martin Luther King holiday. Some of the issues covered are high profile, especially gay marriage and race riots, while others fly below the public radar, especially health care. Although these issues capture a range of primary concerns (see Guth et al. 1997), perhaps, notable issues are missing, especially abortion-related conflicts.

The studies take place in a variety of locales, split almost evenly among big cities, small cities, and rural areas and small towns. Many of the communities are located in the Midwest although there is both southern and western representation. Our contributors base

Table 11.1
Summary of the Diversity of Issues, Communities, and Methods Employed in the Volume's Chapters

Conflict Involved	Community	Region	Methods
Moral Concerns			
Gambling	Rural: W. Michigan	Midwest	Surveys, interviews
Gay marriage	Rural & urban: Nevada	West	Surveys, archives
Gay marriage	Urban: Columbus, OH	Midwest	Surveys, interviews
Social Justice			
Healthcare	Med. city: Omaha, NE	Midwest	Interviews, observation
Homelessness	Small city: Racine, WI	Midwest	Interviews, archives
Public Square			
King holiday	Med. city: Greenville, SC	South	Interviews, observation
Main St. Plaza	Urban: Salt Lake City, UT	West	Surveys, interviews
Race Relations			
Race riots	Urban: Cincinnati, OH	Midwest	Surveys, interviews
Ku Klux Klan	Rural: Siloam Springs, AR	South	Surveys, interviews

their observations on a variety of research methods, drawing on their own strengths and available data, but in practice there is considerable standardization across chapters. Contributors utilize public opinion data (whether gathered by the authors or culled from published sources), interviews of key officials and activists, media reports, and public records.

Lessons from the Case Studies

Since the goal of this volume is to further and comment on religion and politics theory, we will not use this space to present simple summaries of the chapters. Instead, we organize the discussion that follows around large theoretical questions that revolve around the concept of representation.

The vast political potential inherent in American religion is often noted. Faith-based organizations frequently take part in social service activities, work toward racial reconciliation, and engage in other politically relevant action (Ammerman 2005; Chaves 2004). Two-thirds of the population identifies as church attenders, and the United States has about a third of a million houses of worship, myriad groups with a religious tie of some sort, and a thousand denominations or more (Fowler et al. 2004; Kohut et al. 2000). There is, simply put, an enormous amount of political and social capital stored in individuals and organizations with religious ties. We therefore ask these questions: What motivates religious interests to use their political and social capital? When is it unleashed? To what extent are religious interests engaged in trying to solve community problems?

In Table 11.2, we categorize the chapters of this volume according to the timing and extent of religious interest engagement with the conflict or the challenge facing their community. Because immediate involvement by some religious interests was nearly universal, we also include a judgment about the timing of the bulk of the involvement from religious interests. We qualify those judgments below because the chapter discussions merit more than a one-word description.

Why Do Religious Interests Get Involved?

It is typical to ground explanations of the behavior of religious interests in their religious tradition, often categorized as mainline Protestantism, evangelical Protestantism, African-American Protestantism, Catholicism, Judaism, a collection of other, smaller religious traditions, and secularism[4]—although, as Lyman Kellstedt and John Green note, "[I]t has never been clear whether [denominational or traditional] measures refer to ethnic histories, doctrinal beliefs, social status, or social group attachments" (1993: 53). Perhaps these chapters can help illuminate the dominant aspect of the influence of religious traditions.

Table 11.2
How Many and When Did Religious Interests Engage the Conflict?

Conflict Involved	Speed of Initial Engagement	Time from Initial Engagement until Majority Engagement	Extent of Religious Interest Engagement	Centrality of Those Religious Interests Engaged
Moral Concerns				
Gambling	Immediate	Delayed	Most	Peripheral
Gay marriage, NV	Immediate	Immediate	Most	Central
Gay marriage, OH	Immediate	Delayed	Some	Peripheral
Social Justice				
Healthcare	Late	Never	Minimal	Central
Homelessness	Late	Never	Minimal	Central
Public Square				
King holiday	Immediate	Modestly Delayed	Some	Central
Main St. Plaza	Immediate	Immediate	Some	Central
Race Relations				
Race riots	Immediate	Immediate	Many	Mixed
Ku Klux Klan	Immediate	Immediate	Most	Central

Now is not the occasion to present detailed descriptions of the major traditions, especially since others have provided it thoroughly and thoughtfully (Fowler et al. 2004; Wald 2003). And we need not work through every conceivable religious tradition. Instead, we will contrast two religious traditions that have well-established story lines in the literature: mainline Protestants and evangelical Protestants. One major distinction between these two groups is that mainline Protestants emphasize social justice concerns, such as poverty, homelessness, and civil rights, whereas evangelicals focus primarily on moral concerns, such as abortion, school prayer, and homosexuality (Guth et al. 1997). Does that generic pattern hold here?

In matters of race, evangelicals were largely uninvolved in Greenville concerning the Martin Luther King holiday (chap. 7) and were among the least involved in Cincinnati (chap. 9), but they led the charge in Siloam Springs against the Ku Klux Klan rally (chap. 10). We would expect mainline Protestants, for historical and theological reasons, to be out in front on issues of civil rights (Verter 2002), but they were surprisingly uninvolved in Siloam Springs, moderately involved in Cincinnati, and heavily involved at a point in Greenville. On matters of gay rights, mainline Protestants were not silent, but neither were they highly visible actors, preferring to act through community groups such as ministerial organizations. Evangelicals, on the other hand, were highly visible actors in both Nevada (chap. 3) and Ohio (chap. 4) and only partly because it fit the media storyline of a culture war. Evangelicals joined high-profile coalitions and used their own media and growing parachurch networks to reach a wide audience. Of course, the ballot measures in Ohio and Nevada allowed multiple frames, allowing many to engage the issue on their own terms.

Homelessness and health care are issues that exemplify the classic social justice concerns of mainline Protestants (Steensland 2002; Thuesen 2002). Not surprisingly, we find mainline clergy and churches at the forefront in the chapters dealing with these issues. While a baseline level of concern was present, it took organizational entrepreneurs and extensive networks in the community and through the denomination to bring both social programs to life. This development suggests that understanding denominations primarily as the source of long-term socialization or belief systems is to drastically underspecify them. Moreover, clergy and churches from religious traditions beyond white Protestantism joined these community efforts, although not at the same rates as mainline Protestants. Still, the participation of Catholics and African-American Protestants in these antipoverty efforts strains the notion that religious traditions dictate unique concerns.

At another level—the individual level—Sue Crawford (chap. 5) and Laura Olson (chap. 6) each provide another portrait of groups that reveals the tremendous importance of social benefits (Olson 1965)—perhaps in attracting members, but certainly in maintaining their participation. In Omaha, significant portions of the health-care coalition meetings were devoted to sharing between members, which came to be valued in its own right. Olson notes how volunteers developed significant relationships with other volunteers, but also with the homeless people being sheltered. Crawford's participants were quick to point out the productivity lost by devoting time to building social support, a notion confirmed in systematic study (Harrington 2001). In Racine, since the crucial issue was maintaining staffing for an overnight homeless shelter, social benefits were key to sustaining the program. Without looking at the individual level and asking the right questions, these benefits might be considered a denominational effect since they were distributed via church ties.

The lesson that comes across most impressively from these chapters is the diversity of motivations tied to the location of the conflict. James Guth and colleagues (chap. 7) open their discussion of the conflict over observing a Martin Luther King holiday as follows: "Greenville County, South Carolina, is exactly the sort of place to observe 'culture wars' first hand." Little in the chapter, however, fits a typical culture war discussion. African Americans were divided on the final compromise; Bob Jones University took several different positions throughout the conflict; moderate evangelicals and Catholics sat on their hands; and most, including some African-American religious leaders, resented the intrusion of outside interests. Many advocated the holiday to protect the community's economic future—the same reasons why the community mobilized against the Klan in Siloam Springs (chap. 10). It is important to recall that many of the arguments offered by Siloam Springs clergy were not primarily theological but instead explicitly about the integrity of the community. Meanwhile, business interests played a significant role in resolving the dispute over Main Street Plaza in Salt Lake City (chap. 8), in part to prevent the city from sustaining an economic black eye.

James Penning and Andrew Storteboom's observation (chap. 2) that political involvement was greatest in communities situated closest to the proposed west Michigan casino highlights the importance of information networks but also how salience raises the prospect of a positive response to cues to become involved. That finding is bolstered in a dramatic way by Anand Sokhey's (chap. 9) explicit finding that geographic distance from the riot's center in Cincinnati weakened concern and activism.

Separately, the social and political construction of the Main Street Plaza controversy (chap. 8) almost automatically pitted Mormons against non-Mormons in Salt Lake City. The political context of the Salt Lake area has long featured a political divide between

Mormons and non-Mormons because the Church of Jesus Christ of Latter-day Saints is such a dominant religious, political, and social force in Utah. Non-Mormons were immediately mobilized against the sale of Main Street Plaza to the LDS Church, in a perfect illustration of James Madison's pluralism at work. The resolution of this conflict was as much a story of papering over the underlying fault lines between Mormons and non-Mormons in Salt Lake City as it was a productive end to a concrete dispute.

Other chapters illustrate the ways in which the specific complexion of the community affects the roster of religious groups that become involved in a political conflict. Franklyn Niles (chap. 10) notes that mainline Protestant churches, a distinct minority in Siloam Springs, were uninvolved in the anti-Klan rallies. By no means were mainline Protestants unsupportive of anti-Klan efforts; instead, mainline clergy were inactive in the local ministerial organization because of a previous theological shift and, therefore, were uninvolved in planning the response to the Klan. In other communities, however, we find that mainline Protestants have sustained a higher public profile, especially when they have strength in numbers (as chaps. 5 and 6 indicate).

The density of interests in a community affects the visibility of religious interests. Take the example of ministerial organizations. A ministerial organization set the agenda in Greenville's conflict over the King holiday; ministerial organizations had a key role in networking clergy in Cincinnati and west Michigan; one attracted attention in the battle over the ballot measure in Nevada; but they were almost nowhere to be found in Columbus in the fight over the Issue 1 ballot measure (see Neiheisel, Djupe, Sokhey, and Niles 2005). Why was this the case?

We would argue that several factors contribute to the level of prominence displayed by these religious interests. In part, ministerial organizations will be most active and efficacious when the level of conflict coincides with their own constituency. When this coincidence occurs, government officials will more likely seek out their opinions and assistance; ministerial organization members feel more attached to and informed about their own communities; and fewer competing groups exist. In Columbus (chap. 4), there are dozens of ministerial organizations, but none are coincident with the level of the conflict (in the case of Issue 1, the State of Ohio). Even though some ministerial organizations took positions on Issue

1 and communicated those views to the public in various ways, they attracted little, if any, attention. In Nevada (chapter 3), the sole Las Vegas ministerial organization (which is where the conflict over the ballot measure was centered) was much more closely matched to the relevant constituency (Las Vegas ministerial organization, Las Vegas-centered political conflict). Moreover, Ohio is much more politically organized from top to bottom than is Nevada, leaving less room for the voices of organizations with few resources.

Olson's and Crawford's chapters highlight a variant on these ideas by emphasizing that religious interests will act to fill a void in the community as long as some other conditions are satisfied as well (see Crawford 1995; Crawford, Olson, and Deckman 2001; Djupe and Gilbert 2003; Olson, Crawford, and Deckman 2005). Without a local government dealing with homelessness or providing adequate health care, clergy and their churches gave deeply of themselves to meet a need. At the end of the story in Racine, the community had taken over the homeless shelter and had displaced the network of churches providing the service, largely with their blessing, in a blatant confirmation of this relationship.

When Do Religious Interests Get Involved?

One obvious place to start answering the question of when religious interests join a political battle is with the point at which all that will become involved have become involved. For instance, in the gambling conflict in Michigan (chap. 2), in which the Michigan Alliance Against Casinos (MAAC) was involved early on against the proposed casino, most religious interests seemingly did not engage the issue until late in the game. Any widespread engagement on the part of clergy and churches was reactionary and came well after the casino had been proposed. When the issue finally reached religious groups, most showed some sign of interest and engagement so that the delay probably did not result from substantial variance in motivation. Instead, the policy process early on was too amorphous for most religious interests to engage. Once clear points of contact were established (town halls, petitions, legislative votes, and elections), religious interests had an easier time latching on and directing their energies. Moreover, a collection of organizations, including business groups, ministerial organizations, and explicitly anti-casino groups worked to involve affected communities, which were targeted easily through the conservative religious congregations to which most of west Michigan's residents belong.

At the other end of the spectrum are conflicts in which the response was immediate and most religious interests were engaged early. A wide variety of situations fit this category, including the Main Street Plaza controversy in Salt Lake City (chap. 8), the gay marriage debate in Nevada (chap. 3), and the Ku Klux Klan rally in Siloam Springs (chap. 10). In the first case, the controversy directly affected an identifiable and organized religious interest (the LDS Church) but that direct connection was not the case in the latter two situations. In Nevada, the LDS Church was at the forefront of a move to change the Nevada constitution. Since they were agenda-setters, with the cooperation of other religious organizations, involvement was immediate. Moreover, since Nevada's population is so transient, religious interests functioned in a relative organizational vacuum compared to other states such as Ohio (chap. 4). It is noteworthy that a ministerial organization covering Las Vegas was a player in the Nevada constitutional debate while ministerial organizations were largely absent from the struggle in Ohio.

In Siloam Springs (chap. 10), the Klan set the agenda for the community, and local clergy (after discussion with local elected officials) took the lead in organizing a "non-response" to the rally. Although the character of the response was religious rather than political (prayer rallies and church services), the justifications were framed in terms of protecting the community from potential violence and harmful stereotypes.

In the cases of racial conflict, the response was predictably bifurcated in scope and timing. In Greenville (chap. 7), the African-American community consistently pushed to remedy the anachronistic absence of a holiday honoring Martin Luther King Jr. The Baptist Ministers Fellowship was instrumental in putting the King holiday on the agenda, and it almost goes without saying that black religious leaders were present at the County Council meetings that affirmed Greenville's traditional stance against the holiday. The white religious community either never participated (especially Catholics and evangelical Protestants) or joined the fray with a flurry of activity after the council vote to urge reconsideration (as was the case with many mainline Protestant churches).

Many in the African-American religious community responded to the riots in Cincinnati (chap. 9) with voice and action through their organizations and congregations. They did not encounter an overflow of support from white religious interests, although some were active in significant ways. Sokhey concludes that geographic distance from the affected community insulated many in the Cincinnati religious community, in a modern illustration of the "suburban captivity of the churches" (Winter 1966). And if they did not respond early, reactions to the boycott of the city kept them from involvement.

In several cases, the response of the religious community was delayed, and a majority of religious interests never got involved at all. The chapters on health care (chap. 5) and homelessness (chap. 6) exemplify this pattern. Of course, the lack of adequate health care and housing in these two cities was persistent. Neither reached an identifiable crisis point, nor did either community challenge generate outward conflict. Religious interests eventually became involved because there was a persistent need for services that no one else was addressing; elsewhere, Crawford and Olson have referred to this practice as gap filling (Crawford 1995; Crawford, Olson, and Deckman 2001; Olson, Crawford, and Deckman 2005). Factors common to other chapters affected the timing of religious interests' involvement in Omaha and Racine. Involvement may be linked to networks supplying information, either via community ties (homelessness in Racine) or denominational identity (health care in Omaha), and by the actions of entrepreneurs (Lutheran clergy in Omaha and a religiously motivated lay activist in Racine).

Timing is important for many reasons, especially since joining late means that some other force had the opportunity to set the agenda, frame the issue, and perhaps formulate alternative solutions (Kingdon 1995). Thus, it is important to identify the forces that lead religious interests to join the fray at specific times.

A classic explanation of who joins the conflict and when (Hoge and Zulueta 1984) is that religious interests choose to engage issue conflicts that are especially salient to them. We have already seen above that motivations seem to be rather flexible and depend heavily on a link to the community, which is another, and far less common, form of salience in a religious context. All of the issues discussed in the chapters in this volume either are or could be salient to religious interests, and salience by itself seems to make little difference to the timing of entry except as the issue affects a community (for example, the African-American community, as shown in several chapters).

One of the most important activities of interest groups is program monitoring (Heinz et al. 1993; Nownes and Freeman 1998; Salisbury 1990; Schlozman and Tierney 1983), which means that groups and individuals who are thoroughly networked to interest groups will respond more rapidly than those who are socially isolated. Moreover, the time until entry is reduced if the interested party has a diverse network, allowing information to travel further and more quickly through society (Granovetter 1973). While ministerial organizations may not engage in a tremendous amount of political action in the organization's name (Niles and Djupe 2006), at the very least they serve as crucial network nodes, disseminating information widely to those with the resources to act (see, especially, chaps. 9 and 10).

The existence of a group presupposes an entrepreneur (Salisbury 1969), though not all groups begin due to the efforts of an individual (Walker 1991). Entrepreneurs need not be organizational leaders, but they certainly may be identified as individuals on the front lines of some issue of concern. Examples of group entrepreneurship are ubiquitous in this volume. They include Donna Bumpus, the organizer of the homelessness initiative in Racine; Revs. Robert Johnson and Damon Laaker, who founded the Omaha health-care coalition; the clergyperson who reformed the Siloam Springs ministerial organization; and Rev. Damon Lynch III in Cincinnati. Much of the activity of religious interests discussed in the chapters would not have happened when it did without the work and strategic planning of entrepreneurs.

To What Extent Do Religious Interests Get Involved?

The above discussion focuses on environmental effects at the group and individual levels. We now move to the system (community) level to investigate the patterns of religious interest representation. The fundamental issues here involve (1) the types of organized interests (individuals, clergy, churches, denominations, or other types of membership organizations) that play a public role; (2) whether the religious composition of those groups matches the population; and (3) the extent to which cooperation and competition occur between or among interests.

Table 11.3 specifies the dominant religious interest type that engaged the conflict in each community included in this volume. It is important to note that these specifications are generalized

Table 11.3
Summary of the Dominant Types of Religious Interests Playing Public Roles in these Conflicts

Conflict Involved	Community Type	Dominant Interest Type 1	Dominant Interest Type 2	Dominant Interest Type 3
Moral Concerns				
Gambling	Rural	Ministerial org.	Civic orgs.	Clergy
Gay marriage, NV	Rural/ urban	Civic/ interfaith org.	Ministerial org.	
Gay marriage, OH	Urban	Civic orgs.	Ministerial orgs.	Clergy
Social Justice				
Healthcare	Med. City	Select clergy	Mainline churches	
Homelessness	Sm. City	Ecumenical org.	Select churches	
Public Square				
King holiday	Med. city	Ministerial orgs.	Black clergy	Mainline clergy
Main St. Plaza	Urban	Civic/ interfaith org.	Clergy	
Race Relations				
Race riots	Urban	Civic org.	Black clergy	
Ku Klux Klan	Rural	Ministerial org.	Evangelical clergy	Evangelical churches

approximations and that data availability impedes us from making authoritative declarations. Still, what we are able to discern is revealing and at least suggestive.

One pattern that emerges from Table 11.3 is the extent to which the scope of the conflict affects the relative prominence of different types of actors. In rural areas and small towns, ministerial organizations are quite prominent, and clergy play visible roles. The same is true regarding issues of limited conflict such as homelessness and health-care; in such cases, clergy and churches are the dominant actors. As the scope of the issue expands, so too does the extent of community participation (Schattschneider 1960). If the scope expands and the conflict draws in nonreligious actors, clergy may necessarily play a smaller role. The King holiday (chap. 7) and Main Street Plaza (chap. 8) controversies illustrate this point well. While these issues were certainly salient to religious interests, they affected the entire community, so business interests played important roles brokering compromises and pressing for particular outcomes.

In fact, one of the intriguing findings throughout the case studies is the extent to which business interests work alongside (sometimes with and sometimes against) religious interests (see the thorough discussion in Berry, Portney, and Thomson 1993). This cooperation of many different interests has a tendency to offend Madisonian sensibilities preferring fragmented interests.

The second concern about the extent of the public presence of religious interests involves representativeness: do the prominent religious interests look like (and represent the interests of) the rest of the community? This question has no easy answer, and the answers provided are likely to be controversial. Still, three aspects of the communities in conflict seem to structure representativeness: community size, intermediation by government, and the governmental arena.

In Siloam Springs (chap. 10), eventually in west Michigan (chap. 2), and probably in Nevada (chap. 3), the interests involved fairly closely resembled and therefore reflected those of the religious population (which is a fairer standard of comparison than the entire population). In larger communities, religious populations are larger and more varied, so any particular faith-based organization cannot claim to represent any sizable proportion of the religious population. It is therefore by nature much more difficult to gather a group that is representative of the population in large communities. Instead, it is common to see the presence of civic interest groups that deal (or were formed to deal) with the issues involved in the conflict, like the Cincinnati Black United Front in Cincinnati and Citizens for Community Values in Columbus.

Government involvement in setting up commissions in Cincinnati, Greenville, and Salt Lake City ensured that the dominant interests in each conflict were represented. In all three cases, of course, religious interests were represented, but so were various secular and business interests. The commissions wielded a good deal of clout in Salt Lake City, but less so in Cincinnati and even less in Greenville. As Guth and colleagues note in chapter 7, the Greenville County Council rejected the proposal developed by the Greenville public commission, perhaps because the public commission was formed to broker between the county commission and the attentive public rather than conflict within the county commission. By and large, local government involvement seems to have an interest in setting up a representative group to work through difficult and divisive issues.

The particular governmental arena within which the conflict is hashed out seems to affect the representativeness of the prominent interests. Anthony Nownes and Patricia Freeman (1998) detail the proportions of groups that target the different branches of government, showing the prominence of the legislature, the inaccessibility of the courts, and the fact that resources tend to buy access. Elections are still perhaps the most representative option, but campaigns are certainly not. In this venue, acknowledged religious interests largely cede the public square to traditional interest groups, political parties, and candidates. The campaign around the gay marriage ballot initiatives in 2004 was quite costly in Ohio, but less so in Nevada (and hence more inclusive of religious interests there). Primary elections in South Carolina and Michigan, the first without much explicit religious interest mobilization, the latter with it, nominated candidates more in line with demonstrated public desires. Legislative hearings are cheap avenues of communication to government, though not all groups are invested and mobilized to participate in them (chap. 7). In circumstances in which the government plays no role, entry is perhaps easiest, but the consequences are often expensive. For example, volunteering one's church as a homeless shelter is a significant investment of capital and therefore attracts little participation (chap. 6).

The third concern involves the level of cooperation or competition among religious interests. The expectation is that there would be little cooperation, and what little there is would be isolated within religious traditions. Religious particularism, under which groups or individuals refuse to work with others because of their religious beliefs or practices, has long inhibited the ability of religious communities to speak with one voice. The ecumenical movement was an attempt to overcome this, but the predicted reformation (Miller

1957) never materialized (however, one could argue that the erosion of denominationalism is an intermediate step: Wuthnow 1988). Under what circumstances does religious particularism crop up?

Several of our chapters address this issue. In Siloam Springs (chap. 10), mainline Protestants were moved out of the ministerial organization when the dominant evangelicals wrote a more particularistic constitution; hence the mainline congregations were not particularly involved in the anti-Klan efforts. The LDS Church worked with evangelicals and others in Nevada (chap. 6), but they had a non-Mormon leader and only interacted at the elite level. Actual laity from different religious traditions did not need to collide, which might have produced more sparks. The most dramatic illustration of working together yet apart comes from Racine (chap. 6). There, an ecumenical group of churches hosted the homeless without much, if any, interaction among participating churches, allowing particular theological understandings to drive individual churches' actions without challenge. Meanwhile, a diverse group of religious and civic leaders in Salt Lake City was able to formulate a compromise, overcoming tensions within the city split between Mormons and non-Mormons. Of course, the issue itself may have contributed to this ability, as the Alliance for Unity was created before the plaza conflict emerged to bridge religious and cultural divides; it just so happened that the plaza conflict addressed the Alliance's mission directly. Otherwise, ministerial organizations seem to exhibit some resistance to shifting their mission to resolving or addressing conflict in the community unless the conflict threatens the community (as in chap. 10).

Discussion and Conclusion

On the whole, statistical tests allow us to affirm which relationships do not exist. Without the confidence to declare how the world does work based on a handful of case studies, perhaps we have more confidence in winnowing the range of plausible explanations, or at least the attributes of plausible explanations.

The unequivocal claim resulting from this volume is the necessity of including the community in analyses of religion and politics in consequential ways. We have found that the community (the system level) exerts direct force on the behavior of groups and individuals, as well as indirect force by shaping the motivations, resources, and mobilization of groups and individuals. This finding regarding the importance of system-level effects dovetails nicely with research that uses varying units of analysis, such as the individual (Djupe and Gilbert 2006), the clergy and church (Djupe and Gilbert 2002b, 2003; Olson 2000), and the candidate (Green, Guth, and Hill 1993). This is not to mention the large literatures outside of religion and politics that find effects contingent on environmental stimuli.

Readers may have noticed our conscious effort to introduce comment by the interest group literature, which has not been typical in the religion and politics literature. We have done so because the interest group literature has shifted its focus from the individual and group levels, under the influence of Olson (1965), back to the system level. At a minimum, that literature has included system-level variables in its analysis. "Interest group systems" are no more than what we have studied here: politically salient communities. Further, contributors to this volume attempted to be comprehensive in their consideration of religious interests. Such a focus demands answers to certain questions of significant theoretical and normative importance, and we hope this volume helps to elevate them. We believe that religion and politics scholars should attempt to address the density of religious interests involved, their diversity, and how they represent their interests in consideration of the presence of other interests in their milieu. Do they act? What do they do? Do they cooperate with other interests? Moreover, an explicitly multilevel agenda is necessary in the exploration of religious interests that are more or less integrated horizontally and vertically.

Employing this structure of inquiry produces a number of salutary benefits. First, we may feel more confident that the results of such studies have produced generalizable results. Second, such attempts facilitate communication across the field, which is currently fragmented by the usual suspects: method, scope, and theory. Third, generalizable results about the representation of religious interests at the system level create opportunities to examine their relation to governmental outputs, putting the Holy Grail in sight.

Notes

CHAPTER 1

1 For more information about the Public Religion Project conducted by the Martin Marty Center at the University of Chicago Divinity School with funding from the Pew Charitable Trusts, see http://marty-center.uchicago.edu/research/publicreligion.shtml.

CHAPTER 2

1 Throughout this paper, the term *Indian* is used instead of Native American. We do this both because the term *Indian* is less cumbersome and because most media accounts of the controversy examined here, as well as most self-references by Native American participants in the conflict, use the term.

2 Two of the respondents indicated a lack of awareness of the casino controversy and were, therefore, dropped from most of the analysis.

3 In each even-numbered year, the Michigan legislature holds a brief session, called a lame-duck session because it tends to contain fairly large numbers of legislators serving their final terms (due to retirement, electoral defeat, or term limits).

4 Four other members of Michigan's 110-member House also failed to vote on the measure.

5 A number of members of the 110-member House and 38-member Senate did not vote on each resolution. In 2001, five Democratic

and two Republican House members did not vote. In 2002, three Democratic and two Republican House members failed to vote. In that same year, two Democratic Senators and one Republican Senator did not vote. While House Speaker Rick Johnson voted in favor of the casino resolution in both 2001 and 2002, Senate Majority Leader Dan DeGrow voted against the resolution in the 2002 Senate vote.

6 It is interesting to note, however, that the aggregate totals do mask some individual vote switching in the House. Among the fifty-one supporters of the 2001 resolution, the 2002 vote was forty-five "yes," two "no," and four "did not vote." Among the fifty-two opponents of the 2001 resolution, the 2002 vote was forty-two "no," nine "yes," and one "did not vote." Among those who did not vote in 2001, the 2002 vote was four "yes" and three "no."

7 Michigan campaign finance laws provide no limit on the amount an individual can contribute to an individual PAC. An independent PAC, however, is permitted to give ten times what a traditional PAC can give to a candidate . . . up to $34,000 for a gubernatorial candidate and up to $10,000 for a legislative candidate in any given election cycle (Hornbeck, Cain, and Heinlein 2002).

8 The first category included clergy from Assemblies of God, Baptist, Seventh-Day Adventist, Wesleyan, Church of God, Nazarene, United Brethren in Christ, and non-denominational churches. The second category included Congregationalists, Lutherans, Presbyterians, Catholics, United Methodists, and Episcopalians. There were too few Catholic respondents (4) to create a separate Catholic category. Catholics are grouped with Mainline Protestants because they tend to represent long-established, hierarchical, liturgical churches. While the RCA is sometimes categorized as a mainline denomination, its Western Michigan churches tend to be culturally and theologically conservative, much like members of the CRC in the same region.

9 Birkholz did, in fact, deliver the letter, although it took considerable effort on her part to get a hearing with the incoming governor (Birkholz 2003).

CHAPTER 3

1 The U.S. Constitution, Article IV, Section 1 reads: "Full faith and credit shall be given in each state to the public acts, records and

judicial proceedings of every other state. And the Congress may by general laws prescribe the manner in which such acts, records, and proceedings shall be proved, and the effect thereof."

2 In 2003, the Massachusetts Supreme Judicial Court struck down a state law prohibiting same-sex marriages, and subsequently ruled that so-called "civil unions" would not satisfy the equal protection provisions of the Massachusetts state constitution (Cauchon 2003). In the following year, the mayor of San Francisco (again on equal protection grounds) directed the city clerk to issue marriage licenses to gay couples. While the City of San Francisco eventually was enjoined from issuing such licenses, several thousand gay couples had been legally married prior to the injunction by the state supreme court (Dao 2004).

3 The Defense of Marriage Act (DOMA) defines "marriage" as the union of one man and one woman and does not require states, under the Constitution's Full Faith and Credit Clause, to recognize any union as a marriage other than those between one man and one woman. The major implication of the act's passage was a flood of legislation at the state level. Since the passage of DOMA, thirty-nine states now have laws that prohibit gay and lesbian couples from marrying. Prior to the law's passage, only Maryland, New Hampshire, Wisconsin, and Wyoming had laws or court rulings that prohibited same-sex marriages. To date, there has been no legal challenge posed to DOMA because the condition that would activate the legislation (the sanctioning of same-sex marriages by a state) has been in effect only since Massachusetts legalized same-sex marriages. However, if the proposed Marriage Protection Act were to be passed by Congress and signed into law, the federal courts would be excluded from hearing such cases, which would have the effect of upholding DOMA by making it impervious to judicial interpretation.

4 In contrast to state legislatures and executives, state courts have proven to be a more accommodating venue for proponents of gay rights. Indeed, the decision of the Massachusetts Supreme Judicial Court stimulated the recent escalation of the gay marriage debate. At this time, only California, Hawaii, New Jersey, and Vermont provide privileges to same-sex couples that are similar to, but short of, marriage.

5 In the run up to the 2004 election, Nevada experienced unprecedented voter registration and mobilization efforts because of

the state's "battleground" status in the presidential race. These efforts, coupled with the state's growth between 2000 and 2004, resulted in an increase in voter turnout from 612,685 in 2000 to 831,563 in 2004 (Nevada Secretary of State, Elections Department 2000, 2004).

6 Mormon doctrine officially opposes gambling, but Mormon involvement in the gaming industry is justified by the legality of gaming in Nevada (Willis 1998a).

7 Not surprisingly, the influence of the LDS Church has led to criticism that church members, through tight-knit networking, control various business and political entities to such a degree that non-Mormons are shut out of opportunities. Although LDS Church officials deny any talk of a "Mormon Mafia," "speculation abounds in Clark County that certain government sectors are dominated by [Mormons], and that it is even difficult for non-Mormons to land jobs in those agencies" (Willis 1998b).

8 Unfortunately, we are unable to determine the proportion of these resources that members of the LDS Church contributed because the church officially distanced itself from the campaign and instead sought to exert its influence by encouraging its individual members to contribute to the Coalition for the Protection of Marriage.

9 A pre-election poll conducted by the Coalition for the Prediction of Marriage indicated that 55 percent of 18- to 24-year-olds supported the initiative, compared to 74 percent of citizens over the age of 65 (Willis 2000c).

10 For example, in the 2004 initiative campaign to amend Missouri's constitution to define marriage as being between a man and a woman, opponents of the measure spent $450,000, while pro-amendment forces spent only $19,000 (Parker 2004). Nonetheless, the measure passed with 71 percent of the vote.

CHAPTER 4

We thank Laura Olson, Wendy Cadge, and Thomas Nelson for helpful comments at early stages of the project. We also acknowledge and thank Eric Spengler, Adam Crowther, Jon F. Chesky, and Aaron Beastic for their help in survey preparation and data entry. Data gathered for this paper were funded by a small grant from the Denison University Research Foundation; any opinions, findings, conclusions, or recommendations expressed in this chapter are those of the authors and do not necessarily reflect the views of the DURF.

1 For the sake of comparison, it is worth noting that these figures are rather small when placed next to the sums spent by the two main candidates running for the U.S. Senate from the state of Ohio. In the Ohio Senate race, Republican incumbent George V. Voinovich spent $9,866,160, and Democratic challenger Eric D. Fingerhut spent $1,161,315 (Center for Responsive Politics 2005).

2 Incidentally, partly because of his spirited support of Issue 1, Blackwell is now the favored candidate of Christian conservatives determined to assert themselves in the Ohio Republican party as the 2006 race for the governorship approaches (Dao 2004).

3 The memo, made available by the Alliance Defense Fund through a letter of memorandum addressed to pastors in June 2004, was available on the Ohio Campaign to Protect Marriage website <http://www.ohiomarriage.com/contactus.shtml>.

4 These percentages are averages of those reported for four evangelical and four mainline Protestant denominations, respectively (Guth et al. 1997: 83).

CHAPTER 5

This research was funded by a Louisville Institute Religious Institutions Sabbatical Grant and further aided by sabbatical support from Creighton University.

CHAPTER 6

I would like to thank Bob Olson and Mary Olson for extremely valuable assistance throughout this project. Thanks are also due to all the individuals from the REST program who agreed to be interviewed for this project, to Jason Taylor for research assistance, and to Paul Djupe for valuable comments on an earlier draft of this chapter.

1 Information about Racine comes from the author's own knowledge of the city and the following Internet sites: "Racine, Wisconsin: The Belle City of the Lakes" <http://racine.wi.net>; "Racine, Wisconsin" <http://en.wikipedia.org/wiki/Racine,_Wisconsin>; and "SC Johnson: A Family Company" <http://www.scjohnson.com>.

2 For a general discussion of the history of welfare reform in Wisconsin, see Mead (2005); Thompson (1996).

3 For applications of resource mobilization theory to the study of religion and political protest, see Findlay (1993); Morris (1984); Smith (1996).

CHAPTER 8

Katherine Chipman, a student research assistant at Brigham Young University (BYU), aided in the research for this paper. The research was also supported by the award of a John Topham and Susan Redd Butler Faculty Fellowship by the Charles Redd Center for Western Studies at BYU. Kelly Patterson, Howard Christensen, and Joseph Olsen of BYU were all instrumental in collecting the exit poll data used in the paper.

1 Throughout this paper, LDS Church, Mormons, and LDS will be used interchangeably as shortened references to the Church of Jesus Christ of Latter-day Saints and its members.

2 An easement is a right of use (as distinguished from right of possession). In this case, the public easement grants the public access to the plaza, though not without restriction, which is the subject of the litigation.

3 According to the data collected by the Glenmary Research Center of religious adherents, the state of Utah is 66 percent Mormon, while Salt Lake County is only 56 percent Mormon (Jones, Doty, Grammich, Horsch, Houseal, Lynn, Marcum, Sanchagrin, and Taylor 2002). Glenmary data do not include figures for Salt Lake City alone. However, Mormons represented only about 44 percent of the Salt Lake City electorate in 2003 (see Table 8.1), and typically Mormons are slightly overrepresented in statewide exit poll data.

4 The vast majority of the newspaper articles on the Main Street Plaza controversy were written by Brady Snyder of the *Deseret Morning News* and Heather May and Rebecca Walsh of the *Salt Lake Tribune.*

5 For more information on the methodology of the Utah Colleges Exit Poll, see <http://exitpoll.byu.edu> and Grimshaw, Christensen, Magleby, and Patterson (2004).

6 Religious affiliation is measured by the question, "What, if any, is your religious preference? 1. Protestant, 2. Catholic, 3. LDS/Mormon, 4. Jewish, 5. Other, 6. No preference/No religious affiliation, 7. Prefer not to say. Religious activity is measured by self-reported responses to the question: "How active do you consider

yourself in the practice of your religious preference: very active, somewhat active, not very active, or not at all active."

7 The exact question wording was: "Some groups are able to influence public policy while others are not. On a scale of 1 to 5, with 1 being not very powerful and 5 being very powerful, please evaluate each of the following groups in Salt Lake City."

8 $F=10.402$, $p<0.001$. In addition to the mean differences in perception of power between LDS and non-LDS voters, 64.4 percent of all voters rated the LDS Church as "very powerful" by ranking the church 5 on the 1–5 scale. The group with the second highest perceived power, the ACLU, was given a 5 by only 21.3 percent of voters.

9 In addition to the numerous newspaper accounts, for another version of the sequence of events see Guliuzza (2002).

10 First Unitarian Church's pastor Tom Goldsmith also articulated this position (2002).

11 Five months later, the ACLU filed a lawsuit in state court that challenged the restrictions placed on Main Street. This lawsuit, filed in April 2000, questioned the way the sale was approved, noting changes in the street closure ordinance they thought required the plaza to be treated like a public park. In an attempt to eliminate the ACLU's basis for this lawsuit, the City Council ratified and clarified their decision to sell Main Street in May 2000.

12 Utah's other major daily paper, the *Deseret News*, is owned by the LDS Church.

13 In a Dan Jones and Associates poll conducted for the *Deseret News* on December 18–20, 2002, in the days after the compromise was announced, Salt Lake City residents were asked to choose between various options before the City Council; 33 percent favored trading the easement for the land and another 22 percent favored simply selling or giving the easement to the LDS Church. In a separate question specifically about the proposed compromise, 36 percent strongly favored the deal and another 36 percent somewhat favored the compromise. The data for this poll were provided to the authors by Dan Jones.

14 The question asked was, "Salt Lake City and the LDS (Mormon) Church recently settled on the Main Street Plaza dispute. The settlement gives the Church the right to prohibit protesters on

the plaza and gives the city land and money for a community center. Do you agree or disagree with the settlement?"

15 Voters were asked, "In your opinion, how has the controversy over the Main Street Plaza issue affected relations between people of different religions in Utah? 1. Made better, 2. No change, 3. Made worse, 4. Don't know/No opinion."

CHAPTER 9

1 This quote is commonly attributed to Mark Twain, but there is some debate over its authenticity.

2 For this study, I counted all churches in Hamilton County, Ohio as "Cincinnati-area churches." Hamilton County includes more than just Cincinnati, and the Yellow Pages lists some churches outside the county.

3 Though the N was low, the sample turned out to be closely representative of the religious presence in Cincinnati. Using the 1990 listing of U.S. churches and church membership (Bradley, Green, Jones, Lynn, and McNeill 1992), I compared the response rates for different faiths with actual church numbers in the community. While Catholic clergy and Jewish rabbis closely mirrored established estimates (Catholic parishes accounted for approximately 16 percent of Cincinnati-area churches, and the sample was approximately 15 percent Catholic), mainline Protestants were slightly overrepresented in relation to the actual presence of mainline Protestant churches in the community. Unfortunately, evangelical Protestant clergy were a substantially underrepresented group, making up only about 25 percent of my sample, although they constitute nearly 40 percent of the churches in the greater Cincinnati religious community. The sample was more representative when it came to the city's African-American presence. Black churches make up approximately 13 percent of the religious presence in the Cincinnati-area, and approximately 16 percent of the clergy in my sample came from predominantly black churches. None of the area mosques returned a survey.

4 Throughout the remainder of the paper, I will refer to, for instance, predominantly black churches as simply black churches to preserve the economy of speech.

CHAPTER 10

1 Despite the prominence of MOs in America's social and political history, and the ubiquitous role they play in the professional life of clergy in the United States (see Ammerman 2005; Djupe and Gilbert 2003: 149–53), scholars have generally ignored the role of MOs in community politics, leaving us woefully uninformed about one of the most common ways that clergy engage politics: collectively with other clergy (for important exceptions see Ammerman 1997, 2005; McRoberts 2003; Wolcott 1982). At the same time, while recognizing the important role social context plays in shaping individual clergy behavior (Crawford and Olson 2001b; Djupe and Gilbert 2002a, 2003; Gilbert 1993; Huckfeldt, Plutzer, and Sprague 1993; Jelen 1993b), little research has been devoted to exploring how context might shape collective clergy behavior.

2 In the 1800s, Siloam Springs was known for the supposed healing properties of its many hot springs, all of which do not currently flow.

3 Sociodemographic data discussed in this section are drawn from the 2000 United States Census, available in Gaquin and DeBrandt (2002, 2003).

4 According to a recent Chamber of Commerce survey, residents of Siloam Springs "cherish the progressive, friendly atmosphere, beautiful scenery, strong municipal services, and safe family environment" (Mero 2001a).

5 Even after the Klan rally, the Yoakum family continued to harass city residents. According to news reports, the family has "regularly appeared brandishing Confederate flags and various handmade signs, including the recent: 'Siloam, your fire department drowned our son, and now they think it's funny'" (Mero 2001b).

6 It important to note that many of the clergy interviewed did not actually recall how they learned about the Klan rally or who initiated the planning process. To be sure, clergy received much of their information from the media, as well as from their colleagues. For example, one SSMA member recalled learning about the rally from news reports (CI3), while another minister mentioned that he found out about the event from the "issue guys" in the SSMA (CI2). Still, in my conversations with clergy, it is clear that, at least initially, they received many of their cues

directly from city officials, as evidenced by the language they used and strategies they employed.

7 According to clergy estimates, out of sixty congregations in Siloam Springs, fewer than ten ministers regularly participated in SSMA meetings.

8 Church of Siloam Springs is a name coined by SSMA leaders and used when referring collectively to congregations in Siloam Springs.

9 According to Zald and Ash-Garner, a social movement is a "purposive and collective attempt of a number of people to change societal institutions and structures" (1987: 123). In general, social movements attempt to change society in accordance with a set of normative values concerning social relations. Religious groups are especially likely to give rise to social movements because, according to Zald and McCarthy, they include "face-to-face groups . . . constituted around some commonly held beliefs" (1987: 69).

10 Research mobilization theory posits that a SMO is a "a bounded group of individuals harnessed together . . . [being] open to new pressures from the environment as it gives back resources to that environment and, simultaneously, attempts to affect its constituent parts and its environment." (Zald and Ash-Garner 1987: 123).

CHAPTER 11

1 For instance, we do not have a study focusing on a community in the Northeast, nor do we have representative examples of all community types (cities, suburbs, and rural areas/towns) from each region. We are also missing many issues that may or may not engage religious interests, particularly abortion, but also immigration, religion in schools, and others.

2 This finding holds across a general activity measure in Burns, Schlozman, and Verba (2001) and McKenzie (2004), as well as a turnout measure in Wielhouwer (2000), although McKenzie does report a turnout effect.

3 Such relationships are "autoregressive," according to Huckfeldt, Johnson, and Sprague (2004).

4 See Steensland, Park, Regnerus, Robinson, Wilcox, and Woodberry (2000) for a useful discussion of how specific religious denominations are placed into these categories.

References

"Aboard the Underground Railroad: Harriet Beecher Stowe House." 2005. *National Park Service.* http://www.cr.nps.gov/nr/travel/underground/oh1.htm.

Adams, Noah. 2001. "Cincinnati: Searching for a Resolution." *National Public Radio: All Things Considered*, November 1. http://www.npr.org/programs/atc/features/2001/nov/cincinnati/011101.cincinnati.html.

Albrecht, Brian. 2005. "Issue 1 Conflicts with Domestic Abuse Law, Judge Says." *Cleveland Plain Dealer*, March 24: A1.

Aldridge, Kevin. 2002. "Boycott Group Won't Pare Down Demands." *Cincinnati Enquirer*, May 5. http://www.enquirer.com/editions/2002/05/05/loc_group_wont.html.

Aldridge, Kevin, and Robert Anglen. 2002. "Group Offers to End Boycott." *Cincinnati Enquirer*, May 8. http://www.enquirer.com/editions/2002/05/08/loc_group_offers_to_end.html.

Alltucker, Ken, and Kevin Aldridge. 2004. "Events Revive as Boycott Wanes." *Cincinnati Enquirer*, September 19. http://www.enquirer.com/editions/2004/09/19/loc_loc1aboycott.html.

Alongi, Paul. 2003a. "Jackson Rejects Calls to End Protest." *Greenville News*, March 17.

———. 2003b. "MLK Panel Unlikely to Meet Deadline." *Greenville News*, March 3.

Ammerman, Nancy T. 1997. *Congregation and Community.* New Brunswick, NJ: Rutgers University Press.

———. 2002. "Connecting Mainline Protestant Churches with Public Life." In *The Quiet Hand of God: Faith-Based Activism and the Public Role of Mainline Protestantism*, ed. Robert Wuthnow and John H. Evans. Berkeley: University of California Press.

———. 2005. *Pillars of Faith: American Congregations and Their Partners.* Berkeley: University of California Press.

Anderson, Ross C. "Rocky." 2002. "Meeting the Challenges of the Main Street Plaza Controversy." *Teaching Ethics* 3: 85–88.

———. 2005. Telephone interview, December 22.

"Arts Association, Coalition for Just Cincinnati Drop Suits." 2003. *Business Courier*, February 11. http://www.bizjournals.com/cincinnati/stories/2003/02/10/daily24.html.

Assensoh, A. B., and Yvette Alex-Assensoh. 2001. "Inner-City Contexts, Church Attendance, and African-American Political Participation." *Journal of Politics* 63: 886–901.

Babbie, Earl. 2004. *The Practice of Social Research.* 10th ed. Belmont, CA: Wadsworth/Thomson.

Babula, Joelle. 2002. "Clergy Speak Out Against Anti-Gay Marriage Efforts." *Las Vegas Review-Journal*, October 9.

Balser, Deborah. 1997. "The Impact of Environmental Factors on Factionalism and Schism in Social Movement Organizations." *Social Forces* 76: 199–229.

"Baptist Crusade Takes Aim at Mormons, Other 'Cults'." 2000. *Las Vegas Review-Journal*, January 23.

Barnett, Ron. 2003a. "King Holiday Proposals Submitted." *Greenville News*, March 27.

———. 2003b. "Methodist Pastors Push MLK Holiday." *Greenville News*, March 4.

———. 2003c. "Ministers Urge End to King Protests." *Greenville News*, March 13.

———. 2003d. "MLK Day Called A Sign of Clash of Cultures." *Greenville News*, March 6.

Beatty, Kathleen Murphy, and Oliver Walter. 1989. "A Group Theory of Religion and Politics: The Clergy as Group Leaders." *Western Political Quarterly* 42: 129–46.

Bell, Becky, and Melissa L. Jones. 2000. "Siloam Springs Rally Inspires Protest, No Violence." *Arkansas Democrat-Gazette*, August 6: A6.

Benson, Peter L., and Dorothy L. Williams. 1982. *Religion on Capitol Hill: Myths and Realities.* New York: Oxford University Press.

Bernick, Bob Jr. 2005. "Utah Tax Cut Likely Next Year." *Deseret News,* September 24: A1.

Berry, Jeffrey M., Kent E. Portney, and Ken Thomson. 1993. *The Rebirth of Urban Democracy.* Washington, DC: Brookings Institution.

Bills, Dale K. 2002. "The Main Street Plaza: An LDS Response." *Teaching Ethics* 3: 89–91.

Birkholz, Patricia. 2003. Interview, Lansing, MI, March 27.

Bischoff, Laura A. 2004a. "Former Porn Addict Leads State Crusade against Gay Marriage; Burress Architect of Proposed Amendment." *Dayton Daily News,* October 17: A20.

———. 2004b. "Issue 1 Race Getting too Close to Call." *Dayton Daily News,* October 24: A1.

Black, Amy E., Douglas L. Koopman, and David K. Ryden. 2004. *Of Little Faith: The Politics of George W. Bush's Faith-Based Initiatives.* Washington, DC: Georgetown University Press.

Blizzard, Samuel. 1956. "The Minister's Dilemma." *Christian Century* 73: 508–9.

Block, Dustin. 2003a. "County Comes to Rescue over Shelter's Laundry Bills." *Racine Journal Times,* March 26: 1C.

———. 2003b. "Homeless Part of Thomas' Campaign." *Racine Journal Times,* February 27: 1C.

———. 2003c. "Laundry Bills Burying Homeless Shelter." *Racine Journal Times,* March 19: 1C.

———. 2005a., "Census Paints Sobering Picture of the Homeless Situation in Racine County." *Racine Journal Times,* March 26: 1B.

———. 2005b. "Homeless Program Laid to Rest." *Racine Journal Times,* May 14: 11A.

Blumhofer, Edith L., ed. 2002. *Religion, Politics and the American Experience: Reflection on Religion and American Political Life.* Tuscaloosa: University of Alabama Press.

Bonnette, Sarah G. 2002. "County Council Member Requests King Holiday." *Greenville News,* October 2.

———. 2003a. "MLK Day Vote Put Off." *Greenville News,* February 4.

———. 2003b. "MLK Holiday Not Part of County Plan." *Greenville News,* January 18.

———. 2003c. "Sit-in Rekindles '60s Spirit." *Greenville News,* February 6.

———. 2003d. "Thousands Urge Greenville to Establish King Holiday." *Greenville News*, February 19.

Boorsma, Todd. 2003. Interview, Grand Rapids, MI, April 21.

Bowers, Cynthia. 2002. "Seven Days: Cincinnati a Year after the Riots." *CBS Sunday Morning*, April 7.

Boyte, Harry. 1981. *Backyard Revolution*. Philadelphia: Temple University Press.

Bradford, Michelle. 2001. "Siloam Springs Klansman Accused of Harassment, Cops of Misconduct." *Arkansas Democrat-Gazette*, August 7: B1.

Bradley, Martin, Norman Green Jr., Dale Jones, Mac Lynn, and Lou McNeill. 1992. *Churches and Church Membership in the United States 1990*. Atlanta: Glenmary Research Center.

Brady, Henry E., Kay Lehman Schlozman, and Sidney Verba. 1999. "Prospecting for Participants: Rational Expectations and the Recruitment of Political Activists." *American Political Science Review* 93: 153–68.

Branam, Chris. 2000. "Siloam Springs Silent Marchers out To Dissuade KKK from Rally" *Arkansas Democrat-Gazette*, August 1: B2.

Brewer, Paul R. 2003. "The Shifting Foundations of Public Opinion about Gay Rights." *Journal of Politics* 65: 1208–20.

Brown, John. 2001. "Chamber Opposes Proposed Wayland Casino." Press release, Grand Rapids Area Chamber of Commerce, June 20.

Brown, T. C. 2004. "Issue 1 Foes Report Money Problem." *Cleveland Plain Dealer*, December 11: B3.

Buchanan, Michael. 2003a. "King Holiday Not Among County Employees' Picks." *Greenville News*, July 16.

———. 2003b. "King Supporters Protest at Councilman's Home." *Greenville News*, June 4.

Buhler, David. 2005. Interview, Salt Lake City, November 11.

Bumpus, Donna. 2003. Interview, Racine, WI, July 29.

Burke, Michael. 2003. "Steps toward a Solution." *Racine Journal Times*, November 14: 1A.

Burns, Nancy, Kay Lehman Schlozman, and Sidney Verba. 2001. *The Private Roots of Public Action*. Cambridge, MA: Harvard University Press.

Button, James W., Barbara A. Rienzo, and Kenneth D. Wald. 1997. *Private Lives, Public Conflicts: Battles over Gay Rights in American Communities*. Washington DC: CQ Press.

Buttweiler, Joe. 2002. "Racine Emergency Shelter Taskforce Begins New Season Helping Homeless." *Racine Journal Times*, October 5: 1B.

Byrnes, Timothy A. 1991. *Catholic Bishops in American Politics.* Princeton: Princeton University Press.

Byrnes, Timothy A., and Mary C. Segers, ed. 1992. *The Catholic Church and the Politics of Abortion: A View from the States.* Boulder: Westview.

Cadge, Wendy. 2002. "Vital Conflicts: The Mainline Denominations Debate Homosexuality." In *The Quiet Hand of God: Faith-Based Activism and the Public Role of Mainline Protestantism*, ed. Robert Wuthnow and John H. Evans. Berkeley: University of California Press.

Calhoun-Brown, Allison. 1996. "African-American Churches and Political Mobilization: The Psychological Impact of Organizational Resources." *Journal of Politics* 58: 935–53.

———. 1997. "Still Seeing in Black and White: Racial Challenges for the Christian Right." In *Sojourners in the Wilderness: The Christian Right in Comparative Perspective*, edited by Corwin E. Smidt and James M. Penning. Lanham, MD: Rowman & Littlefield.

———. 1998. "While Marching to Zion: Otherworldliness and Racial Empowerment in the Black Community." *Journal for the Scientific Study of Religion* 37: 427–39.

Campbell, David E. 2004. "Acts of Faith: Churches and Political Engagement." *Political Behavior* 26: 155–80.

Campbell, David E., and J. Quin Monson. 2003. "Following the Leader? Mormon Voting on Ballot Propositions." *Journal for the Scientific Study of Religion* 42: 605–19.

Campbell, Ernest Q., and Thomas F. Pettigrew. 1959. *Christians in Racial Crisis: A Study of Littlerock's Ministry.* Washington, DC: Public Affairs Press.

Canham, Matt. 2004. "Mormon Portion of Utah Population Steadily Shrinking." *Salt Lake Tribune*, July 28: A1.

"Casino Plan Stalls, Tribe Sues State." 2001. *Detroit News*, January 22.

Cauchon, Dennis. 2003. "Mass, About to Alter Gay Marriage Debate." *USA Today*, December 26.

Cavendish, James C. 2000. "Church-based Community Activism: A Comparison of Black and White Catholic Congregations." *Journal for the Scientific Study of Religion* 39: 371–84.

———. 2001. "To March or not to March: Clergy Mobilization Strategies and Grassroots Antidrug Activism." In *Christian Clergy in*

American Politics, edited by Sue E. S. Crawford and Laura R. Olson. Baltimore: Johns Hopkins University Press.

Cavendish, James C., Michael R. Welch, and David C. Leege. 1998. "Social Network Theory and Predictors of Religiosity for Black and White Catholics: Evidence of a 'Black Sacred Cosmos'?" *Journal for the Scientific Study of Religion* 37: 397–410.

Center for Responsive Politics. 2005. "2004 Race: Ohio Senate." http://www.opensecrets.org/races/summary.asp?ID=OHS2&Cycle=2004.

Chaves, Mark. 1999. "Religious Congregations and Welfare Reform: Who Will Take Advantage of Charitable Choice?" *American Sociological Review* 64: 836–46.

———. 2001. "Religious Congregations and Welfare Reform: Assessing the Potential." In *Can Charitable Choice Work? Covering Religion's Impact on Urban Affairs and Social Services*, edited by Andrew Walsh. Hartford, CT: The Leonard E. Greenberg Center for the Study of Religion in Public Life.

———. 2004. *Congregations in America*. Cambridge, MA: Harvard University Press.

Christensen, Carlton. 2005. Telephone interview, November 11.

Church of Jesus Christ of Latter-day Saints. 2002. "Realizing a Vision: A Perspective from the Church of Jesus Christ of Latter-day Saints." Public relations information packet distributed by the LDS Church, November 14.

Cincinnati Community Action Now. 2002. http://www.cincinnati-can.org.

"Cincinnati Signs Pact with U.S. over Police." 2002. *Cable News Network*, April 13: http://archives.cnn.com/2002/LAW/04/12/ashcroft.rights/.

"Clark County Demographics Study." 2004. http://www.co.clark.nv.us/comprehensive_planning.

Clark, Peter B., and James Q. Wilson. 1961. "Incentive System: A Theory of Organization." *Administrative Science Quarterly* 6: 129–66.

Clark, Stephen. 2005. Interview via e-mail (November–December).

Cnaan, Ram A. 1999. *The Newer Deal: Social Work and Religion in Partnership*. New York: Columbia University Press.

———. 2002. *The Invisible Caring Hand: American Congregations and the Provision of Welfare*. New York: New York University Press.

Cnaan, Ram A., and Gaynor I. Yancey. 2000. "Our Hidden Safety Net." In *What's God Got to Do with the American Experiment?* edited by E.

J. Dionne and John J. DiIulio. Washington, DC: Brookings Institution.

Coalition for the Protection of Marriage. 2004. http://www.protectmarriagenv.org.

Colquhoun, Ross, and Brian Martin. 2001. "Constructing Social Action." *Philosophy and Social Action* 27: 7–28.

Cook, Elizabeth Adell, Ted G. Jelen, and Clyde Wilcox. 1992. *Between Two Absolutes: Public Opinion and the Politics of Abortion*. Boulder: Westview.

Cook, Tony. 2006. "City Had a Bloody 2005." *Cincinnati Post*, January 3. http://news.cincypost.com/apps/pbcs.dll/article?AID=/20060103/NEWS01/601030354.

Cooperman, Allen, and Thomas B. Edsall. 2004. "Evangelicals Say They Led Charge for the GOP." *Washington Post*, November 7: A1.

Crain, Robert. 1969. *The Politics of School Desegregation*. New York: Doubleday.

Crawford, Sue E. S. 1995. "Clergy at Work in the Secular City." Ph.D. diss., Indiana University.

Crawford, Sue E. S., and Laura R. Olson, ed. 2001a. *Christian Clergy in American Politics*. Baltimore: Johns Hopkins University Press.

———. 2001b. "Clergy as Political Actors in Urban Contexts." In *Christian Clergy in American Politics*, edited by Sue E. S. Crawford and Laura R. Olson. Baltimore: Johns Hopkins University Press.

Crawford, Sue E. S., Laura R. Olson, and Melissa M. Deckman. 2001. "Understanding the Mobilization of Professionals." *Nonprofit and Voluntary Sector Quarterly* 30: 321–50.

Dahl, Robert A. 1956. *A Preface to Democratic Theory*. Chicago: University of Chicago Press.

Danielson, Mary Beth. 2001. "R.E.S.T. Shelters Us All." *Racine Journal Times*, January 19: 1C.

Dao, James. 2004. "State Action is Pursued in Same-Sex Marriage." *The New York Times*, February 24.

———. 2005. "Movement in the Pews Tries to Jolt Ohio." *The New York Times*, March 27: A14.

Davids, Carolyn, ed. 2001. "Grand Rapids in Controversy over Casino." *Calvin College Chimes*, February 15.

Deckman, Melissa M. 2004. *School Board Battles: The Christian Right in Local Politics*. Washington, DC: Georgetown University Press.

DiMaggio, Paul J., John H. Evans, and Bethany Bryson. 1996. "Have Americans' Social Attitudes Become More Polarized?" *American Journal of Sociology* 102: 690–755.

Djupe, Paul A. 2001. "Cardinal O'Connor and His Constituents: Differential Benefits and Public Evaluations." In *Christian Clergy in American Politics*, edited by Sue E. S. Crawford and Laura R. Olson. Baltimore: Johns Hopkins University Press.

Djupe, Paul A., and Christopher P. Gilbert. 2002a. "The Political Voice of Clergy." *Journal of Politics* 64: 596–609.

———. 2002b. "Politics in Church: Byproduct or Central Mission?" Paper presented at the annual meeting of the American Political Science Association, Boston.

———. 2003. *The Prophetic Pulpit: Clergy, Churches, and Communities in American Politics*. Lanham, MD: Rowman & Littlefield.

———. 2004. "The Local Roots of Aggregate Opinion Structures." Paper presented at the annual meeting of the American Political Science Association, Chicago.

———. 2005. "The Political Cohesion of Churches." Paper presented at the annual meeting of the Midwest Political Science Association, Chicago.

———. 2006. "The Resourceful Believer: Generating Civic Skills in Church." *Journal of Politics* 68: 116–27.

Djupe, Paul A., and J. Tobin Grant. 2001. "Religious Institutions and Political Participation in America." *Journal for the Scientific Study of Religion* 40: 303–14.

Djupe, Paul A., and John C. Green. 2007. "The Politics of American Muslims." In *From Pews to Polling Places: Political Mobilization in the American Religious Mosaic*, edited by J. Matthew Wilson. Washington, DC: Georgetown University Press.

Djupe, Paul A., Eric L. McDaniel, and Jacob R. Neiheisel. Forthcoming. "The Politics of the Religious Minorities Vote in the 2004 Elections." In *Religion and the Bush Presidency*, edited by Mark J. Rozell and Gleaves Whitney. Washington, DC: Georgetown University Press.

Djupe, Paul A., Laura R. Olson, and Christopher P. Gilbert. 2005. "Sources of Clergy Support for Denominational Lobbying in Washington." *Review of Religious Research* 47: 86–99.

Drake, Cynthia J. 2002. "House Hopefuls Air Views." *Holland Sentinel*, July 31.

Dreisbach, Daniel L. 2003. *Thomas Jefferson and the Wall of Separation between Church and State.* New York: New York University Press.

Drummond, Susie Kasinski. 2003. "No REST for the Homeless." *Racine Journal Times,* May 3: 11A.

Dykes, David. 2003. "Jackson Vows to Continue Push for MLK Holiday." *Greenville News,* March 2.

Earle, John R., Dean D. Knudsen, and Donald W. Shriver Jr. 1976. *Spindles and Spires: A Re-Study of Religion and Social Change in Gastonia.* Atlanta: John Knox Press.

Edelman, Murray. 1964. *The Symbolic Uses of Politics.* Urbana: University of Illinois Press.

Edison-Swift, Anne. 2001. "National Casino Study Bolsters Rival Sides in Debate." *Capital News Service,* September 28.

Ehrenhalt, Alan. 1991. *The United States of Ambition: Politicians, Power, and the Pursuit of Office.* New York: Random House.

Eisinger, Peter. 1973. "The Condition of Protests in American Cities." *American Political Science Review* 81: 11–28.

Engler, John. 2002. Unpublished letter to Majority Leader Dan DeGrow and Speaker Rick Johnson, December 30.

Entman, Robert M. 1993. "Framing: Toward Clarification of a Fractured Paradigm." *Journal of Communication* 43: 51–59.

Euchner, Charles C. 1996. *Extraordinary Politics: How Protest and Dissent Are Changing American Democracy.* Boulder: Westview.

Evans, John H. 2003. "Have Americans' Attitudes Become More Polarized? An Update." *Social Science Quarterly* 84: 71–90.

Ewing, Josh. 2005. Telephone interview, October 14.

Fantin, Linda. 2002. "Hard-Core Rockyites Are on the Decline." *Salt Lake Tribune,* December 16: B1.

Fee, John E. 2002. "Main Street Plaza: An Opportunity to Rebuild." *Teaching Ethics* 3: 97–100.

Findlay, James F. Jr. 1993. *Church People in the Struggle: The National Council of Churches and the Black Freedom Movement, 1950–1970.* New York: Oxford University Press.

Findsen, Owen. 1999. "Beecher's Students Debated Slavery." *Cincinnati Enquirer,* February 14. http://www.enquirer.com/editions/1999/02/14/loc_mbeechers_students.html.

Fiorina, Morris P. 2005. *Culture War? The Myth of a Polarized America.* New York: Pearson Longman.

Flanigan, William H., and Nancy H. Zingale. 2002. *Political Behavior of the American Electorate.* 10th ed. Washington DC: CQ Press.

Flannery, Gregory. 2003. "Burning Questions: What's Wrong with the Cincinnati Police?" *City Beat,* April 16–22. http://citybeat.com/2003-04016/bq.shtml.

Flores, Terry. 1997. "Jobs, Prison Dominate Concerns." *Racine Journal Times,* February 11: 1B.

Flowers, Lana. 2000a. "Churches Walk for Unity as Klan Rally Nears." *Morning News of Northwest Arkansas,* August 2: A9.

———. 2000b. "Klan Rally Ends Early, Peacefully." *Morning News of Northwest Arkansas,* August 6: A7.

———. 2000c. "Local Law-Enforcement Agencies Will Keep Eye on Klan Situation." *Morning News of Northwest Arkansas,* July 22: A2.

Fowler, Robert Booth, Allen D. Hertzke, Laura R. Olson, and Kevin R. den Dulk. 2004. *Religion and Politics in America: Faith, Culture, and Strategic Choices.* 3rd ed. Boulder: Westview.

Franklin, Amy. 2000. "Michigan Facing another Casino Compact Dilemma." *Detroit News,* December 25.

Freeman, Jo. 1975. *The Politics of Women's Liberation: A Case Study of an Emergent Social Movement and Its Relation to the Policy Process.* New York: David McKay.

Friends of the Gun Lake Indians (FOGLI). 2001. "The Vote on House Resolution 167." http://www.fogli.org/167.htm.

———. 2003. "Jobs! Tribe! Casino!" http://www.fogli.org/economicbenefits.htm.

Galbincea, Barb, and Sandy Theis. 2004. "Heights Officials, Colleges, Take 'Sue Me' Stance on Marriage Law." *Cleveland Plain Dealer,* December 2: A1.

Gaquin, Deirdre A., and Katherine A. DeBrandt. 2002. *2002 County and City Extra: Annual Metro, City and County Data Book.* 11th ed. Lantham, MD: Kraus.

———. 2003. *Places, Towns and Townships,* 3rd ed. Lantham, MD: Kraus.

Gardner, Marilyn. 2003. "Small Towns Confront an Urban Problem." *Christian Science Monitor,* March 7: 5.

Garretson, Craig. 2001. "On 4th Night, All Quiet: Curfew Brings Calm to City Streets." *Cincinnati Post,* April 13. http://www.cincypost.com/2001/apr/13/curfew041301.html.

Gilbert, Christopher P. 1993. *The Impact of Churches on Political Behavior: An Empirical Study.* Westport, CT: Greenwood.

Gilder Lehrman Center for the Study of Slavery, Resistance, and Abolition. 2003. "Historic Reenactment of the Lane Slavery Debates of 1834." http://www.yale.edu/glc/events/lane.htm.

Giles, Michael W., and Marilyn K. Dantico. 1982. "Political Participation and the Neighborhood Social Context Revisited." *American Journal of Political Science* 26: 144–50.

Gimpel, James G. 1998. "Grassroots Organizations and Equilibrium Cycles in Group Mobilization and Access." In *The Interest Group Connection*, edited by Paul S. Herrnson, Ronald G. Shaiko, and Clyde Wilcox. Chatham, NJ: Chatham House.

Goetz, Kristina. 2001. "What Comes Next? Good Examples Few." *Cincinnati Enquirer*, December 30. http://www.enquirer.com/unres2001/race7.html.

Goldsmith, Tom. 2002. "Main Street Plaza: An Ethical Perspective." *Teaching Ethics* 3: 93–95.

———. 2005. Telephone interview. November 23.

Goudreau, Rosemary, and Tim Bonfield. 2002. "Clinton Offers to Help City: Racial Peace Would Be Visit's Aim." *Cincinnati Enquirer*, May 5. http://www.enquirer.com/editions/2002/05/05/loc_clinton_offers_to.html.

Granovetter, Mark. 1973. "The Strength of Weak Ties." *American Journal of Sociology* 78: 1360–80.

Gray, Virginia, and David Lowery. 1992. "Reflections on the Study of Interest Groups in the States." Paper presented at the annual meeting of the American Political Science Association, Chicago.

———. 1993. "The Diversity of State Interest Group Systems." *Political Research Quarterly* 46: 81–97.

———. 1996a. "Environmental Limits on the Diversity of State Interest Organization Systems: A Population Ecology Interpretation." *Political Research Quarterly* 49: 103–18.

———. 1996b. *The Population Ecology of Interest Representation: Lobbying Communities in the American States*. Ann Arbor: University of Michigan Press.

Green, John C. 1999. "The Spirit Willing: Collective Identity and the Development of the Christian Right." In *Waves of Protest: Social Movements since the Sixties*, edited by Jo Freeman and Victoria Johnson. Lanham, MD: Rowman & Littlefield.

Green, John C., James L. Guth, and Kevin Hill. 1993. "Faith and Election: The Christian Right in Congressional Campaigns 1978–1988." *Journal of Politics* 55: 80–91.

Green, John C., James L. Guth, Corwin E. Smidt, and Lyman A. Kellstedt. 1996. *Religion and the Culture Wars: Dispatches from the Front.* Lanham, MD: Rowman & Littlefield.

Green, John C., James L. Guth, and Clyde Wilcox. 1998. "Less than Conquerors: The Christian Right in State Republican Parties." In *Social Movements and American Political Institutions*, edited by Anne N. Costain and Andrew S. McFarland. Lanham, MD: Rowman & Littlefield.

Green, John C., Mark J. Rozell, and Clyde Wilcox, eds. 2000. *Prayers in the Precincts: The Christian Right in the 1998 Elections.* Washington, DC: Georgetown University Press.

———. 2003. *The Christian Right in American Politics: Marching to the Millennium.* Washington, DC: Georgetown University Press.

Green, John C., Corwin E. Smidt, James L. Guth, and Lyman A. Kellstedt. 2004. "The American Religious Landscape and the 2004 Presidential Vote." http://www.uakron.edu/bliss/research.php.

Grimshaw, Scott D., Howard B. Christensen, David B. Magleby, and Kelly D. Patterson. 2004. "Twenty Years of the Utah Colleges Exit Poll: Learning by Doing." *Chance* 17: 32–38.

Guliuzza, Frank. 2002. "Showdown on Main Street: Salt Lake City, the Mormon Church, and Freedom of Expression." *Teaching Ethics* 3: 77–84.

Gunderson, Gary. 1995. *Toward a Movement: Why Faith and Health Leaders Can Change the World.* Columbia: South Carolina Christian Action Council.

———. 2004. *Boundary Leaders: Leadership Skills for People of Faith.* Minneapolis: Fortress.

Guth, James L. 2001. "Reflections on the Status of Research on Clergy in Politics." In *Christian Clergy in American Politics*, edited by Sue E. S. Crawford and Laura R. Olson. Baltimore: Johns Hopkins University Press.

Guth, James L., and John C. Green, ed. 1991. *The Bible and the Ballot Box: Religion and Politics in the 1988 Election.* Boulder: Westview.

Guth, James L., John C. Green, Corwin E. Smidt, Lyman A. Kellstedt, and Margaret M. Poloma. 1997. *The Bully Pulpit: The Politics of Protestant Clergy.* Lawrence: University of Kansas Press.

Guth, James L., Lyman A. Kellstedt, John C. Green, and Corwin E. Smidt. 2002. "A Distant Thunder? Religious Mobilization in the 2000 Elections." In *Interest Group Politics*, edited by Allan J. Cigler and Burdett A. Loomis. 6th ed. Washington DC: CQ Press.

Guth, James L., Lyman A. Kellstedt, and Corwin E. Smidt. 1998. "Thunder on the Right? Religious Interest Group Mobilization in the 1996 Election." In *Interest Group Politics*, edited by Allan J. Cigler and Burdett A. Loomis. 5th ed. Washington, DC: CQ Press.

Guth, James L., Lyman A. Kellstedt, Corwin E. Smidt, and John C. Green. 1998. "Thunder on the Right? Religious Interest Group Mobilization in the 1996 Election." In *Interest Group Politics*, edited by Allan J. Cigler and Burdett A. Loomis. 5th ed. Washington, DC: CQ Press.

Gutsche, Robert. 2005a. "Friday is 1st District Decision Day." *Racine Journal Times*, July 9: 2B.

———. 2005b. "HALO Shelter Set To Open." *Racine Journal Times*, October 30: 1A.

Hadden, Jeffrey K. 1969. *The Gathering Storm in the Churches*. Garden City, NY: Doubleday.

Haga, Chuck. 2004. "Election May Hinge on Same-Sex Marriage Issue." *Minneapolis-St. Paul Star Tribune*, October 28: 1A.

Hammond, James T. 2000. "Hodges Signs King Day Into Law." *Greenville News*, May 2.

Hampel, Paul, Denise Hollinshed, and Tim O'Neill. 2001. "Problems are Hauntingly Familiar; Condition and Tensions That Caused Riots There Also Exist in St. Louis." *St. Louis Post-Dispatch*, April 15: A1.

Harmon, Steven. 2002a. "Casino Foes Make Case to Washington." *Grand Rapids Press*, December 13.

———. 2002b. "Casino Supporters Take Shot at Lame Duck." *Grand Rapids Press*, December 5.

———. 2002c. "Late Push for Casino Angers Foes." *Grand Rapids Press*, December 10.

———. 2002d. "Polpourri '02." *Grand Rapids Press*, December 15.

Harmon, Steven, and Peter Luke. 2002. "Casino Supporters See Vote as Hitting Economic Jackpot." *Grand Rapids Press*, December 11.

Harrington, Brooke. 2001. "Organizational Performance and Corporate Social Capital: A Contingency Model." In *Social Capital of Organizations*, vol. 18, edited by Shaul M. Gabbay and Roger Th. A. J. Leenders. New York: JAI.

Harris, Fredrick C. 1999. *Something Within: Religion in African-American Political Activism*. New York: Oxford University Press.

Hayworth, Chad. 2000. "Siloam Springs Ku Klux Klan To Hold Parade, Rally in August." *Arkansas Democrat-Gazette*, June 17: B1.

Heinlein, Gary. 2001. "Casino Plan Stalls, Tribe Sues State." *Detroit News*, January 6.

Heinz, John P., Edward O. Laumann, Robert L. Nelson, and Robert H. Salisbury. 1993. *The Hollow Core*. Cambridge, MA: Harvard University Press.

Held, Tom. 2005. "State's Poverty Rate Rises Fastest in Nation." *Milwaukee Journal Sentinel*, August 31: 3A.

Hertzke, Allen D. 1988. *Representing God in Washington: The Role of Religious Lobbies in the American Polity*. Knoxville: University of Tennessee Press.

———. 1993. *Echoes of Discontent: Jesse Jackson, Pat Robertson, and the Resurgence of Populism*. Washington, DC: CQ Press.

"High Rollers Join West Michigan Casino Fight." 2002. *Gambling Magazine*, September 13.

Hill, Chris. 2001. "Bill May Extend Rights for Gays." *Las Vegas Sun*, March 27.

Himes, Kenneth R., ed. 2005. *Modern Catholic Social Teaching: Commentaries and Interpretations*. Washington, DC: Georgetown University Press.

Hofrenning, Daniel J. B. 1995. *In Washington But Not of It: The Prophetic Politics of Religious Lobbyists*. Philadelphia: Temple University Press.

———. 1999. "Religious Interest Groups: Pragmatism, Purism, and the Life of Faith." Paper presented at the annual meeting of Christians in Political Science, Grand Rapids.

Hogan, John. 2004a. "Casino No Joke to '23 Is Enough'." *Grand Rapids Press*, June 8.

———. 2004b. "Tribal Casino Plans in Jeopardy." *Grand Rapids Press*, December 9.

Hoge, Dean R., and Ernesto Zulueta. 1984. "Salience as a Condition for Various Social Consequences of Religious Commitment." *Journal for the Scientific Study of Religion* 24: 21–38.

Hoover, Dan. 2003. "GOP Leaders Scold Council for MLK Vote." *Greenville News*, April 2.

Horn, Dan. 2001a. "Summer of Blood: Guns Rule the Streets." *Cincinnati Enquirer*, December 30. http:// www.enquirer.com/unrest 2001/race4.html.

———. 2001b. "Tests of Justice: Officers Acquitted." *Cincinnati Enquirer*, December 30. http://www.enquirer.com/unrest2001/race5.html.

———. 2001c. "The Trigger: Shooting 'Ignites Furious Response'." *Cincinnati Enquirer,* December 30. http://www.enquirer.com/unrest2001/race2.html.

Hornbeck, Mark. 2002. "House Directs Engler to Negotiate New Casino." *Detroit News,* December 11.

Hornbeck, Mark, Charlie Cain, and Gary Heinlein. 2002. "Investors Donated Thousands to 45 of 51 Who OK'd Project." *Detroit News,* December 10.

Huckfeldt, Robert, Paul Allen Beck, Russell J. Dalton, and Jeffrey Levine. 1995. "Political Environments, Cohesive Social Groups, and the Communication of Public Opinion." *American Journal of Political Science* 39: 1025–54.

Huckfeldt, Robert, Paul E. Johnson, and John Sprague. 2004. *Political Disagreement: The Survival of Diverse Opinions within Communication Networks.* New York: Cambridge University Press.

Huckfeldt, Robert, Eric Plutzer, and John Sprague. 1993. "Alternative Contexts of Political Behavior: Churches, Neighborhoods, and Individuals." *Journal of Politics* 55: 365–81.

Huckfeldt, Robert, and John Sprague. 1995. *Citizens, Politics, and Social Communications: Information and Influence in an Election Campaign.* New York: Cambridge University Press.

Hunter, Floyd. 1953. *Community Power Structure.* Chapel Hill: University of North Carolina Press.

Hunter, James Davison. 1991. *Culture Wars: The Struggle to Define America.* New York: Basic Books.

Hunter, Kennith G., Laura Ann Wilson, and Gregory G. Brunk. 1991. "Social Complexity and Interest-Group Lobbying in the American States." *Journal of Politics* 53: 488–503.

Iacoboni, Donna. 2005. "Second Judge Cites Amendment in Domestic Violence Ruling." *Cleveland Plain Dealer,* March 25: B2.

"Indian Casino in Allegan County Clears Hurdle." 2001. WWMT-TV, June 28.

"Irate Secchia Goes After GOP Leader over Casino Support." 2002. *Grand Rapids Press,* May 21.

Janofsky, Michael. 2005. "When Cleaner Air Is a Biblical Obligation." *The New York Times,* November 7: A18.

Jansen, Mark. 2003. Interview, Grand Rapids, February 21.

Jelen, Ted G. 1991. *The Political Mobilization of Religious Beliefs.* Westport, CT: Praeger.

———. 1993a. "The Political Consequences of Religious Group Attitudes." *Journal of Politics* 55: 178–90.
———. 1993b. *The Political World of the Clergy*. Westport, CT: Praeger.
———, ed. 1995. *Perspectives on the Politics of Abortion*. Westport, CT: Praeger.
———. 2001. "Clergy as Political Leaders: Notes for a Theory." In *Christian Clergy in American Politics*, edited by Sue E. S. Crawford and Laura R. Olson. Baltimore: Johns Hopkins University Press.
Jelen, Ted G., and Clyde Wilcox. 1995. *Public Attitudes Toward Church and State*. Armonk, NY: M. E. Sharpe.
Jennings, James. 2005. "Black Faith-Based Coalitions in Boston: Civic Advantages and Challenges." In *Black Churches and Local Politics: Clergy Influence, Organizational Partnerships, and Civic Empowerment*, edited by R. Drew Smith and Fredrick C. Harris. Lanham, MD: Rowman & Littlefield.
Jensen, Benjamin R., and Laura R. Olson. 2002. "Are Mormons Culture Warriors? Mormon Participation in Local Political Debate over Gay Marriage." Paper presented at the annual meeting of the Society for the Scientific Study of Religion, Salt Lake City.
Johnson, Alan. 2004a. "Financial Facts Few As Issue 1 Survives Court Action." *Columbus Dispatch*, October 22: 10D.
———. 2004b. "Gay-Marriage Ban; Twenty in GOP Backing Issue 1; Lawmakers at Odds with Party Leaders." *Columbus Dispatch*, October 20: 1D.
———. 2004c. "Same-Sex Marriage Ban; Big Business, OSU among Those against Amendment." *Columbus Dispatch*, September 30: 1A.
———. 2005. "Domestic Partners; Miami Benefits Against the Law, Parent's Suit Says." *Columbus Dispatch*, November 30: 1E.
Johnson, Robert. 2003. Interviews, Omaha, NE.
Jones, Dale E., Sherri Doty, Clifford Grammich, James E. Horsch, Richard Houseal, Mac Lynn, John P. Marcum, Kenneth M. Sanchgrin, and Richard H. Taylor. 2002. *Religious Congregations and Membership in the United States, 2000*. Nashville: Glenmary Research Center.
Kanigher, Steve. 2000a. "Candidate Tackle Issues." *Las Vegas Sun*, October 11.
———. 2000b. "Marriage Question Heats Up Ballot Issues." *Las Vegas Sun*, October 21.

Kellstedt, Lyman A., and John C. Green. 1993. "Knowing God's Many People: Denominational Preference and Political Behavior." In *Rediscovering the Religious Factor in American Politics*, ed. David C. Leege and Lyman A. Kellstedt. Armonk, NY: M. E. Sharpe.

Kellstedt, Lyman A., John C. Green, James L. Guth, and Corwin E. Smidt. 1994. "Religious Voting Blocs in the 1992 Election: The Year of the Evangelical?" *Sociology of Religion* 55: 307–26.

Kenny, Christopher B. 1992. "Political Participation and Effects from the Social Environment." *American Journal of Political Science* 39: 259–67.

Kertscher, Tom. 2003. "Becker Lays out Plan to Buff Up City's Image." *Milwaukee Journal Sentinel*, April 5: 7A.

"Key Findings from Nevada Exit Polls." 2000. *Las Vegas Review-Journal*, November 7.

Killackey, Brent. 2003. "REST Prepared for Residents from Kenosha." *Racine Journal Times*, October 5: 1B.

Kingdon, John W. 1995. *Agendas, Alternatives, and Public Policies*. 2nd ed. New York: HarperCollins.

Kirkbride, Rob. 2003. "Chamber Tries to Stack the Deck against a Casino." *Grand Rapids Press*, February 17.

Kitschelt, Herbert. 1986. "Political Opportunity Structures and Political Protest: Anti- Nuclear Movements in Four Countries." *British Journal of Political Science* 16: 57–85.

Klandermans, Bert. 2001. "Why Social Movements Come into Being and Why People Join Them." In *The Blackwell Companion to Sociology*, edited by Judith Blau. Malden, MA: Blackwell.

Knape, Chris. 2003a. "Casino Foes Place Businesses' Loss at $92 Million." *Grand Rapids Press*, February 18.

———. 2003b. "Lake Band Draws Full House of Casino Support." *Grand Rapids Press*, March 26.

———. 2003c. "Report: Casino Would Hit Kent Hardest." *Grand Rapids Press*, March 13.

———. 2004a. "'23 Is Enough' Ups the Ante." *Grand Rapids Press*, June 9.

———. 2004b. "Casino Gets Key Approval for Land." *Grand Rapids Press*, March 20.

Knight, Jennifer. 2002. "Forbuss Camp Blames Question 2 for Loss in Board of Regents Race." *Las Vegas Sun*, November 11.

Knuteson, John. 1996. "R.E.S.T. Provides a Home for the Homeless, with Your Help." *Racine Journal Times*, April 7: 8A.

Kohut, Andrew, John C. Green, Scott Keeter, and Robert C. Toth. 2000. *The Diminishing Divide: Religion's Changing Role in American Politics.* Washington, DC: Brookings Institution.

Kooiman, Jerry. 2003. Interview, Grand Rapids, March 31.

Kuipers, Sen. Wayne. 2003. Interview, Lansing, MI, March 27.

Laaker, Damon. 2003. Interviews, Omaha, NE.

Layman, Geoffrey. 2001. *The Great Divide: Religious and Cultural Conflict in American Party Politics.* New York: Columbia University Press.

Layman, Geoffrey C., and Thomas M. Carsey. 1998. "Why Do Party Activists Convert? An Analysis of Individual-Level Change on the Abortion Issue." *Political Research Quarterly* 51: 723–49.

Layman, Geoffrey C., and John C. Green. 2005. "Wars and Rumors of Wars: The Contexts of Cultural Conflict in American Political Behavior." *British Journal of Political Science* 36: 61–89.

Lazare, Daniel. 2001. "Cincinnati and the X-Factor." *Columbia Journalism Review,* May/June. http://archives.cjr.org/year/01/4/cincinnati.asp.

Leege, David C. 1988. "Catholics and the Civic Order: Parish Participation, Politics, and Civic Participation." *Review of Politics* 50: 704–31.

Leege, David C., Kenneth D. Wald, Brian S. Krueger, and Paul D. Mueller. 2002. *The Politics of Cultural Differences: Social Change and Voter Mobilization Strategies in the Post-New Deal Period.* Princeton: Princeton University Press.

Legislative Service Bureau. 2001. *Casino Gaming and the Role of the Michigan Legislature.* Research report, vol. 16, no. 1. Lansing, MI: Michigan Legislative Service Bureau.

Leighley, Jan E. 1990. "Social Interaction and Contextual Influences on Political Participation." *American Politics Quarterly* 18: 459–75.

———. 1996. "Group Membership and the Mobilization of Political Participation." *Journal of Politics* 58: 447–63.

Lienesch, Michael. 1982. "Right-Wing Religion: Christian Conservatism as a Political Movement." *Political Science Quarterly* 97: 403–25.

Lincoln, C. Eric, and Lawrence H. Mamiya. 1990. *The Black Church in the African-American Experience.* Durham, NC: Duke University Press.

Lipsky, Michael. 1968. "Protest As a Political Resource." *American Political Science Review* 62: 1144–58.

Lisotta, Christopher. 2004. "Enemies of the States." *Advocate,* October 26.

Livezey, Lowell W., ed. 2000. *Public Religion and Urban Transformation: Faith in the City.* New York: New York University Press.

Loftus, Jeni. 2001. "America's Liberalization in Attitudes toward Homosexuality, 1973–1998." *American Sociological Review* 66: 762–82.

Lowery, David, and Virginia Gray. 1995. "The Population Ecology of Gucci Gulch, or the Natural Regulation of Interest Group Numbers in the American States." *American Journal of Political Science* 39: 1–29.

Luke, Peter. 2002. "House OKs Another Casino." *Grand Rapids Press,* December 11.

MacDonald, Heather. 2001. "What Really Happened in Cincinnati." *City Journal* 11: 28–43.

Maisel, L. Sandy, and Ira N. Forman. 2001. *Jews in American Politics.* Lanham, MD: Rowman & Littlefield.

Marty, Martin E. 2000. *Politics, Religion, and the Common Good: Advancing a Distinctly American Conversation about Religion's Role in Our Shared Life.* San Francisco, CA: Jossey-Bass.

Maurer, Dave. 2003. "United Way Task Force Looks at Homelessness." *Racine Journal Times,* March 2: 2D.

May, Heather. 2002a. "City Not Obligated on Plaza." *Salt Lake Tribune,* December 23: D1.

———. 2002b. "Rocky Walked a Fine Line in Working Out Plaza Deal." *Deseret News,* December 20: A1.

McAdam, Doug. 1982. *Political Process and the Development of Black Insurgency.* Chicago: University of Chicago Press.

McAdam, Doug, John D. McCarthy, and Mayer N. Zald. 1996. *Comparative Perspectives on Social Movements: Political Opportunities, Mobilizing Structures, and Cultural Framings.* New York: Cambridge University Press.

McCarthy, John D. 1987. "Pro-Life and Pro-Choice Mobilization: Infrastructure Deficits and New Technologies." In *Social Movements in an Organizational Society,* ed. Mayer N. Zald and John D. McCarthy. Somerset, NJ: Transaction.

McCarthy, John D., and Mayer N. Zald. 1977. "Resource Mobilization and Social Movements: A Partial Theory." *American Journal of Sociology* 82: 1212–41.

McKenzie, Brian D. 2004. "Religious Social Networks, Indirect Mobilization, and African-American Political Participation." *Political Research Quarterly* 57: 621–32.

McRoberts, Omar. 2003. *Streets of Glory: Church and Community in a Black Urban Neighborhood.* Chicago: University of Chicago Press.

Mead, Lawrence M. 2005. *Government Matters: Welfare Reform in Wisconsin.* Princeton: Princeton University Press.

Meehan, Chris. 2003. "Ministers Speak Out against Casino." *Grand Rapids Press,* January 13.

Meier, Kenneth J. 1994. *The Politics of Sin.* Armonk, NY: M. E. Sharpe.

Melmer, David. 2001. "Gun Lake Pact on Hold." *Indian Country,* July 25.

Mero, Robin. 2001a. "Survey: Residents Want More Options." *Morning News of Northwest Arkansas,* January 5: A2.

———. 2001b. "Tension Mounts in Siloam Springs." *Morning News of Northwest Arkansas,* August 7: A1.

Meyer, David S., and Debra C. Minkoff. 2004. "Conceptualizing Political Opportunity." *Social Forces* 82: 1457–92.

Michaud, Ann. 2001. "Cincinnati Cleans Up, Amid Many Black-White Questions." *Boston Globe,* April 29: A6.

Mikita, Carole. 2003. "Evangelical Ministers Rally in Support of LDS Community." *KSL TV News,* October 21. http://tv.ksl.com/index.php?nid=5&sid=54312.

Milicia, Joe. 2001. "Cincinnati Continues Curfew to Prevent Further Riots." *Associated Press,* April 13.

Miller, Arthur, Patricia Gurin, Gerald Gurin, and Oksana Malanchuk. 1981. "Group Consciousness and Political Participation." *American Journal of Political Science* 25: 494–511.

Miller, Joseph Q. 1957. *Christian Unity: Its Relevance to the Community.* Strasburg, VA: Shenandoah Publishing.

Miller, Robert M. 1957. "The Protestant Churches and Lynching, 1919–1939." *Journal of Negro History* 42: 118–31.

Moe, Terry. 1980. "A Calculus of Group Membership." *American Journal of Political Science* 24: 593–632.

Moen, Matthew C. 1992. *The Transformation of the Christian Right.* Tuscaloosa: University of Alabama Press.

———. 1994. "From Revolution to Evolution: The Changing Nature of the Christian Right." *Sociology of Religion* 55: 345–57.

Morris, Aldon D. 1984. *The Origins of the Civil Rights Movement: Black Communities Organizing for Change.* New York: Free Press.

Morris, Aldon D., and Carol McClurg Mueller, eds. 1992. *Frontiers in Social Movement Theory.* New Haven: Yale University Press.

Morris, Barbara. 1998. "Regional Patterns of Interest Groups in the American States." Paper presented at the annual meeting of the Midwest Political Science Association, Chicago.

Morrison, Jane Ann. 2002a. "Gay Rights Activists Let Pledge Signers Slide." *Las Vegas Review-Journal*, September 10.

———. 2002b. "Political Notebook: Question 2 Factions Put Focus on Hospital Visitation Rights." *Las Vegas Review-Journal*, October 28.

Mueller, Carol McClurg. 1992. "Building Social Movement Theory." In *Frontiers of Social Movement Theory*, edited by Aldon Morris and Carol McClurg Mueller. New Haven: Yale University Press.

National Conference of State Legislatures. 2004. "Supermajority Vote Requirements." http://www.ncsl.org/programs/legman/SupermajVote.htm.

National Underground Railroad Freedom Center. 2005. "Glimmer of Hope in Cincinnati Attitudes on Race? Freedom Center Sponsored Survey Suggests Younger Blacks and Whites More Willing to Talk About Race Divide." http://www.freedomcenter.org/index.cfm?fuseaction=home.viewPage&page_id=E3E231FA-D0B7-88DE-94038CC2B785056E.

Neff, Erin. 2002a. "Political Notebook: Early Voting Expected to Draw Half the Electorate." *Las Vegas Sun*, November 1.

———. 2002b. "Political Notebook: Rumors Fly After One Public Poll Withheld." *Las Vegas Sun*, October 18.

———. 2002c. "Vandals Strike Signs Again." *Las Vegas Sun*, October 1.

Neiheisel, Jacob R., Paul A. Djupe, Anand E. Sokhey, and Franklyn C. Niles. 2005. "Quick, Bar the Gates! Issue 1 and Religious Communities." Paper presented at the annual meeting of the American Political Science Association, Washington, DC.

Nevada Secretary of State. 2004a. "Coalition for the Protection of Marriage Contributions, Expenses, and Financial Disclosures, Period 1 Summary." http://sos.state.nv.us.

———. 2004b. "Coalition for the Protection of Marriage Contributions, Expenses, and Financial Disclosures, Period 2 Summary." http://sos.state.nv.us/000Contributions.

———. 2004c. "Equal Rights Nevada Contributions, Expenses, and Financial Disclosures, Period 1 and 2 Summary." http://sos.state.nv.us.

———. 2004d. "Equal Rights Nevada Contributions, Expenses, and Financial Disclosures, Period 3 Summary." http://sos.state.nv.us.

Nevada Secretary of State, Elections Department. 2000. "Voter Turnout Official 2000 General Election Results." http://sos.state.nv.us.

———. 2004. "Voter Turnout Official 2004 General Election Results." http://sos.state.nv.us.

Niles, Franklyn C. 2003. "Piety and Politics: The Christian Right and American Politics in the Twentieth Century and Beyond." In *Political Perspectives: Essays on Government and Politics*, ed. Kenneth L. Manning and John Fobanjong. Dubuque, IA: Kendall/Hunt.

Niles, Franklyn C., and Paul A. Djupe. 2006. "The Public Presence of Religious Interests: Ministerial Organizations in American Politics." Paper presented at the annual meeting of the Western Political Science Association, Albuquerque.

"No Casino in Allegan County." 2002. *Grand Rapids Press*, December 9.

Noll, Mark A. 1990. *Religion and American Politics: From the Colonial Period to the 1980s*. New York: Oxford University Press.

Nownes, Anthony J., and Patricia Freeman. 1998. "Interest Group Activity in the States." *Journal of Politics* 60: 86–112.

Oldfield, Duane M. 1996. *The Right and the Righteous: The Christian Right Confronts the Republican Party*. Lanham, MD: Rowman & Littlefield.

Oldmixon, Elizabeth Anne. 2005. *Uncompromising Positions: God, Sex, and the U.S. House of Representatives*. Washington, DC: Georgetown University Press.

Olson, Amy. 2003. "Smith Ousted in Mayoral Primary." *Racine Journal Times*, February 18: 1A.

Olson, Laura R. 2000. *Filled with Spirit and Power: Protestant Clergy in Politics*. Albany: State University of New York Press.

———. 2007. "Whither the Religious Left? Religiopolitical Progressivism in Twenty-first Century America." In *From Pews to Polling Places: Political Mobilization in the American Religious Mosaic*, edited by J. Matthew Wilson. Washington, DC: Georgetown University Press.

Olson, Laura R., and Sue E. S. Crawford. 2001. "Clergy in Politics: Political Choices and Consequences." In *Christian Clergy in Politics*, edited by Sue E. S. Crawford and Laura R. Olson. Baltimore: Johns Hopkins University Press.

Olson, Laura R., Sue E. S. Crawford, and Melissa M. Deckman. 2005. *Women with a Mission: Religion, Gender, and the Politics of Women Clergy*. Tuscaloosa: University of Alabama Press.

Olson, Laura R., Karen V. Guth, and James L. Guth. 2003. "The Lotto and the Lord: Religious Influences on the Adoption of a Lottery in South Carolina." *Sociology of Religion* 64: 87–110.

Olson, Mancur Jr. 1965. *The Logic of Collective Action.* Cambridge, MA: Harvard University Press.

Ostling, Richard N., and Joan K. Ostling. 1999. *Mormon America: The Power and the Promise.* San Francisco: Harper.

Packer, Adrienne. 2000. "Maxfield Edges Tarkanian." *Las Vegas Sun,* November 8.

Padgett, Beth. 2003. "County Missed Opportunity on MLK Day." *Greenville News,* January 26.

Parker, Kathleen. 2004. "Missourians Turn Out to Vow 'I Don't'." *Las Vegas Review Journal,* August 20.

Parks, Wendy. 1999. "Emergency Shelter Program Needs Community's Support." *Racine Journal Times,* September 4: 1B.

Penning, James M. 2005. "A War on the Home Front? The Christian Right in the 2004 Michigan Elections." Paper presented at the Annual Meeting of the Southern Political Science Association, New Orleans.

Pew Forum on Religion and Public Life. 2004. "How the Faithful Voted." http://pewforum.org/events/index.php?EventID=64.

Pfau, Christopher. 1998a. "Homeless Shelter Sites Ready for Cold Weather." *Racine Journal Times,* September 17: 1C.

———. 1998b. "R.E.S.T. Leader Never Takes Break." *Racine Journal Times,* June 29: 1A.

———. 1998c. "State's Welfare Change May Push More to Racine Shelters." *Racine Journal Times,* August 24: 1B.

———. 1998d. "Task Force Leader Seeks Permanent Homeless Shelter Funds." *Racine Journal Times,* June 29: 1A.

Pignanelli, Frank. 2005. Telephone interview, November 21.

Piven, Frances Fox, and Richard A. Cloward. 1977. *Poor People's Movements: Why They Succeed, How They Fail.* New York: Pantheon.

"Plan for Single-Site Homeless Shelter Delayed Until Spring." 2004. *Racine Journal Times,* November 30: 1B.

Pope, Liston. 1942. *Millhands and Preachers: A Study of Gastonia.* New Haven: Yale University Press.

Pratt, Timothy. 2002. "Ads May Add Something in Translation." *Las Vegas Sun,* October 31.

Prendergast, Jane. 2002. "Cincinnati's Riots One Year Later: Violence Up, Arrests Down." *Cincinnati Enquirer*, April 7. http://www.enquirer.com/oneyearlater/.

Price, Matthew J. 2000. "Place, Race, and History: The Social Mission of Downtown Churches." In *Public Religion and Urban Transformation: Faith in the City*, ed. Lowell W. Livezey. New York: New York University Press.

Putnam, Robert D. 2000. *Bowling Alone: The Collapse and Revival of American Community*. New York: Simon & Schuster.

Quinley, Harold E. 1974. *The Prophetic Clergy: Social Activism among Protestant Ministers*. New York: Wiley.

"Racine, Wisconsin." 2005. http://en.wikipedia.org/wiki/Racine,_Wisconsin.

"Racine, Wisconsin: The Belle City of the Lakes." 2005. http://racine.wi.net.

Ralston, Jon. 2000. *The Anointed One: An Inside Look at Nevada Politics*. Las Vegas: Huntington Press.

Reed, Ralph. 1994. *Politically Incorrect*. Dallas: Word.

Reens, Nate. 2001. "Casino Compact Gains Momentum." *Holland Sentinel*, June 29.

Reese, Laura A. and Ronald E. Brown. 1995. "The Effects of Religious Messages on Racial Identity and System Blame among African Americans." *Journal of Politics* 57: 24–43.

"REST Shelter News Marks Beginning, Not an End." 2005. *Racine Journal Times*, April 20: 6A.

Richardson-Moore, Deb. 2003a. "Black Churches Mobilize." *Greenville News*, January 28.

———. 2003b. "Clergy Mixed on King Holiday." *Greenville News*, February 10.

———. 2003c. "White Clergy Circulate Petition for King Holiday." *Greenville News*, February 26.

Riley, Brendan. 2002. "State's Catholic Bishops Throw Support behind Question 2." *Las Vegas Review-Journal*, October 3.

Roebuck, Lucas. 2003. "Benton County's Growth Minute Compared to I-540 Corridor." *Siloam Springs Herald Leader*, July 30.

Roelofs, Ted. 2003. "Casino Issue Is Not Granholm's Deal." *Grand Rapids Press*, January 1.

———. 2004a. "Casino Foes Say Hefty Fine Should Serve as Warning." *Grand Rapids Press*, June 18.

———. 2004b. "Public Vote Eased Casino Decision." *Grand Rapids Press*, December 10.

Rogers, Ben. 2000. "Gay Marriage Issue Divides Nevada." *Las Vegas Review-Journal*, July 17.

Roozen, David A., William McKinney, and Jackson W. Carroll. 1984. *Varieties of Religious Presence*. New York: Pilgrim.

Rosenstone, Steven J., and John Mark Hansen. 1993. *Mobilization, Participation, and Democracy in America*. New York: Macmillan.

Rothenberg, Lawrence. 1988. "Organizational Maintenance and the Retention Decision in Groups." *American Political Science Review* 82: 1129–52.

Rowland, Darrel. 2004. "Gay Marriage Ban; Issue 1 is Winning in Landslide." *Columbus Dispatch*, October 4: 1A.

Rozell, Mark J., and Clyde Wilcox, eds. 1995. *God at the Grass Roots 1994*. Lanham, MD: Rowman & Littlefield.

———, eds. 1997. *God at the Grass Roots 1996*. Lanham, MD: Rowman & Littlefield.

Ryan, Cy. 2000. "Catholics Told to Vote Their Conscience on Marriage Ban." *Las Vegas Review-Journal*, October 17.

Salisbury, Robert H. 1969. "An Exchange Theory of Interest Groups." *Midwest Journal of Political Science* 13: 1–32.

———. 1990. "The Paradox of Interests in Washington, DC: More Groups, Less Clout." In *The New American Political System*, ed. Anthony King. 2nd ed. Washington, DC: American Enterprise Institute.

Salt Lake City Council Public Hearings. 2002. Main Street Plaza Hearings. Ten hours. Videorecording.

Saxton, Nancy. 2005. Telephone interview, November 21.

"SC Johnson: A Family Company." 2005. http://www.scjohnson.com.

Schattschneider, E. E. 1942. *Party Government*. New York: Holt, Rinehart & Winston.

Schlozman, Kay Lehman, and John T. Tierney. 1983. "More of the Same: Washington Pressure Activity in a Decade of Change." *Journal of Politics* 45: 351–77.

———. 1986. *Organized Interests and American Democracy*. New York: Harper & Row.

Sebelius, Steve. 2002. "Big Guns Join the Fight Against Bigotry." *Las Vegas Review-Journal*, October 13.

Sells, Jeffrey E., ed. 2005. *God and Country: Politics in Utah*. Salt Lake City: Signature Books.

Shagonaby, John. 2001. "Gun Lake Band of Pottawatomie Indians Announces Casino Location and Economic Impacts on Allegan County, Michigan." Gun Lake Band press release, June 5.

Shapiro, Walter. 2004. "Presidential Election May Have Hinged on One Issue: Issue 1." *USA Today*, November 5: 6A.

Sharp, Elaine B. 1986. *Citizen Demand-Making in the Urban Context*. Tuscaloosa: University of Alabama Press.

———, ed. 1999. *Culture Wars in Local Politics*. Lawrence: University Press of Kansas.

Sheen, Fulton. 2003. Interview, Lansing, MI, March 27.

Sides, Phyllis. 2004. "HALO Hopes to Unite Homeless Groups." *Racine Journal Times*, October 5: 1A.

———. 2005a. "Grant Will Aid Homeless Shelter Project." *Racine Journal Times*, August 6: 1A.

———. 2005b. "HALO's First Goal: Raising Funds." *Racine Journal Times*, April 3: 15A.

Siegel, Jim. 2004. "Media Blitz Begins for Ohio's Issue 1." *Cincinnati Enquirer*, October 26.

Siloam Springs Area Christian Ministerial Fellowship Constitution. 2000.

Siloam Springs Area Ministerial Association Constitution. 1975.

Smidt, Corwin E., and James M. Penning, eds. 1997. *Sojourners in the Wilderness: The Christian Right in Comparative Perspective*. Lanham, MD: Rowman & Littlefield.

Smidt, Corwin E., and James M. Penning. 2004. "Stepping off the Bully Pulpit? The Changing Politics of American Clergy." Paper delivered at the Symposium on Religion and Politics, Calvin College.

Smith, Christian. 1996. *Resisting Reagan: The U.S.-Central America Peace Movement*. Chicago: University of Chicago Press.

Smith, Jane I. 1999. *Islam in America*. New York: Columbia University Press.

Smith, R. Drew, and Fredrick C. Harris, eds. 2005. *Black Churches and Local Politics: Clergy Influence, Organizational Partnerships, and Civic Empowerment*. Lanham, MD: Rowman & Littlefield.

Snedeker, Lisa. 2000. "Coalition Says 'Protection of Marriage' Ballot Question Discriminatory." *Las Vegas Review-Journal*, September 11.

Snow, David A. 2004. "Framing Processes, Ideology, and Discursive Fields." In *The Blackwell Companion to Social Movements*, edited by

David A. Snow, Sarah A. Soule, and Hanspeter Kriesi. Malden, MA: Blackwell.

Snow, David A., and Robert D. Benford. 1992. "Master Frames and Cycles of Protest." In *Frontiers of Social Movement Theory*, edited by Aldon D. Morris and Carol McClurg Mueller. New Haven: Yale University Press.

Snow, David A., Louis A. Zurcher, and Sheldon Ekland-Olson. 1980. "Social Networks and Social Movements: A Microstructural Approach to Differential Recruitment." *American Sociological Review* 45: 787–801.

Snyder, Brady. 2002a. "Huntsman Tries to Mediate and is Still Hopeful." *Deseret News*, December 6: A1.

———. 2002b. "No Main Street Plaza Resolution." *Deseret News*, December 11: A1.

Spencer, Carrie. 2004. "Experts: Issue One Impact to be Felt More in Homes than Workplaces." *Associated Press*, November 4.

"Spotlight on the Cincinnati Police." 2006. The Public Library of Cincinnati and Hamilton County. http://www.cincinnatilibrary.org/features/police.asp.

Stark, Rodney, Bruce D. Foster, Charles Y. Glock, and Harold E. Quinley. 1971. *Wayward Shepherds: Prejudice and the Protestant Clergy*. New York: Harper & Row.

Steensland, Brian. 2002. "The Hydra and the Swords: Social Welfare and Mainline Advocacy, 1964–2000." In *The Quiet Hand of God: Faith-Based Activism and the Public Role of Mainline Protestantism*, edited by Robert Wuthnow and John H. Evans. Berkeley: University of California Press.

Steensland, Brian, Jerry Z. Park, Mark D. Regnerus, Lynn D. Robinson, W. Bradford Wilcox, and Robert D. Woodberry. 2000. "The Measure of American Religion: Toward Improving the State of the Art." *Social Forces* 79: 291–318.

Steggart, Frank X. 1975. *Community Action Groups and City Governments: Perspectives from Ten American Cities*. Cambridge, MA: Ballinger.

Steinkraus, David. 2004. "REST Finds a Place to Call Home." *Racine Journal Times*, April 19: 1A.

Sterling, Amy. 1997. "Frigid Weather Brings Crowds to Area Shelters." *Racine Journal Times*, October 22: 1A.

Stolarz, Christina. 2001. "Allegan County Indian Casino Would Be State's 18th." *Capital News Service*, February 23.

Szobody, Ben. 2004. "3 GOP Newcomers Elected To Council." *Greenville News,* November 3.

———. 2005. "King Day Quietly Moves a Step Closer in County." *Greenville News,* February 1.

Szobody, Ben, and Anna B. Brutzman, 2005. "King Holiday Passes." *Greenville News,* February 2.

Tarrow, Sidney. 1996. "States and Opportunities: The Political Structuring of Social Movements." In *Comparative Perspectives on Social Movements,* edited by Doug McAdam, John D. McCarthy, and Mayer N. Zald. New York: Cambridge University Press.

———. 1998. *Power in Movement,* 2nd ed. New York: Cambridge University Press.

Tatalovich, Raymond, and Byron Daynes. 1988. "What Is Social Regulatory Policy?" In *Social Regulatory Policy: Moral Controversies in American Politics,* edited by Ray Tatalovich. Boulder: Westview.

Taylor, Marilyn. 2003. *Public Policy in the Community: Public Policy and Politics.* New York: Palgrave Macmillan.

Taylor, Verta, and Nancy Whittier. 1992. "Collective Identity in Social Movement Communities: Lesbian Feminist Mobilization." In *Frontiers of Social Movement Theory,* edited by Aldon D. Morris and Carol McClurg Mueller. New Haven: Yale University Press.

Tenuta, Marci Laehr. 2003. "Helping Hands." *Racine Journal Times,* November 22: 1C.

Theis, Sandy. 2004a. "Group Wants Constitutional Ban on Gay Marriage." *Cleveland Plain Dealer,* October 24: T51.

———. 2004b. "Issue 1 TV Ads Cite Harm to Seniors; Amendment's Backers Rebut Claim." *Cleveland Plain Dealer,* October 26: B4.

Thomas, Alice. 2004. "Issue 1 Approval Saddens Gays; Some Feeling Rejected, Insulted by State Ban on Same-Sex Marriage." *Columbus Dispatch,* November 6: 1B.

Thomas, Clive S., and Ronald J. Hrebenar. 1994. "Interest Group Power in State Politics." *Comparative State Politics* 15: 7–18.

———. 1999. "A Reappraisal of Interest Group Power in the American States." Paper presented at the Annual Meeting of the American Political Science Association, Atlanta.

Thomas, Ron. 2003. Interview, Racine, Wisconsin, July 29.

Thompson, Tommy G. 1996. *Power to the People: An American State at Work.* New York: HarperCollins.

Thuesen, Peter J. 2002. "The Logic of Mainline Churchliness: Historical Background since the Reformation." In *The Quiet Hand of God:*

Faith-Based Activism and the Public Role of Mainline Protestantism, edited by Robert Wuthnow and John H. Evans. Berkeley: University of California Press.

Tinsley, Jesse. 2004. "Ministers Raise Voices in Support of Issue 1." *Cleveland Plain Dealer,* October 12: B1.

"Tribe Seeks Deputy Coverage for Proposed Casino." 2002. *Holland Sentinel,* May 23.

Truman, David. 1951. *The Governmental Process.* New York: Alfred A. Knopf.

Tunison, John. 2002. "Lawmakers Hope Engler Leaves Without Signing Casino Pact." *Grand Rapids Press,* December 29.

Tunkieicz, Jennie. 2001. "Are Poor Better Off Under W-2?" *Milwaukee Journal Sentinel,* April 15: 5A.

———. 2004a. "Permanent Homeless Shelter in the Works." *Milwaukee Journal Sentinel,* April 24: 6B.

———. 2004b. "Racine Homeless Groups Unite under HALO." *Milwaukee Journal Sentinel,* September 9: 4B.

———. 2005a. "$2 Million Raised for Racine Shelter." *Milwaukee Journal Sentinel,* September 28: 5B.

———. 2005b. "276 Homeless People Recorded in Racine County One-Day Census." *Milwaukee Journal Sentinel,* March 23: 3B.

———. 2005c. "$750,000 Grant Will Help Clear Brownfields for Shelter." *Milwaukee Journal Sentinel,* August 5: 4B.

———. 2005d. "Area Shelters Taking in Record Numbers." *Racine Journal Times,* March 26: 2B.

———. 2005e. "Judge Counts Homeless Voters; Challenger May Appeal." *Milwaukee Journal Sentinel,* July 16: 3B.

Turner, Ralph. 1970. "Determinants of Social Movement Strategy." In *Human Nature and Collective Behavior: Papers in Honor of Herbert Blumer,* edited by Tamotsu Shibutani. Englewood Cliffs, NJ: Prentice Hall.

United States Census Bureau. 2001. "Nation's Household Income Stable in 2000, Poverty Rate Virtually Equals Record Low." http://www.census.gov/Press-Release/www/2001/cb01-158.html.

———. 2003. *Statistical Abstract of the United States.* Washington, DC: United States Department of Commerce.

———. 2005. "State and County Quick Facts: Franklin County, Ohio." http://quickfacts.census.gov/qfd/states/ 39/39049.html.

Utah Colleges Exit Poll [data]. 2002. Center for the Study of Elections and Democracy, Brigham Young University, Provo, UT [producer and distributor].

———. 2003. Center for the Study of Elections and Democracy, Brigham Young University, Provo, UT [producer and distributor].

Verba, Sidney, Kay Lehman Schlozman, and Henry E. Brady. 1995. *Voice and Equality: Civic Voluntarism in American Politics.* Cambridge, MA: Harvard University Press.

Verter, Bradford. 2002. "Furthering the Freedom Struggle: Racial Justice Activism in the Mainline Churches since the Civil Rights Era." In *The Quiet Hand of God: Faith-Based Activism and the Public Role of Mainline Protestantism*, edited by Robert Wuthnow and John H. Evans. Berkeley: University of California Press.

Vogel, Ed. 2000. "Survey Shows Nevadans Oppose Same-Sex Unions." *Las Vegas Review-Journal*, June 17.

Voorhees, Harold. 2003. Telephone interview, March 9.

Wagner, Angie. 2000. "Buchanan Says Opponents Ignoring Moral Issues." *Las Vegas Review-Journal,* October 27.

Wald, Kenneth D. 2003. *Religion and Politics in the United States,* 4th ed. Lanham, MD: Rowman & Littlefield.

Wald, Kenneth D., James W. Button, and Barbara A. Rienzo. 2001. "Morality Politics vs. Political Economy: The Place of School-based Health Centers." *Social Science Quarterly* 82: 221–34.

Wald, Kenneth D., Dennis E. Owen, and Samuel S. Hill. 1988. "Churches as Political Communities." *American Political Science Review* 82: 531–48.

———. 1989. "Evangelical Politics and Status Issues." *Journal for the Scientific Study of Religion* 28: 1–16.

———. 1990. "Political Cohesion in Churches." *Journal of Politics* 52: 197–215.

Wald, Kenneth D., Adam L. Silverman, and Kevin S. Fridy. 2005. "Making Sense of Religion in Political Life." *Annual Review of Political Science* 8: 121–43.

Waldkoening, Gilson A.C., and William O. Avery. 1999. *Cooperating Congregations: Portraits of Mission Strategies.* Indianapolis: Alban Institute.

Walker, Jack. 1991. *Mobilizing Interest Groups in America.* Ann Arbor: University of Michigan Press.

Walsh, Katherine Cramer. 2004. *Talking About Politics: Informal Groups and Social Identity in American Life*. Chicago: University of Chicago Press.

Walsh, Rebecca. 1999. "Suit Crashes LDS Block Party." *Salt Lake Tribune,* November 17: C1.

Washington, Vanita. 2003. "Clinton Council Approves King Holiday." *Greenville News*, March 26.

Wells, Garrison. 2002a. "Casino Trio Could Hit Jackpot." *Grand Rapids Press*, December 22.

———. 2002b. "Suit Accuses Tribal Gaming Backers of Subversion." *Grand Rapids Press*, September 16.

———. 2002c. "Tribe Details Allegan County Casino Plans." *Gazette News Service*, November 29.

———. 2003. "GR Group Challenges Casino Evaluation." *Grand Rapids Press*, February 14.

Whaley, Sean. 2000a. "Likely Voters Asked: Measures Supported." *Las Vegas Review-Journal*, September 18.

———. 2000b. "Nevada Voters: Questions Unlikely to Influence Races." *Las Vegas Review-Journal,* October 30.

———. 2000c. "Poll: Questions Likely to Pass." *Las Vegas Review-Journal,* November 2.

Whaley, Sean, and Ed Vogel. 2002. "Poll: Minds Made Up on Two Ballot Measures." *Las Vegas Review-Journal,* October 28.

"Why We Are Against Issue 1." 2004. *Cincinnati Enquirer,* October 17. http://www.enquirer.com/editions/2004/10/17/editorial_ed2a.html.

Wielhouwer, Peter W. 2000. "Releasing the Fetters: Parties and the Mobilization of the African-American Electorate." *Journal of Politics* 62: 206–22.

Wilcox, Clyde. 1989. "Evangelicals and the Moral Majority." *Journal for the Scientific Study of Religion* 28: 400–14.

———. 1992. *God's Warriors: The Christian Right in 20th Century America.* Baltimore: Johns Hopkins University Press.

Wilcox, Clyde, Ted G. Jelen, and David C. Leege. 1993. "Religious Group Identifications: Toward a Cognitive Theory of Religious Mobilization." In *Rediscovering the Religious Factor,* edited by David C. Leege and Lyman A. Kellstedt. Armonk, NY: M. E. Sharpe.

Wilcox, Clyde, and Barbara Norrander. 2002. "Of Moods and Morals: The Dynamics of Opinion on Abortion and Gay Rights." In *Under-*

standing Public Opinion, edited by Barbara Norrander and Clyde Wilcox. 2nd ed. Washington, DC: CQ Press.

Wilcox, Clyde, and Robin Wolpert. 2000. "Gay Rights in the Public Sphere: Public Opinion on Gay and Lesbian Equality." In *The Politics of Gay Rights*, ed. Craig A. Rimmerman, Kenneth D. Wald, and Clyde Wilcox. Chicago: University of Chicago Press.

Wildavsky, Aaron. 1987. "Choosing Preferences by Constructing Institutions: A Cultural Theory of Preference Formation." *American Political Science Review* 81: 3–21.

Williams, Rhys H., ed. 1997. *Cultural Wars in American Politics: Critical Reviews of a Popular Myth*. Hawthorne, NY: De Gruyter.

———. 2000. "Introduction: Promise Keepers, a Comment on Religion and Social Movements." *Sociology of Religion* 61: 1–10.

Willis, Stacy J. 1998. "Mormons Knit LV's Fabric." *Las Vegas Sun*, October 7.

———. 2000a. "Protestants Labor with Stance on Question 2." *Las Vegas Sun*, October 30.

———. 2000b. "Pushing Morals of Marriage Issue." *Las Vegas Sun*, May 8.

———. 2000c. "Question 2 Opponents Appeal to Young Voters." *Las Vegas Sun*. October 30.

Winter, Gibson. 1966. *The Sub-Urban Captivity of the Churches: An Analysis of Protestant Responsibility in the Expanding Metropolis*. New York: Macmillan.

Winternitz, Felix. 2001. "Gallery of Emotions; 'Civil Unrest in Cincinnati' Exhibit Seeks to Turn Hatred into Understanding." *Dayton Daily News*, July 21.

"With Friends Like These," 2002. *Salt Lake Tribune*, December 21: A19.

Witte, John. 2005. *Religion and the American Constitutional Experiment*, 2nd ed. Boulder, CO: Westview.

Wolcott, Roger T. 1982. "The Church and Social Action: Steelworkers and Bishops in Youngstown." *Journal for the Scientific Study of Religion* 21: 71–79.

Wood, Richard L. 2002. *Faith in Action: Religion, Race, and Democratic Organizing in America*. Chicago: University of Chicago Press.

Woods, Dennis James. 2005. *Love and Charity: The Life and Story of Louise Hunter and the Love and Charity Homeless Shelter*. Baltimore: Publish America.

Wuthnow, Robert. 1988. *The Restructuring of American Religion: Society and Faith since World War II.* Princeton: Princeton University Press.

———, ed. 1994. *"I Come Away Stronger": How Small Groups Are Shaping American Religion.* Grand Rapids: Eerdmans.

———. 2000. "The Moral Minority." *American Prospect* 11, May 22.

———. 2003. "Can Religion Revitalize Civic Society? An Institutional Perspective." In *Religion as Social Capital: Producing the Common Good*, ed. Corwin E. Smidt. Waco, TX: Baylor University Press.

———. 2004. *Saving America? Faith-Based Services and the Future of Civil Society.* Princeton: Princeton University Press.

Wuthnow, Robert, and John H. Evans, eds. 2002. *The Quiet Hand of God: Faith-based Activism and the Public Role of Mainline Protestantism.* Berkeley: University of California Press.

Young, Gwendolyn. 2003. "MLK Holiday Issue Concerns Business Leaders." *Greenville News*, February 17.

Zacher, Jason. 2003a. "Black Leaders Say No Compromise." *Greenville News*, March 29.

———. 2003b. "Business Leaders Endorse King Holiday." *Greenville News*, April 1.

———. 2003c. "Council Meeting Calm Under Tight Security." *Greenville News*, March 19.

Zacher, Jason, and Ron Barnett. 2003a. "Council Recommends County Employees Choose Paid Holidays." *Greenville News*, April 2.

———. 2003b. "County Council Won't Revisit King Day." *Greenville News*, April 16.

———. 2003c. "Tensions Rise Over King Holiday." *Greenville News*, March 5.

Zajac, Andrew and Tim Jones. 2004. "Heavy Turnout Aided GOP in Ohio." *Chicago Tribune*, November 3. http:www.chicagotribune.com/news/specials/elections/chi- 041103ohio,1,4564747.story?

Zald, Mayer N., and Roberta Ash-Garner. 1987. "Social Movement Organizations: Growth, Decay, and Change." In *Social Movements in an Organizational Society*, ed. Mayer N. Zald and John D. McCarthy. Somerset, NJ: Transaction.

Zald, Mayer N., and John D. McCarthy. 1979. *The Dynamics of Social Movements: Resource Mobilization, Social Control, and Tactics.* Cambridge, MA: Winthrop.

———. 1987. "Religious Groups as Crucibles of Social Movements." In *Social Movements in an Organizational Society*, edited by Mayer N. Zald and John D. McCarthy. Somerset, NJ: Transaction.

Zaller, John R. 1989. "Bringing Converse Back In: Modeling Information Flows in Political Campaigns." In *Political Analysis*, edited by James A. Stimson, vol. 1. Ann Arbor: University of Michigan Press.

———. 1992. *The Nature and Origins of Mass Opinion*. New York: Cambridge University Press.

About the Contributors

MICHAEL W. BOWERS is vice provost for academic affairs and professor of political science at the University of Nevada, Las Vegas. He is author of *The Sagebrush State: Nevada's History, Government, and Politics* (University of Nevada Press, 2006), now in its third edition, and *The Nevada State Constitution: A Reference Guide* (Greenwood, 1993).

JOSHUA COPELAND is a recent graduate of Furman University.

SUE E. S. CRAWFORD is associate professor of political science at Creighton University. She is coauthor of *Women with a Mission: Religion, Gender, and the Politics of Women Clergy* (University of Alabama Press, 2005) and coeditor of *Christian Clergy in American Politics* (The Johns Hopkins University Press, 2001).

DAVID F. DAMORE is assistant professor of political science at the University of Nevada, Las Vegas. He is an expert on public opinion and congressional politics.

PAUL A. DJUPE is associate professor of political science at Denison University. He is coauthor of *The Prophetic Pulpit: Clergy, Churches, and Community in American Politics* (Rowman & Littlefield, 2003) and *Religious Institutions and Minor Parties in the United States* (Praeger, 1999), and coeditor of *The Encyclopedia of American Religion and Politics* (Facts on File, 2003).

JAMES L. GUTH is William R. Kenan Jr. Professor of Political Science at Furman University. He is coauthor of *The Bully Pulpit: The Politics of Protestant Clergy* (University Press of Kansas, 1997), *Religion and the Culture Wars: Dispatches from the Front* (Rowman & Littlefield, 1996), and *The Bible and the Ballot Box: Religion and Politics in the 1988 Elections* (Westview, 1991).

TED G. JELEN is professor of political science at the University of Nevada, Las Vegas. Recent books include (as coauthor) *A Wall of Separation? Debating the Public Role of Religion* (Rowman & Littlefield 1998), (as editor) *Sacred Markets, Sacred Canopies: Essays on Religious Markets and Religious Pluralism* (Rowman & Littlefield, 2002), and (as coeditor) *Religion and Politics in Comparative Perspective: The One, the Few, and the Many* (Cambridge University Press, 2002).

LYMAN A. KELLSTEDT is professor of political science emeritus at Wheaton College. He is coauthor of *The Bully Pulpit: The Politics of Protestant Clergy* (University Press of Kansas, 1997) and *Religion and the Culture Wars: Dispatches from the Front* (Rowman & Littlefield, 1996), and coeditor of *Rediscovering the Religious Factor in American Politics* (M. E. Sharpe, 1993).

J. QUIN MONSON is assistant professor of political science and assistant director of the Center for the Study of Elections and Democracy at Brigham Young University. He is coeditor of *Dancing Without Partners: How Candidates, Parties, and Interest Groups Interact in the Presidential Campaign* (Rowman & Littlefield, 2006) and *Electing Congress: New Rules for an Old Game* (Prentice Hall, 2006).

JACOB NEIHEISEL is an undergraduate student at Denison University.

FRANKLYN C. NILES is associate professor of political science at John Brown University. An expert on American political behavior, elections, political parties, religion and politics, his work has been published in the *Journal for the Scientific Study of Religion* and *Political Perspectives: Essays on Government and Politics* (Kendall/Hunt, 2005).

KARA L. NORMAN is a recent graduate of Brigham Young University.

LAURA R. OLSON is professor of political science at Clemson University. Recent books include (as coauthor) *Women with a Mission: Religion, Gender, and the Politics of Women Clergy* (University of Alabama Press, 2005) and *Religion and Politics in America: Faith, Culture, and Strategic Choices* (Westview, 2003), and (as coeditor) *The Encyclopedia of American Religion and Politics* (Facts on File, 2003) and *Christian Clergy in American Politics* (The Johns Hopkins University Press, 2001).

JAMES M. PENNING is professor of political science at Calvin College. He is coeditor of *Sojourners in the Wilderness: The Christian Right in Comparative Perspective* (Rowman & Littlefield, 1997) and coauthor of *Evangelicalism: The Next Generation* (Baker, 2002) and *Divided by a Common Heritage: The Christian Reformed Church and the Reformed Church in America at the Beginning of the Millennium* (Eerdmans, 2006).

CHRISTINE ROWLAND is a recent graduate of Furman University.

ANAND EDWARD SOKHEY is a Ph.D. candidate in political science at The Ohio State University. His research interests include American political behavior, public opinion, religion and politics, and methodology.

ANDREW STORTEBOOM is a recent graduate of Calvin College.

Index